DATE DUE

SOCIAL RESEARCH TODAY

Series editor
Martin Bulmer

Social impact assessment: method and experience in Europe, North America and the Developing World

Henk A. Becker

Professor of Sociology
Utrecht University

UCL
PRESS

First published in 1997 by UCL Press

UCL Press Limited
1 Gunpowder Square
London
EC4A 3DE

and

1900 Frost Road, Suite 101
Bristol
Pennsylvania 19007–1598

The name of University College London (UCL) is a registered
trade mark used by UCL Press with the consent of the owner.

British Library Cataloguing in Publication Data
A catalogue record for this book is available from the British Library.

ISBNs: 1-85728-346-5 HB
      1-85728-347-3 PB

Typeset in Palatino by Wilmaset Ltd, Birkenhead, Wirral
Printed and bound by TJ International Ltd, Padstow, UK

Contents

CONTENTS

Figures

Preface

People have always tried to avoid decisions they might regret later. The earliest manifestation of this may have been consulting the oracle at Delphi. In the eighteenth century, the search for least-regret strategies became a branch of applied research, and since that time co-operation between decision-makers and social scientists has gradually increased. Scientists have learned to assist decision-makers by pretesting their plans and by helping them select the strategy that promises the most benefit for the least sacrifice. Over time, the pretesting of human action has evolved into a distinct type of policy-oriented social research: impact assessment. Impact assessment has had a chequered history, mainly because the predictability of future impacts is often relatively low. The ex-post evaluation of impact assessments has been developed and applied to exploring the limits of forecasting the consequences of strategic decisions.

This book provides an overview of how pretesting interventions in human life courses, organizations and society as a whole, has developed over time. It describes the methodology, the methodological pitfalls, and goes on to elaborate experiences. Its prospective readership includes advanced undergraduates, graduate students, practising social researchers seeking to familiarize themselves with developments in new areas, and nonspecialists who want to extend their knowledge of social research.

In the early 1980s, the then Department of Science Policy in the Netherlands launched a programme to stimulate policy-oriented social research and to improve its relationship with policy-makers in

xi

government, business and nonprofit organizations in the Netherlands. Although this programme was wound down in the mid-1980s, having run its course, a number of research institutes and university departments have continued to work along the lines originally established, and this book is one of the outcomes of that enterprise.

Earlier versions of some of the chapters intended for this book have been discussed at the annual conferences of the International Association for Impact Assessment (IAIA). I am particularly grateful for comments I have received from colleagues at the conferences held in Washington (1992), Shanghai (1993), Quebec City (1994), Durban (1995) and Estoril (1996). I owe a great deal to the IAIA for providing a stimulating environment that made possible the exchange of professional experiences.

I wish to extend my thanks to those who helped me in so many different way during the preparation of this book. I owe a considerable debt of gratitude to Frank Vanclay for extensively commenting on, and revising, earlier drafts of the manuscript. I am also grateful to Martin Bulmer and Alan Porter for many helpful suggestions. I wish to thank the members of the Department of Sociology at Utrecht University and the Interuniversity Center for Social Science Theory and Methodology (ICS) for the many discussions we shared on social impact assessment. My thanks also go to Astrid Zaat for her valuable assistance in searching for literature and for preparation of this book. Parts of the book have been used in teaching and I am grateful to more than 20 cohorts of sociology, environmental science and policy science students for their comments. These have been a substantial help in structuring the text. However, the responsibility for the arguments put forward here is mine.

Henk A. Becker
Utrecht

CHAPTER 1

The quest for least-regret strategies

1.1 Introduction

This textbook synthesizes a wide range of experiences reported over the years by many social impact assessors and has benefited substantially from the experience of many colleagues. However, it is in no way a routine instruction in social impact assessment (SIA) methodologies. It is my belief that each problem presented to a social impact assessor requires an approach that combines well-known procedures with new trial-and-error approaches. For this reason I doubt very much whether a standardized overall methodology for this type of policy-oriented social research will ever appear.

This is not only a textbook but also a *context-book*. Methods for SIA will be presented in the context of insights derived from sociology, demography, the political sciences and related disciplines. During the last few decades, the social sciences have made considerable progress and social impact assessors have incorporated these achievements into their projects. In particular, the social sciences have increased our understanding of individual behaviour, of the objectives of individuals, and of the action space individuals have at their disposal. The methodology of social science research also provides many new insights, but as yet we do not see much of this being applied in SIA.

Most people usually imagine large development projects like dams and reservoirs when they hear the words *social impact assessment*. These schemes, often commissioned by national governments, usually have dramatic consequences for villagers, their homes and their fields. There are indeed many SIAs which explore the social consequences of these types of development projects and a number of them will be discussed in this book. However, there are many types of SIA. Another kind is legal IA. For example, European integration will have consequences for social security policies in the member states. The member states have to prepare for deregulation and for new legal provisions, and in this connection social impact assessors are actively assessing the consequences of deregulation and re-regulation (see De Kemp & Sips 1994). We also find SIA in commercial enterprises. Management teams apply *strategic learning* to explore shifts in the social environment of their organizations, to design new strategies and to simulate the consequences of these shifts for the activities of their organization, their customers and their competitors (see Schwarz 1992; Senge 1990).

What is implied by the term *impact assessment* in the general sense? Impact assessment (IA) can be defined as *the process of identifying the future consequences of a current or proposed action*. This kind of policy-oriented social research is also called ex-ante evaluation, the pre-testing of actions, or the analysis of consequences. One of the major sub-fields of impact assessment is SIA. I define social impact assessment as *the process of identifying the future consequences of a current or proposed action which are related to individuals, organizations and social macro-systems*.

This definition is similar to the description of SI assessment by the Inter-organizational Committee on Guidelines and Principles (1994). The committee defined social impacts as *the consequences for human populations of any public or private action – that alters the way in which people live, work, play, relate to one another, organize to meet their needs, and generally cope as members of society*. According to the committee, the term also includes cultural impacts involving changes in the norms, values and beliefs that guide and rationalize their cognition of themselves and their society (ibid 1994: 1).

In its monograph, the Inter-organizational Committee defined SIA in terms of

> efforts to assess or estimate, in advance, the social consequences
> likely to follow from specific policy actions (including programs,
> and the adoption of new policies), and specific government
> actions (including buildings, large projects and leasing large

tracts of land for resource extraction), particularly in the context of the US National Environmental Policy Act of 1969 (NEPA).

Although the *Guidelines and Principles* is an important document, it was developed for the regulatory system in the USA. Moreover, it implies that SIA did not exist prior to the passage of the NEPA. I do not agree and will argue that SIA is not restricted to the context of environmental impact assessment but operates as a type of IA in its own right.

This book is intended as an introduction to SIA, and sets it in an international perspective. I focus on the following issues, that can also be read as questions:

1. The major characteristics of SIA.
2. The historical development of SIA.
3. The main methods used in SIA.
4. The experiences gained from SIA in Europe, North America and a number of developing countries and the pitfalls encountered.
5. The state of the art in contemporary SIA.
6. The normative and practical aspects of SIA which give rise to concern.

In discussing SIA as one of the subfields of IA, attention has to be paid to its many relationships with the other major components of IA. First, *environmental impact assessment* (EIA) must be mentioned. This has already been mentioned in the context of the National Environmental Policy Act of the USA. This law has served as a model for similar legislation concerning the protection of the environment in various judicial systems throughout the world. A typical example of an EIA is the ex-ante evaluation of the environmental consequences of building a new industrial plant and the questions its development raise, such as, will it pollute ground water and air in the region?

Secondly, we have to take a look at *technology assessment* (TA). This type of analysis was developed in the 1960s and reflects concern about the unintended consequences of technology on society. In the USA, TA was formalized in 1972 with the establishment of the Office of Technology Assessment, an agency that concentrated on US Government policy concerns (see Vanclay & Bronstein 1995: xi). In recent years, TA has been institutionalized in most other western countries but lacks the legal basis entrenching environmental IA. Early in 1996 the US Office of

Technology Assessment was forced to close its doors, although this kind of policy-oriented research can be expected to continue in other organizational settings. A characteristic example of TA is the ex-ante evaluation of innovations in telecommunication.

Thirdly, I want to draw attention to *economic impact assessment*. This involves the impact of actions on economic structures and processes, including changes in local employment, business activities, earnings and income (Leistritz 1995: 129). A key activity in economic IA is input-output analysis, that is, providing estimates that reflect expenditure patterns in regional or national economies.

IA is closely related to the evaluation of actions situated in the past. The analysis of past actions has acquired so much prominence that it is often called just *evaluation research*. Two main types of ex-post evaluation can be distinguished. If intermediate outcomes of the analysis are used to improve the action, it is known as a formative evaluation, whereas if the final outcomes of the analysis are used to judge the action it is known as a summative evaluation. There is a substantial body of literature on ex-post evaluation research, and the practitioners of this kind of research have established an international professional association of their own. The link between ex-ante and ex-post evaluation is illustrated by the emergence of *programme evaluation*. This type of policy-oriented research introduces an integrated analysis of interventions that span two or more stages. Each stage of the programme is accompanied by both ex-ante and ex-post evaluation, and in addition to this the programme as a whole is subjected to an ex-ante and an ex-post evaluation. As an example of a programme I take a nation-wide educational reform that spans three years. Each year can be taken as a stage in the programme, consisting of interventions, and both types of evaluation research. I will elaborate on ex-post evaluation and programme evaluation later on.

There also exists close links between IA and advisory activities, because designing and ranking of actions in IA represents advice to a central actor. This implies that in this book I can draw upon the literature on scientists engaged in advisory activities, counselling and planned social change (inter alia Becker 1976). For example, I will discuss the difference between a suggestion for action made by a lay person and professional advice for action formulated by a scientist. I will also discuss the difference between a professional manager running a reorganization and a scientist assisting the manager in accomplishing the reorganization. The scientific adviser could be a sociologist, an economist, but also a mathematician or a natural scientist. When I formulate scientific advice, I am presenting an intervention hypothesis, because I predict that action A will have the consequences $x1 \ldots xn$. Intervention hypotheses can be tested by empirical research, by deriving predictions and confronting the predictions with observations. I will also discuss in which situations scientific advisers or counsellors represent a worthwhile investment.

In this chapter, some of the main ideas related to SIA developed later in this book will be introduced. The discussion is informal and is intended to prepare the way for the more detailed arguments that follow. Unfortunately some overlap between this and later discussions cannot be avoided. I begin by providing an example, and next I describe the main characteristics of SIA projects and go on to present a conceptual model for SIA that focuses on the relationships between SIA and the social sciences. I also examine the main types of SIA.

1.2 A case of SIA

To illustrate SIA and its utilization in policy-making, I take a life insurance company in a western country. This fictitious corporation sells life insurance to private customers. It also sells investment arrangements to individuals who want to use these investments as a source of income when they retire. I shall discuss a board meeting of this corporation, including the documents presented by staff departments in preparation of decision-making. On the agenda there is an issue related to an expansion of the market for life insurance and investment arrangements. A second issues deals with a merger with another life insurance company. The third issue requires a decision on a proposal for kindergarten provisions for young children of female employees of the company.

The document about the first issue on the agenda starts by analyzing the problem. The corporation is confronted with a new law on pensions. Until recently employees had to become members of a pension scheme created by their employer. The premiums for the pension rights were deduced from the income tax. Now a law has been passed that permits employees to arrange for their income in old age either by participating in a pension scheme offered by their employer or by paying a specified sum each month into an investment arrangement. In both cases the monthly payment can be deduced from income tax. The new law confronts life insurance companies with a substantial increase of their market opportunities. Our corporation estimates an increase of 30–40 per cent of its annual sales during a period of about five years. The corporation will have to expand its organization. The document discusses two policy options and their consequences. One option would be to employ more personnel. Another alternative would be to engage temporary manpower. The second alternative will enable the company to retrench without firing personnel as soon as the market shrinks. The policy document presents an SIA. Is also discusses economic and fiscal consequences.

The second issue on the agenda relates to a process of reorganization that started two years ago with a policy decision to merge with another life insurance company. In both companies a process of planned change was initiated that follows the rules of strategic learning. In both firms workshops were held to design new corporate strategies and to analyze their consequences, taking macro-change into consideration. The next step in the merger will be negotiations between the two partners concerning the new structure after the merger. Option one is a highly centralized organization and a co-ordinated set of departments. Option two is a decentralized organization with relatively autonomous departments and a light co-ordination by a central corporate board. Which option will lead to the most favourable effects for both partners in the merger? The policy document presents an SIA, describing just one step in a process of strategic learning.

The third issue on the agenda looks at kindergarten facilities for the offspring of female employees. The corporation wants to hire a certain number of *positions* in a kindergarten in operation near its main office building. The policy document drafted in preparation of this decision provides an overview of the number of female employees and the number of children they have under the age of four. At the last moment the staff department has realized that an announcement of the advent of kindergarten facilities will result in a baby boom starting nine months after the communication. Female employees that have postponed pregnancies because kindergarten facilities were lacking will decide to have their babies now. The policy document presents an informed guess about the demand for positions related to (a) children already born, and (b) children to be born after the announcement of the child care facilities. It also estimates how long the baby boom will last and how the corporation can cope with the leave of absence of female employees before and after the birth of their babies. It is evident that this policy document is an SIA.

This example illustrates that the board of the corporation has to take social impacts into consideration before arriving at a decision on each of the three issues. The issues are too complex to be decided upon without an assessment of impacts. It is also evident that the decisions have to be based on both hard and soft information.

1.3 A profile of SIA

As orientation, I will begin by sketching a profile of SIA. Figure 1.1 gives a flow-chart of the initial and main phases of a large-scale project. Later, in Chapter 6, I will discuss this flow-chart in more detail and specify guidelines for instant projects and medium-size projects. Because SIA deals with the consequences of a current or future action, we first have to take a closer look at the action itself. An action is launched to mitigate or eliminate a problem. A problem is the discrepancy between a desired situation or process and an actual situation or process. Who decides whether a discrepancy requires action to mitigate or eliminate it? This question leads to specifications being made by the central decision-maker in the problem. Next we have to discover the nature of the problem and why it has been judged serious enough to merit action. Perhaps the problem is located in substantial shortcomings in the host social system. We have, however, to guard against false problems. Taking action sometimes only makes the problem worse, and in such a situation action is a waste of time and money.[1]

Carrying out a rigorous problem analysis at the beginning of an assessment project is an extremely complex procedure, and is perhaps the most difficult activity in the whole project. Assessors often discover that they only see the problem clearly at the end of a project. Even

---

THE INITIAL PHASE IN AN SIA PROJECT
1. Problem analysis and communication strategy
2. Systems analysis
3. Baseline analysis
4. Trend analysis and monitoring design
5. Project design

THE MAIN PHASE IN AN SIA PROJECT
1. Scenario design
2. Design of strategies
3. Assessment of impacts
4. Ranking of strategies
5. Mitigation of negative impacts
6. Reporting
7. Stimulation of implementation
8. Auditing and ex-post evaluation

N.B.
(a) In a SIA project two or more steps will often be taken simultaniously. This is explained in Chapters 3 and 4
(b) In Chapters 3 and 4 each step will be divided into a number of substeps
(c) In Chapter 6 the flow-chart will be differentiated into instant projects, medium-size projects and large-scale projects

Figure 1.1   Flow-chart of a large-scale SIA project.

discovering the identity of the central actor may prove difficult, often because more than one actor is involved. We are accustomed to referring to a central actor who launches an action directed at a target system. However, in many social systems the target system reciprocates by launching action itself. The problem analysis report has to meet very high standards.

Problems that may require input from an SI assessor are in most cases situated at the meso- or macro-level. At the meso-level, we may encounter processes or situations in organizations or social networks that are unsatisfactory to one or more actors involved. These actors define the problem as a focal issue for intervention (Blake & Mouton 1976). At the macro level, a social problem can be defined as *an alleged situation that is incompatible with the values of a significant number of people who agree that action is needed to alter the situation* (Rubington & Weinberg 1981). An alleged situation is a situation that is said to exist. People talk about it. The allegation, however, need not actually be true. People may be afraid of risks that are in fact minimal. Incompatibility of values is also a complex matter. Different people hold different values, and the same person may hold conflicting values. For these reasons, different people consider different things to be social problems. How many people are *a significant number*? In studying social problems on a macro-level, we usually deal only with socially troublesome or deleterious situations that are recognized as problems by the general public. Sometimes, the SI assessor will feel obliged to take the role of the social critic, maybe as a single person opposing social injustice. In that case, the number of individuals being concerned is (still) extremely small.

A communication strategy must be designed at the very beginning of the assessment project. Some assessors are convinced that every SIA project requires full public participation in the decision-making process.[2] This may make sense if we are dealing with regional development or the process of reorientation in an organization. Full participation of all parties, however, would be absurd in situations where actions were being considered to control illegal activity or where secrecy was required because an organization had not yet fully committed itself. For example, it would not be appropriate to involve criminal organizations in an impact assessment. A political party probably would not have full public participation if it were to commission an SIA to consider the impacts of a range of positions it might take on certain issues so that it could have information before adopting a final policy position. This would be especially true if the issue was particularly controversial. However, general communication with everyone involved in the action is wise, and should be followed to the end of the assessment project.

We now have to analyze the social system we are dealing with. Having already mentioned the central actor and the target actor, we must go on to identify the other actors involved. We have to define the boundaries of the system, its subsystems and related phenomena outside the system's boundaries. System analysis provides a conceptual model of the system. The hard core of a conceptual model of a social system is a survey of actors, their behaviour, their objectives and their action space. The action space is the amount of room left for manoeuvre after the constraints faced by the actors have been taken into consideration. Designing a conceptual model for a SIA project is difficult, as we will see in the next paragraph.

In most cases, the problem to be mitigated or eliminated and the social system hosting the problem will have a history.[3] A critical account of this history is called the *baseline analysis*. The impact assessor goes back in time – sometimes years, sometimes decades – and reconstructs what has happened as far as the problem is concerned. In order to come as close as possible to a causal analysis, description has to be combined with explanation and interpretation. Insight into the developments that caused the problem are a necessary precondition for designing adequate mitigating strategies.

After analyzing the past, we have to explore the future. In the preliminary phase of an SIA project, future analysis is restricted to a critical inventory of trends. We focus on the extrapolation of developments we can forecast in a relatively precise and reliable way. Here we can take the example of the cohort replacement of individuals born in a particular year. If we are discussing a country that has been free of war and natural disasters, mortality can be predicted in an accurate way. The greying of North America and Europe, for example, can be explored by trend analysis.

Exploring the future also requires designing and institutionalizing a monitoring system that will provide information about the development of action and its intended and unintended consequences. Monitoring intervention is important because, more often than not, decisions for interventions are implemented in ways that differ from the formulation of the decision that initiated them. It is no coincidence that the body of scientific literature on implementing policy decisions has grown substantially in recent years.[4]

Towards the end of the initial phase, we have to make a critical review of how far we have come in our explorations. Are the decision-makers and impact assessors prepared to launch the main phase of the project? If they are, then research questions and the overall design of the project has to be elaborated with great care.

In the main phase of the project, the first step is scenario design. Scenarios are sketches of possible future contexts for the actor system and the target system. In most cases, three to five scenarios provide an adequate basis for simulating what might happen to the systems we are interested in. If we want to introduce more *noise* into the systems, we add one or more *critical incidents*. Designing scenarios is both a scientific and an artistic enterprise, and in designing them we require a theoretical model of the processes to be simulated. For this reason, designing scenarios and in a broader perspective impact assessment projects, is a kind of *art-science*.[5]

The following step is to design strategies that might mitigate or eliminate the problem. Strategies are plans for the action the central actor has in mind. Designing strategies also belongs to the area of art-science. In most cases, three to five strategies are all we need to prepare the intervention. In preparing complex interventions, it is advisable to specify strategies, tactics and operational plans.

Assessing impacts involves a number of simulations. Here strategies are tested by confronting them with the various scenarios, and, if necessary, with each of the critical incidents as well. The simulations can be based on the data from previous projects and ex-post evaluations. The outcomes of these simulations are insights into the strong and weak aspects of each of the strategies specified for each scenario. We have to keep in mind that impact assessment, including SIA, is a kind of simulation. We pretest actions in an artificial setting in order to gather information about possible consequences.

One of the outcomes of the simulation must be a ranking of strategies. A strategy that shows many favourable outcomes under one scenario may be a disaster in another. Strategies are ranked per scenario and per critical incident, from a least-regret strategy to a most-regret strategy, and there are a number of techniques for ranking scenarios. If it is possible to quantify costs and benefits in monetary terms, cost-benefit analysis will be preferred. If, however, negative and positive aspects cannot be expressed in monetary terms, it is better to apply multiple-criteria analysis.

After the first round of simulations, we will probably have found many weaknesses in the current or proposed action and we will hesitate to launch the action because we are discontented with its negative consequences. This hesitation leads to a redesigning of the action in order to mitigate its negative impacts. After the strategies have been redesigned, we again simulate their fate and rank them once more. Iteration sometimes requires ten or more rounds of redesigning, simulation and ranking.

Finally the products of the SIA project are ready for reporting. In most cases, multiple reporting is necessary in order to reach all appropriate audiences. Reporting ranges from executive summaries and press releases to full-scale reports and workshops. In SIA, written reports are gradually becoming less important than oral and audiovisual presentations. In the course of strategic learning, policy-makers may be confronted with the outcomes of the assessments of *scenario-to-strategy workshops*. The latter approach implies that communication has taken place between decision-makers and impact assessors at regular intervals during the project.

The hallmark of good advice is its impact. The same applies to the results of a SIA project. During the project, the assessor stimulates participation by decision-makers and other relevant social actors. The stimulation of implementation continues after the assessment project. Often members of staff units in the action system will be made responsible for a longer-term stimulation of the implementation, where, for example, the monitoring process is continued and strategic learning is institutionalized.

Finally, the auditing of an SIA project will provide information on its performance, its cost-effectiveness and the fit between plan and actual process. If government financing is involved, auditing will be prescribed formally and the National Audits Court will comment on the project. Closely related to auditing is ex-post evaluation. The beneficiary of the evaluation report will be the scientific community or, in our case, the impact assessment community. Maybe the project yields new insights into SIA methodology or the organization of projects in this kind of policy-oriented research.

The term *policy-oriented research* emphasizes that we are dealing with a certain type of research. In most cases, however, an SIA project is more than research. This is particularly apparent when the research project is integrated into a process of strategic learning.

1.4 Towards a conceptual model of SIA

The social sciences have not yet produced a fully elaborated, generally accepted conceptual and theoretical model. This does not mean, however, that they stand empty-handed as far as concepts and theories are concerned. They already have some preliminary conceptual and theoretical models available, and these can be used in SIA projects. I will summarize one of these models, illustrate it by giving an example and go on to deal with another preliminary model. Finally, I will discuss the relationship between the two models.

I want to begin by discussing the model presented in Figure 1.2.[6] First, we have to identify the core relationship in an SIA project. Given the definition of SIA presented earlier, this is the relationship between the current or proposed action and its consequences. In the model this is represented by the relationship between an action originating from one or more individual or collective actors in the action system and the behaviour of one or more individual or collective actors in the target system (arrow 1). The principal theoretical problem involved in this relationship is explaining the behaviour of actors in the target system before and after the action. In most cases we are dealing with differences

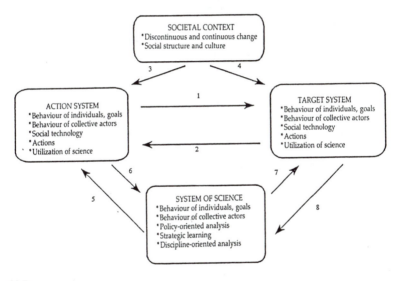

N.B.

(a) Often a target system also acts as an action system, and vice versa, as will be explained in Chapters 3 and 4

(b) Social technology is the sum of policy instruments for the management of organizations, intervention, and collective action, as will be explained in Chapter 6

(c) Utilization of science in an action system or a target system is often facilitated by a staff unit, as will be explained in Chapter 6

Figure 1.2 Overview of a conceptual model for SIA.

in behaviour. Two groups of variables have to be taken into consideration in explaining these behavioural differences. First, we have to look at the goals of the individual actors in the target system and, secondly, we have to look at the constraints that confront them.

The goals of the individual actors are specified in this model as being the pursuit of physical wellbeing and social esteem. Physical wellbeing includes such variables as good health and access to financial resources. Social esteem includes variables relating to compliance with values and social norms, and the actor's relative position in social networks. This description of goals raises a number of questions that I will deal with later. Here I only wish to emphasize that both egoistic and altruistic goals are included in the model.

The constraints of individual actors are specified in the model by taking the variables in the target system and other systems into consideration. In the target system, social technology is listed as a group of resources. By social technology I mean policy instruments for the management of the organization, the launching of interventions and the co-ordination of collective action, for example. Social technology will be discussed in more detail in Chapter 6. Opportunities for the utilization of science can also be seen as resources. In the action system, social technology and opportunities for the utilization of science are also listed as resources.

The behaviour patterns of individual and collective actors are identified in the target system and the action system. Collective actors can be organizations or social networks (such as communities). To refer to actions using the name of a collective actor is, however, a simplification. In all circumstances what is involved is the behaviour of one or more individual actors.[7]

The societal context represents discontinuous change, such as wars, economic booms and depressions. It also represents continuous change, such as modernization in western countries.[8] Furthermore the societal context involves social structure and culture, and its impact can be seen as a constraint on behaviour in both the action system (arrow 3) and the target system (arrow 4).[9] The impact of the societal context on the system of science has not been made explicit in the model because it is arguably not significant for SIA, but I do not mean to imply that the system of science is free of societal context.

Policy-oriented analysis, like impact assessment, ex-post evaluation and basic research are to be found in the system of science. In the model we are only interested in the oriented type of basic research.[10] Here analyses are expected to contribute to the body of knowledge of a particular scientific discipline and serve as basic research in the service of policy-oriented analysis. Furthermore they have to enhance the actor's understanding of social problems in general. The utilization of science in an action system or a target system can be facilitated by an intermediate organization, such as a staff unit. I will discuss the organizational setting of the utilization of the social sciences in Chapter 6.

So far, the model is a relatively empty one and gives very little information on specific social systems. As a next step, we introduce specific theories, at a lower level of abstraction. By drawing on an example, I will try to demonstrate the practical relevance of this explanatory approach. Generally speaking, national governments have two strategies to choose from in their fight against drug addiction. First, the French strategy, which treats dealing in and using all drugs as a criminal offence but which uses discretion in the application of the law as action space or room to manoeuvre. Secondly, the Dutch strategy, which permits limited dealing in and use of soft drugs, such as marijuana, but which treats dealing in hard drugs as a criminal offence, although regards those addicted to them as patients not criminals. What will be the impact of each of these strategies on individual behaviour in the risk population? Which option will be the least-regret strategy for national governments? To answer these questions we introduce specific theories into the model. First, the domino theory that predicts there will be a series of disruptions in society as soon as drugs are legalized. Secondly, the safety valve theory, predicting a containment of drug addiction if individuals are granted a closely defined opportunity to act out or escape disappointments in their private lives and their role in society. In the Appendix the reader is invited to elaborate the model by adding the stepping stone theory, which, for example, predicts that the use of soft drugs will lead to the use of hard drugs.

The model summarized in Figure 1.1 can be used as a frame of reference both for SIA as well as other kinds of IA. The model can also be used for SIA of actions directed at the central actor if, for example, target actors want to retaliate. Furthermore, the model can provide a context for those studies into the way an action system accomplishes its tasks by conducting an ex-post evaluation of the action (arrow 1). The model can also be useful in analyzing how scientific knowledge is used in the action and target systems. These examples illustrate that the model not only covers social impact assessment but other types of social policy analysis as well.[11]

Impact assessors who work with the model summarized above are following the analytical tradition within the social sciences. This implies that they use a covering law approach. The proponents of this paradigm advocate causal analyses but, at the same time, they realize there are severe limitations to causal explanation in social science research. The proponents know that, at best, they can only present quasi-causal analyses. They presume that if they design their analyses to approximate causal analysis as closely as possible, they will arrive at the results that provide the best possible explanation.

If we consider interpretation, we come to the second model I wish to discuss in this section. The godfather of the interpretative tradition is Max Weber. He advocated an approach called *Verstehen*. Briefly, this approach implies taking on the role of the other in order to understand their motives. In interpretative analysis, variables are not studied in a quasi-causal analysis but are explored as part of a *Gestalt*. A prototype of interpretative analysis is *Awareness of Dying* (1974) by Glaser and Strauss.[12] This project examined the quality of dying of cancer patients who were terminally ill and who had only a few months to live. The researchers tried to assess the impact of a number of health care strategies on the quality of dying of those patients in the cancer ward, for example, who was the best person to tell the patient about their approaching death: family members, doctors, nurses or clergy? What had the most beneficial effect – being honest with the patient when the crucial question was asked or beating around the bush? In this example, it was not possible to follow a research approach rooted in the strict requirements of the analytical tradition. Researchers had to feel their way carefully during extensive participant observation.

Weber has formulated strict rules for the process of interpretation in social research. He stipulated that interpretations of social relationships must first be checked according to the usual methods of causal analysis before any understanding, however plausible, can be accepted as a valid explanation of these relationships.[13] In the appendix, the reader will be invited to apply interpretation in social impact assessment to the two main strategies in fighting drug addiction.

A number of social scientists advocate the application of both analytical and interpretive approaches in social science analyses (see also Esser 1993). This does not imply, however, that every project and every publication has to show both of these aspects. Application is advocated for a research line as a whole. A research line is a co-ordinated set of research projects in a specific problem area. In this book the co-ordinated application of the analytic and the interpretative approach in SIA will be strongly advocated.

1.5 Towards a typology of SIA

Impact assessment does not yet have a fully elaborated, generally accepted typology. In most cases, impact assessors use a rather simple typology: environmental IA, technology assessment, economic IA, and SIA. This typology provides a global overview and each IA project can be categorized using this typology. Projects are classified according to the first-order impact they evaluate. There is one exception to this rule. Technology assessment is classified according to the action to be pretested and not the target system at which the action is directed.

In Chapter 5, a close look will be taken at the problem of providing a typology for impact assessment. In the meantime, a typology for the components of SIA is required. This typology has been summarized in Figure 1.3. Three types of SIA can be identified: micro, meso and macro. The types are constructed on the basis of their predominant features. Type 1, micro-SIA, focuses on individuals and their behaviour. Type 2, meso-SIA, focuses on organizations and social networks (including communities), while type 3, macro-SIA, focuses on national and international social systems. The three types can be found in different settings, sometimes exclusively focused on social impacts, while at other times they can be integrated with other forms of IA. They can be project based, or they can be applied to policies, when it is also called strategic IA.

We will begin by considering micro-level projects. In many SIA studies, the target system is generally represented by a number of individuals, their goals and their behavioural choices. Analyzing the consequences of a current or proposed action often requires studying the activities of these individual actors. An example from demographic

---

A. SIA PROJECTS ON A MICRO-LEVEL
Analyzing impacts on the behaviour of large numbers of individuals, as in demographic impact assessment

B. SIA PROJECTS ON A MESO-LEVEL
Analyzing impacts on the behaviour of collective actors, such as organizations and social movements

C. SIA PROJECTS ON A MACRO-LEVEL
Analyzing impacts on social macro-systems, such as national and international political and legal systems

---

N.B.
(a) A project of SIA may fall into more than one of these types, as will be explained in Chapter 5

Figure 1.3 Typology of SIA projects

IA might be the policy-maker in higher education who is interested in the consequences for enrolment of any change in the scholarship system.

This kind of SIA frequently takes the form of a micro-simulation. In a micro-simulation, we focus on micro-units in the target system. In the example cited here, these are individual educational careers. The system studied is simulated by a model which allows the characteristics of individual educational careers to be adjusted from time to time. In other words, a micro-simulation acts on micro-data which represents several thousand individual actors, their goals and their behavioural choices. The use of data from the micro-level have given this simulation model its name.

The essence of micro-simulation lies in a program which focuses on a multi-actor, multi-level and multi-process analysis. A micro-level presentation of individuals and their social, economic and demographic characteristics, together with other relevant spatial and activity attributes, provides the basis for the simulation (Nelissen 1993: 34). Information about individuals is stored in the form of person-period files which are updated for each period.

Secondly, the meso-level: here action is directed at an organization (which is neither too large or too small) or a social network. How does a social impact assessor work? Here I take my example from a gender IA study (Verloo & Roggeband 1996). Will a specific retrenchment policy in the university sector result in decreased career opportunities for female academics? Cuts in a university budget will affect the academics employed in various ways. Older professors who have reached the upper levels of the salary scale for this type of employment will not experience any problem financially. However, other academics, many of whom are female, who are ready to move from their position at the lower end of the salary scale to an intermediate level in the academic hierarchy, may be forced to stay longer in their present position if those intermediate positions are reduced in number.

Thirdly, the macro-level. Again an example can best demonstrate this type of SIA. As I have already mentioned, the European Union (EU) requires the free circulation of workers, and as a result it will be necessary to harmonize social security schemes. A macro-simulation of a number of social security arrangements could be used to analyze the impacts of innovations, for example. The focus will then be on the impact each innovation might be expected to have on wage levels, the percentage of unemployed in the labour force and schemes for financing social security provisions. Macro-level social impact assessments often consist of pretesting a country's legal arrangements.

In most cases, this typology provides an adequate basis for classifying SIA studies. Now and again, a study will have the characteristics of more than one type, and in such cases the study must be classified according to its dominant characteristics. Later, in Chapter 5, I will present a more detailed outline of the classification.

1.6 Outline of the book

The first part of this book is an overview. As we saw, Chapter 1 sketches the quest for least-regret strategies, presents an overview of SIA, the theoretical models to be used in this kind of IA and a typology of SIA studies. Chapter 2 focuses on the history of SIA and discusses it in the context of social policy and policy-oriented social science research.

In the second part of the book, methods for SIA are presented. The methods relate to large-scale projects. Chapter 3 deals with methods used in the preliminary phase of a study and Chapter 4 discusses methods used in the main phase. This part of the book not only presents methods but it also offers descriptions of pitfalls and enables policy-oriented social researchers to carry out SIA studies on their own. The reader receives a textbook that presents methodology in the context of disciplinary requirements, such as explanation and interpretation.

The third part of the book can be seen as an elaboration of the second section. Chapter 5 deals with the main types of SIA and the discussion is broadened from micro-level projects to projects on the medium- and macro-level. The discussion develops further. What auxiliary methods are available and what are their strong and weak points? Chapter 6 elaborates the main features of SIA and deals not only with large-scale projects but also with instant projects and medium-sized projects. Relationships with basic science and with normative discussions relating to policy-oriented social research are explored.

The fourth section of the book documents the experiences of those working with SIA. Chapter 7 deals with experiences in western Europe and North America, and Chapter 8 focuses on the developing countries. The conclusions reached in the book are discussed in Chapter 9 and are related to the questions raised in the first chapter. This final chapter also explores the future of this form of policy-oriented social research. Finally, a number of case studies and exercises are provided to assist in further study.

Notes

1. In *Justice across the Generations*, Epstein (cited by Laslet & Fishkin 1992: 85) argues: "My point is that no special forms of regulation are needed to take into account the problem of justice across generations. Why should anyone want to adopt this leave-bad-enough-alone attitude? Because the alternatives are worse." Later more examples will be provided.
2. See Richard Roberts (1995). This issue will be elaborated later.
3. This raises the problem of defining the period to be covered in the baseline analysis. The starting point is usually taken to be a major event in the history of the problem and/or the social system. In Chapter 6 guidelines will be presented which will be of assistance in choosing a period for baseline analysis.

4. One of the reasons for the increase in the number of analyses being made of the impacts of policy decisions is the increasing incidence of public scandal surrounding the actions of governments, business enterprises and nonprofit organizations. Another reason is the growing legal quest for expost evaluations of government policies.

5. The concept of *art-science* originated in medicine. For many centuries doctors practised medicine as an art. Over the years scientific knowledge about diseases and disabilities increased and gradually a combination of medical knowledge and art-like medical skills emerged. The result is known as an art-science.

6. The explanatory model represented in Figure 1.2 originated from the analytical tradition in the social sciences and for a long time has been known as the rational choice model. Because the term *rational* generated considerable confusion, and because the model has been elaborated over the years, it is now known as the *utilitarian individualistic* model. See inter alia Esser 1993.

7. In the case of an institution such as marriage the contribution of individual actors to its invention, institutionalization and continuation is a rather vague notion. The assumption is called *methodological individualism*.

8. Modernization in western European societies is considered to have taken form towards the end of the eighteenth century. It is generally accepted that modernization in this sense includes political democratization, secularization, industrialization, urbanization, individualization and increased participation in formal education. Later I will discuss these developments further.

9. By social structure I mean allocative arrangements in social systems, such as social hierarchies. By social culture I mean normative or prescriptive arrangements in social systems, like rules for negotiations and communication.

10. See Chapter 6.

11. Policy analysis includes policy assessment. See Boothroyd, *Policy Assessment*, (Vanclay & Bronstein 1995: 83–128). I define policy assessment as ex-ante and ex-post evaluation of policy.

12. In this kind of interpretive analysis, explanation and interpretation involve grounded theories. Further examples will be provided later.

13. See Max Weber, for example, in an anthology of his methodological writings published in 1968 (pp. 169–70).

CHAPTER 2

The historical context of SIA

2.1 Introduction

Understanding SIA requires insight into its roots. Why has SIA emerged as part of policy-oriented social research? What have been the political and economic developments that forced policy-makers to co-operate with impact assessors and related social scientists?

The historical context of SIA exhibits a number of periods. First there was a period of isolated *explorations* by pioneers. Not a real period, in my opinion. Next there was a period of *industrialization* in western countries and *confrontations* within these countries and with countries in other parts of the world. This period ranges from about 1800 to 1945.

Following this, the impact of the Second World War becomes visible. This war has lead to a restructuring of the international order. The restructuring up until about 1965 has increased the demand for scientific research on the consequences of interventions on a macro- and micro-level.

The social criticism of the late 1960s and 1970s demands our attention. Policy-makers have been forced by the protesters to take account of new types of consequences of their interventions, including environmental consequences. Since 1975, the *economic recession* has forced them to act even more carefully. In the period 1966–1985, policy-oriented research, including SIA, became institutionalized in most countries all over the world.

In the mid-1980s, the economic recession became less pressing. However, other constraints gained in strength. The quest for *sustainability* became stronger and stronger. In 1986, a period set in that still reigns in the mid-1990s.

Taking account of the consequences of current and future actions is as old as intelligent life on this planet. When scientific knowledge and know-how were employed to explore these consequences, a new era in the analysis of consequences commenced. There has been some controversy over the candidate for the title of the first social assessor. I would put a case for a Dutchman, Johan de Witt, Grand Pensionary of Holland, as being the inaugurator of SIA. As Weesie (1988) records, in July 1671 the United Provinces were threatened by France and England. The Provinces needed money to enlarge their army and navy. As always, Holland, the richest province in the union, would have to pay the lion's share. However, Holland was not in a good financial shape. It had substantial debts, and war had been all but beneficial for trade. Johan de Witt exerted himself to improve the financial situation. He submitted a memorandum to the Estates of Holland in which he proposed, referring to scientific arguments, to increase the price of annuities sold in Holland. In the seventeenth century, it was common practice for the Estates of Holland to borrow money by selling annuities to its citizens. De Witt computed the expected value, or *mathematical hope* in de Witt's terminology, of such an annuity. He argued that Holland was selling its annuities far too cheaply.

What makes the memorandum of special interest is the method employed by de Witt. While all previous methods for setting the price were based on intuition and on market considerations, de Witt designed a model to calculate a fair price, and had his clerks do extensive calculations. At the heart of his model is an assumption on how delayed and uncertain payments should be discounted. The fair price of an annuity is determined by the expected sum of money to be received, death risks are taken into account and future payments discounted with the market interest rate.

The model of de Witt is essentially still in use in annuity science; only the death risks are now estimated with more advanced statistical techniques. In the English literature, it is sometimes stated that annuity science started in England with the astronomer Halley (1693). Given that de Witt wrote his memorandum in 1671, de Witt is the real founder of annuity science.

Weesie (1988), whose description of the work of de Witt I have used, concludes that the memorandum of 1671 provides the first real application of mathematics to a social problem. I also argue that the memorandum constitutes the first SIA. De Witt produced a demographic IA and a health IA. The model of de Witt combines SIA and economic IA. Further on, we will often meet models that deal with more than one consequence of a current or future action. Now, as then, models tend to relate not only to social impacts.

2.2 Industrialization and confrontation: 1800–1945

At the end of the eighteenth and the beginning of the nineteenth century, a number of *revolutions* took place, in particular the French Revolution, which changed the political scene, and the Industrial Revolution, which changed the structure of the labour force and the nature of settlement, draining the countryside of people to swell the cities. Industrialization is part of the process called modernization. In the western world, this concept represents industrialization plus secularization, that is, reform of the educational system, improvement of medical care and health conditions and an increase in population. Finally, the sciences as a social system were forced to change. The scientific revolution consisted of progress in the natural and medical sciences and their applications, and it led to the emergence of the social sciences. According to their founders, the social sciences had to acquire the same rigour as the natural sciences. They had to formulate scientific laws that permitted precise and reliable predictions. They had to develop methods that would lead to precise and reliable applications of scientific laws. Practical problems would be subjected to causal explanations and to interventions with predictable outcomes.

In this spirit, during 1775–6, the Marquis de Condorcet carried out an analysis that, according to Prendergast (1989), constituted the beginnings of SIA. At the time, Condorcet was an *Inspecteur du navigation*. The 32-year-old mathematician had his doubts about a plan for a canal that would join the towns of Cambrai (on the Escaut) and Saint-Quentin (on the Somme). Two sections of the proposed canal constituted a problem from an engineering point of view, for they were required to tunnel through the hills near Saint-Quentin. The plan also required inundations of the already marshy valleys along the Somme. According to Condorcet, up to 40,000 people would be negatively affected by the inundations, largely by being more susceptible to disease and epidemics. To test his hypothesis, Condorcet conducted a controlled comparison study. During the summer of 1775, he travelled through Picardy and investigated its demographic and social conditions. He selected some 16 parishes in the region as his sample. Eight of these were located on higher grounds and eight near the marshes. His dependent variable was the mortality rate. The selected parishes were similar with respect to soil, wealth of the inhabitants, way of life, predominant occupations, availability of medical assistance, type of public administration and the amount of taxes paid to the government. The results were unequivocal: in the low-lying parishes, the average life expectancy was reduced by one-fifth. Furthermore, the number living into old age was considerably lower. Condorcet recommended that the subterranean canal should not be built. He supported an alternative route that was longer but in the open. Part of Condorcet's plan was realized in 1889.

Prendergast (1989) concluded that Condorcet's canal study was an early specimen of a breed of investigation that has become universal in modern industrial societies: the collection of data for the purpose of making a rational choice between alternatives. The purpose of social science – or, as Condorcet called it, the *social art* – was to use the experimental method to investigate the total consequences of royal action, including impacts on subjects without political rights in the region. "It is a common, everyday science that is being presented here," Condorcet wrote in his social mathematics (1793). It aims, simply, "to evaluate, from the natural relationships of facts among themselves, the ground for believing the truth of a fact that has not been possible to observe immediately" (Prendergast, 1989: 25–37). The tradition of social theory has a different cognitive goal: to comprehend social life (Prendergast 1989). Condorcet looked at demographic and health impacts, and he also conducted an early environmental IA. He evidently is one of the founding fathers of IA.

From France we turn to Britain. The idea of objective scientific inquiry into social conditions and the consequences of government actions to improve those conditions gained support in the 1830s. One of those who were instrumental in this was Edwin Chadwick, who in 1834, became secretary to the Poor Law Commissioners (Bulmer 1982: 3). Chadwick was concerned about the effects of insanitary conditions upon the state of the population. He saw a connection between sanitary problems, illness, poverty and the cost of the Poor Law. If there was a link between them, then a way to reduce the cost of poor relief would be to improve sanitary conditions. In 1842, he published the *Report on the Sanitary Conditions of the Labouring Population*. The report was received with shock by the more well-to-do sections of the population, most of whom were ignorant about how the working classes lived. Bulmer summarizes the purpose of the 1842 Report as follows:

> It described graphically the appalling social and health con-
> ditions in expanding towns; it demonstrated that these con-
> ditions were proportionately worse in towns than in rural areas;
> and it demonstrated the inability of the central and local
> administration to deal with the problems which they faced
> (Bulmer, 1982: 3–4).

Chadwick was not alone in exercising a reforming influence upon mid-Victorian Britain. Some inquiries were undertaken by private individuals, some by and for governments, but generally the same individuals were prominent in government-sponsored inquiries. Backing up the work of these individuals was the work of the statistical societies (particularly those of London and Manchester) founded by citizens active in social reform. The Statistical Society of London became a major forum for the presentation of the results of nineteenth-century statistical social investigation. After 1887, it became the Royal Statistical Society (Bulmer 1982: 7).

Sidney and Beatrice Webb followed a somewhat different approach. The Webbs believed that it was possible to combine scientific research into social institutions with active participation in their operation. The Webbs's methods of work and influences can be illustrated from the history of the Royal Commission on the Poor Laws 1905–9. The Commission, as an independent body reporting to the King, was instructed to inquire into the workings of the Poor Law and also into the means adopted outside the Poor Law "for meeting distress arising from want of employment, particularly during periods of severe industrial depression" (cited by Bulmer 1982: 19). The Commission produced two reports: the Majority Report, signed by the chairperson and fourteen members, which recommended that the role of guardians should be replaced by local authorities; and the Minority Report, signed by Beatrice Webb and three other members (Sidney was not a member of the Commission), which presented an argument that was simple, and novel – destitution, not pauperism, was the problem. The phenomenon of poverty was a social condition resulting from the condition and organization of the economy. What was needed was not moral improvement but social reorganization.

The Webbs' contribution to applied social research included analyses of the consequences of current and future action. They also tried to improve social conditions by using their influence on policy-makers, inter alia, by co-operating with them in royal commissions. Last but not least they developed historical and institutional analysis in the social policy field and stimulated the founding of the London School of Economics and Political Science, which opened in 1895, being devoted to research and not to propaganda (Bulmer 1982:21).

SIA is not only indebted to analyses of health policy and care for the poor but also to research in the military field. The emergence and evolution of war games are obscure, but chess evidently is a symbolic equivalent of warfare. It was originally designed for training in military strategy formation. In the history of modern war games, the year 1798 marks an innovation that has become highly influential. In that year, the *Neue Kriegspiel*, a true war game, was developed in Schleswig in Germany. The game used a map divided into 3,600 squares, each with distinctive topographical features, on which game pieces were moved to represent troop and cavalry manoeuvres. A century later, the war game had split into two types, the rigid *Kriegspiel* and the free *Kriegspiel*. In the rigid version, a game was controlled by very formal rules, charts, maps, tables, and pre-programmed calculation routines, and dice were used to generate random effects. In the free version, most of these paraphernalia were replaced with human referees, a *control team* that ruled on the permissibility of given moves. Both types of game spread rapidly from the military academies in Prussia to other countries, including Britain and the USA. In most of these settings, the free variety was more popular than the rigid one, since the flexibility of using a control team made it easier to administer than the rigid version, which required extensive calculations and data support. During World War II, war games were widely used, particularly by the Japanese and Germans. Most versions combined the rigid and free forms, embodying richly programmed environments and databases but with the addition of human judges as a check on the preset calculation routines (Raser 1969: 46).

From war games to the preparations for the peace treaty that ended World War I is only a small step. In the autumn of 1918, it became obvious that victory was in sight for the Allies. At that time in Britain a young economist, John Maynard Keynes, was head of a new department at the Treasury, which was established to deal with all questions of external finances. The department was called the *A Division*, and became famous in a short time. This division was instructed to prepare the British claims for reparations at the peace negotiations to be held in Paris.

Keynes's division got busy on this topic. His team estimated Germany's prewar foreign trade, her production, the foreign assets, the value of those territories which she was likely to lose, and her colonies. The team also estimated the amount of all those forms of damage that, under the terms of the Armistice, were likely to give rise to claims (Harrod 1951).

Their findings were before the Cabinet at the end of November. Biasing their estimates on the high side, they found that the bill against Germany, in accordance with the Armistice terms, might be about £4,000 million. The Treasury was satisfied with the document and it was presented to the War Cabinet. The War Cabinet was not satisfied. An independent committee was set up. It took the view that Germany should pay for the full cost of the war to the Allies and this was determined to be £24,000 million. It appears that this report was written in total ignorance of the most elementary points. One problem was that these heavy payments would surely compel Germany to compete strongly in British export markets. In fact, if Germany captured half of the British prewar markets and the whole of the French, she still would not be exporting enough goods to meet the bill.

The Cabinet left the matter undetermined. The British delegates went forth to Paris in January 1919 with the Treasury report, a Board of Trades report (which reached similar conclusions) and the report prepared by the independent committee. Keynes went to Paris as principal representative of the Treasury, but without power to speak during the main negotiations. Ultimately the Allies formulated a peace treaty that followed the line of the extreme demands.

The treaty was signed on 28 June 1919, but Keynes had already left Paris. He resigned from his position in the Treasury, retreated to the countryside and wrote a book to describe the whole sad story. *The Economic Consequences of the Peace* was written during August and September at Charleston and appeared on the bookstalls in December 1919. It made him famous in many countries, but he remained an outlaw from British official circles for many years afterwards.

The book presented an assessment of the economic, political and social consequences of the treaty that ended World War I. Keynes argued that the terms of the treaty would prove to be disastrous to both Germany and the Allies. At the end of the book, he developed an alternative policy providing Germany with resources that would enable it to pay a reasonable amount of restitution but also to recover economically and socially from the war and its aftermath. This proposal can be seen as the blueprint for the Marshall Plan that was ultimately put into place after World War II.

After five years of tribulation, Germany obtained lenient terms in the Dawes's Plan and promotion to an equal status in the Locarno Treaty. Germany obtained generous loans from America. With these advantages she enjoyed a period of comparative and not unsubstantial prosperity in the years from 1925 to 1929. Keynes's experiment was tried in the end (Harrod 1951).

Keynes presented an analysis of consequences that has become a landmark in applied social research. *A Revision of the Treaty*, Keynes's second book on the reparations problem, appeared at the beginning of 1922. It had the incisive and lively style of the earlier book, but it is more strictly addressed to the economic issue. In 1936 he published *The General Theory of Employment, Interest and Money*, his magnum opus. This book broke new ground in its analysis of the possibility of a stable equilibrium with high unemployment with no natural forces tending to redress it (Harrod 1951). The book can be seen as a transformation of the analytical model applied in *The Economic Consequences of the Peace* (1919) into a model of a national (and international) economic, political and social system.

The period 1800–1945 has been a period of industrialization and confrontation. Industrialization changed the western countries, reshaping the countryside and creating urban concentrations of unskilled labour. SIA has followed a top-down approach (Condorcet, Chadwick, the Webbs, Keynes). The underdogs still lacked organizations that could take effective action and mobilize countervailing power. The years 1800–1945 have also been the heyday of colonial expansion. There are no examples of activities of colonial powers that have been prepared by SIA or any other type of analysis of consequences. Absolute power does not believe in the need of an analysis of actions that takes social consequences into consideration!

2.3 Restructuring the international order: 1946–1965

SIA is highly dependent on social systems analysis. In the history of the analysis of social systems, the publication in 1947 of *Theory of Games and Economic Behavior* by Von Neumann and Morgenstern is a milestone. A model based on game theory is a mathematical representation of rational decision-making involving two or more actors. Game theory has been widely applied in the social sciences, for example, in models for coalition formation in political science. It is striking to see that, in the theory of games, Von Neumann's axiomatic lottery approach to utility is very similar to de Witt's theory of values, formulated almost three centuries earlier (Weesie 1988: 4).

A second major background development for SIA is the emergence of the system-theoretical approach. This approach begins with some postulated properties of a system, that is, a collection of entities having a structural and functional relation to each other. The theoretical problem is to derive hypotheses about the behaviour of the system (as reflected in the stages through which it passes) from the postulated interdependence of the variables. A relatively simple example is the dynamic theory of the solar system. For example, eclipses of the sun and the moon can be predicted centuries in advance. Sometimes systems are so complex that predictions can be made only roughly. The atmosphere is an example. For this reason, weather predictions cannot be made in a highly reliable and precise way.

Based on the degree of complexity, closed and open systems are distinguished. A closed system is characterized by the absence of systems noise. The behaviour of a closed system can be predicted in a reliable and precise way. An example of a relatively open system, characterized by much systems noise, is the economic system of a region.

In 1956, members of the American Management Association visited the US Naval War College. The visitors were introduced to war games. They came to the conclusion that what is good for the navy might be good for business too. The models could evidently be used in business firms, for predictions and for training purposes. Since 1956, the number of simulations modelling economic processes, dynamics of firms and the behaviour of consumers has shown a steady increase. A state of the art on corporate simulation models available in the USA in 1969 shows that the models have been primarily used to evaluate alternative operating or investment strategies (Gershefski 1970).

During this period, simulation of political processes gained importance. In 1959, the political parties prepared for the US presidential elections of 1960. The Democratic Party decided to have its election campaign pretested by computer simulation. In this simulation, called Simulmatics, data from 50 surveys held between 1952 and 1958 were subjected to a secondary analysis. Added to this data set were the outcomes of 16 surveys held in 1959 and early in 1960. In the simulation, 480 types of voters were distinguished. One of the dilemmas in designing the election strategy was the presentation of Kennedy's membership of the Catholic Church. Strategy one was to admit his membership in a matter-of-fact way. Strategy two was to avoid the issue as much as possible. The computer simulation focused on the reactions of voters that were put under cross-pressure by the dilemma. How would, for example, anti-Catholic Democrats react? The computer simulation predicted that the first strategy would yield the best results for the Democrats, and ultimately Kennedy did win the 1960 presidential elections. After the elections, the computer simulation was evaluated by interviewing a sample of voters. It turned out that the simulation had predicted the reactions of voters under cross-pressure in a relatively precise and reliable way. According to the research team, the favourable results were due to three factors: first, to the availability of powerful psychological and sociological theories on voter behaviour; secondly, to the enormous size of the available database; and thirdly, to the use of (for those times) powerful computers.

In 1966, people realized that two-thirds of the twentieth century had passed. What would the remaining one-third bring? Which threatening developments might be diverted into a less unfavourable direction? In many countries, scientists published explorations of the future, taking the end of the century as their time horizon. A striking example is *The Year 2000* by Kahn and Wiener (1967). The subtitle of this book, *A framework for speculation on the next thirty-three years* illustrates the scenario approach used by Kahn and Wiener:

> Scenarios are hypothetical sequences of events constructed for the purpose of focusing attention on causal processes and decision-points: (1) Precisely how might some hypothetical situation come about, step by step? (2) What alternatives exist, for each actor, at each step, for preventing, diverting or facilitating the process? (1967: 6)

Both authors had been employed by the Hudson Institute, engaged inter alia in military research. This explains why the scenario analysis by Kahn and Wiener has much in common with war games. We can discern the artificial landscapes (scenarios) of the military exercises, full of hidden opportunities and threats. We can also distinguish the alternative strategies the military commander can select, after having evaluated their consequences. The approach elaborated by Kahn and Wiener is typical of the American tradition in scenario analysis. In this tradition, the context for decision-making is represented by a scenario. Within the constraints of the context, the player selects a strategy.

At about the same time, in France, a different tradition of scenario analysis was developed, *inter alia* in the field of regional planning. In the French tradition of scenario analysis, two types of scenarios are used. A *contrast scenario* is a kind of blueprint for the future, in other words, a preferential scenario or sketch of a desirable ultimate situation of the social system at issue, including a strategy to make this design come true. The second type is a *trend scenario*. In the French tradition of scenario analysis, one or more contrast scenarios are combined with a trend scenario. A trend scenario is an extrapolation of troublesome developments in the present. A trend scenario is also called a *scenario de l'inacceptable*, literally a picture of developments that are unacceptable and therefore have to be avoided. A scenario of the unacceptable is a doomsday scenario. Policy-makers are urged to take action in order to avoid the disaster.

Both traditions in scenario analysis have their strong and weak aspects. The American tradition stimulates careful policy formation, avoiding unnecessary risk and uncertainty. This tradition tends to evoke overcautious strategies. A project co-ordinator has to prevent this negative development of the analysis. The French tradition stimulates overbold policy formation and utopian dreaming. The outcomes of scenario and strategy design are not confronted with information about the political, economic, cultural and social environment of the actor. In this tradition, too, the project co-ordinator has to intervene. Utopian dreams can be pretested by confronting them with a set of contextual scenarios. Does the principal actor have enough resources to overcome resistance in the context?

A doomsday scenario on environmental developments appeared in 1962. Rachel Carson's *Silent Spring* was a passionate exposure of the effects of indiscriminate crop dusting with insecticides – the destruction of wild life and the progressive poisoning of the human habitat. Carson was a professional biologist and a gifted journalist. No single book on our environment has done more to awaken and alarm the world. The book contributed substantially to the founding of the ecological movement. Carson assessed the ecological and social consequences of the attacks on the environment in her day. She also sketched *the other road*. In this strategy, she described the consequences of changing to a more responsible handling of nature.

In the early 1960s, western countries were in the middle of an economic boom. As a consequence, governments in North America and western Europe embarked upon large-scale innovation projects and programmes. The War on Poverty programme can be seen as an example of this development. The ambitious programme, designed by President Kennedy and put into action by President Johnson, was initiated in 1964 as *a basic attack on the problems of poverty and waste of human resources*. The main idea behind the programme was that local organizations could model the Anti-War programmes according to their own needs and preferences. However, the program did not have the planned effect, mainly due to the difficulties in attuning national policy aims to local needs. Another reason was the incompetence of federal planners in co-ordinating local activities.

Williams (1971: 3) described this planning process as follows:

Taking young black men from the ghettos to the wilderness of an isolated Job Corps Centre was not a solution in itself, as one had to worry about such mundane problems as curriculum, and accommodating these young men in a Spartan environment lacking female companionship. This atmosphere of confidence and enthusiasm ignored the fact that we had neither the benefit of experience in such programs nor much realization of the difficulties involved in developing effective techniques and getting these techniques to be used in the field.

In his evaluation of the programme, Williams (1971) asks a general question: "Does a decision to start a new program in the field rest on a sound blueprint for action derived from extensive study and testing on a small scale, or from a vaguely delineated desire to solve a problem?" (1971: 5) In the War on Poverty (WoP), the second alternative reigned. A critical missing link was empirical and conceptual information directly addressing questions of programme design, organization and operation, Williams concluded.

The WoP has turned into one of the best-documented planning disasters of this century. Social scientists like Williams have evaluated its failure at great length. The evaluation of these failures has contributed substantially to a major change in social innovation policies in western countries. The methodology for preparing and implementing social innovation projects has been improved. Policy-makers have become more careful in launching planned social change and re-organizations of social systems. The end of the 1960s has become a turning point in western countries in both politics and social research.

In a number of non-western countries, pioneering projects of social impact assessment were launched in the 1950s and 60s. Rogers (1995: 5) describes a number of these projects. One example was a village in Peru where a policy experiment on water boiling failed because the change agent was too *innovation-oriented* and not *client-oriented* enough.

In this period, most of the later *developing countries* still struggled for freedom, trying to get rid of colonial ties. The battle between colonial powers and nationalist forces was a confrontation of naked power. In periods dominated by this kind of warfare, policy-oriented research like

SIA is not likely to occur. As a consequence, in this section only SIA within developed countries is described.

2.4 Cultural protest and economic crisis: 1966–1985

In the USA about 1965, and in western Europe about 1968, a wave of cultural protest emerged. In the USA, the civil rights movement was followed by the student revolt, which in turn was followed by the protest against the war in Vietnam. In western Europe, the student revolt of May 1968 triggered a process of social change that is known as the *cultural revolution*. This movement of cultural protest has only its name in common with the revolutionary activities of the Red Guards in the People's Republic in China. The Cultural Revolution in the West has changed the developed countries drastically. It has also affected the relationship between developed and developing countries. For this reason, the late 1960s marks a major change in both types of countries.

In the USA in the late 1960s, cultural protest included the emergence of the environmental movement, triggered inter alia by Rachel Carson's book. In 1969, pressure from the environmental movement resulted in the passing by the US Congress of the National Environmental Policy Act (NEPA). The act aimed at mitigating the deterioration of the biophysical environment caused by new development. The legal requirements stated in NEPA were to be met by research activities, Environmental Impact Assessments (EIAs). These research activities, in turn, led to reports, Environmental Impact Statements (EISs).

The environmental IA process was meant to ensure political awareness of contentious environmental issues. Also, the procedures required the consideration of alternatives to the project before project approval decisions were made. Furthermore, the consequences of the project had to be taken into consideration, and the EIS had to be published.

For early efforts at EIA, no particular methodologies were specified. As a consequence, the results were far from satisfactory. In an attempt to provide a comprehensive perspective, the emphasis on the biophysical aspects of development was expanded to include socio-economic aspects as well. This triggered the incorporation of SIA in EIA. In later

EIAs, the focus is not only on biophysical, but also on demographic, social and economic aspects of the project at issue.

In 1967, Congressman Daddario called for a new form of policy research that was termed *technology assessment* (TA) which was intended to provide policy-makers with a tool for coping with the impacts of technology on society. It would systematize the identification of positive payoffs from technological innovations and foster their transfer into practice. At the same time, it would isolate potential negative consequences, thus serving as an early warning system. In 1972, the US Office for Technology Assessment (OTA) was established. The OTA was instructed to provide congressional committees with TA reports. In many cases, TA was carried out as a component of EIA (Porter et al. 1980: 33–4).

Joseph Coates (1976: 372), a leader in the TA movement, offered the following definition of a TA: ". . . a class of policy studies which systematically examine the effects on society that may occur when a technology is introduced, extended or modified. It emphasizes those consequences that are unintended, indirect, or delayed."

As a next step, SIA as a component of EIA had to be defined. Wolf (1974) argued that the "analytic problem of SIA is nothing less than that of estimating and appraising the condition of a society organized and changed by large-scale application of high technology". This definition suggests a close link between SIA and TA. As we will see later on, SIA has developed both as a separate type of policy-oriented research and as a component of IA projects primarily focusing on EIA or TA.

Since 1969, the EIA process has become common in the USA, resulting in thousands of EISs. Gradually, the production of EISs has also been introduced in a number of other countries, both in developed and developing regions. Sometimes, the activities of EIA were not yet required by law in the countries involved.

The environmental movement has been strengthened by activities of the Club of Rome. This nongovernmental organization gained an international reputation in 1972 when Dennis Meadows and his team presented *The Limits to Growth*. The book is based on a computer simulation model specifying (a) population growth, (b) food supply, (c) resource depletion, (d) capital investment and (e) pollution. Meadows advocated a number of actions to avoid global disasters, in particular excessive damage to the environment. Population growth and industrialization had reached their limits and both had to be curbed, they argued (Meadows 1972).

In 1978, a Latin American reaction appeared. Herrera et al. published *Catastrophe or a New Society?*. The analysis was published by the Bariloche Foundation, an Argentinean institution. The Bariloche Report introduced an approach that was quite different from the Meadows Report. Herrera et al. attacked poverty in the developing countries and overconsumption in the developed world. The Bariloche Report advocated a global redistribution of scarce goods. It stressed the need for high economic growth in developing countries and a restraint on economic expansion in the developed countries. The computer model in this report was based upon a specification of basic needs of each member of the world's population. The model was run up to the year 2060. Even drastic measures would not have eliminated inequality by that date. However, the increase of inequality in opportunities for an existence above an absolute minimum would be curbed (Herrera et al. 1978).

The cultural revolution in the Western world has, *inter alia*, triggered a movement for public participation. Three types of public participation emerged: first, the dispersal of information to the public; secondly, we find the provision and promotion of opportunities for interaction between the public and those responsible for developing the policy or programme; and thirdly, there is the collection of information which is useful to SIA.

How can the information collected as a result of a public participation process be used best? First, some researchers argue that such subjective information, sometimes combined with expert opinion, can be used directly to structure an explicit weighting scheme which in turn can be applied to objective data. However, such an approach tends to involve unsupported causal assumptions. It also tends to assume a monolithic homogeneous public instead of one made up of diverse and competing groups. Secondly, this information can be used as a complement to objective data and allow the two kinds of information to be synthesized by the decision-maker. The second approach holds the danger that the decision-maker will ignore the information or do the synthesis badly. Critics of public participation, as it has emerged since the 1960s, also object to its potential for elitism. Generally, only a small, interested segment of the population tends to be involved (see Burdge & Vanclay 1995; Roberts 1995).

In the years 1966–85, SIA has gone through a process of unfolding. As we saw in the beginning of the period, SIA was linked to EIA in the USA, and was required by law. Following this, SIA became a component of TA in the USA also. Gradually SIA turned into an institutionalized component of economic and fiscal IA as well. Besides being integrated in other types of IA, SIA continued to operate as a specific type of IA. I will discuss a number of examples of this process of unfolding.

A simulation model of the educational system which was denoted SOM (Simulation Option Model) was developed during 1969–70 at the Paris-based Centre of Educational Research and Innovation, which is affiliated with the Organization for Economic Co-operation and Development (OECD). SOM estimates future student stocks, future outflow from various levels of the educational system, teacher supply and real and monitory resource requirements. In general, the purpose of SOM was to be a tool for explorations of the consequences and implications of alternative educational strategies. The model has been used to explore the consequences of increasing the length of compulsory schooling in the United Kingdom (UK). The raising of the school leaving age from 15 to 16 years was a reform already decided upon. The problem which was dealt with was not the significance of the reform, but the scheduling of the introduction of this reform (Schwartz 1972).

The second example comes from the field of large dam projects. In 1970, the OECD observed that the southern European countries were about to embark upon a large number of irrigation projects without adequate concern for the return they would yield and without attempting to define what markets there might be for the production the projects would make possible. In 1971, an international team of experts, and national teams in seven member countries, were established to develop and test a *Guide to the Economic Evaluation of Irrigation Projects*. As a next step, in 1979 an international expert group was invited to design and pretest a guide to decision-making concerning multipurpose water reservoir projects. This guide had to consider social and environmental aspects as well. The members of the international team visited multipurpose water projects in both developed and developing countries. The site visits were paid to both ongoing and finished projects. A draft for a guidebook was designed. This draft was field tested by potential users in North and South America and in Europe. The final version of the guidebook was published in 1985, both in English and in French (OECD 1985).

The third example comes from the Dutch *Societal Discussion on (Nuclear) Energy Policy* held in the early 1980s. Through this societal discussion, the Dutch Parliament intended to overcome a political stalemate regarding a 1974 government proposal to expand the use of nuclear power. It comprised an 18–month expert-dominated information phase, ending in the Steering Committee's Interim Report. It also comprised a six-month nationwide discussion phase, consisting of several thousand small-group discussions yielding the completion of numerous questionnaires focused on future electric power generation. A number of research projects were conducted, for example, about:

(a) alternative socio-economic scenarios as embedding contexts for total energy demand;
(b) environmental consequences of the various energy scenarios;
(c) perceived risk from different energy sources, especially coal and nuclear energy.

In addition, science courts (called controversy sessions) were held to discuss the desired organization of large-scale gas distribution in the Netherlands; and the meaning and usefulness of risk analysis and risk perception studies. Ultimately, the nuclear disaster at Chernobyl terminated the debate in the Netherlands about nuclear energy (Vlek 1986).

During this period, much energy was put into improving SIA methodology. In 1974, Charlie Wolf formulated a simple model of the interactions in the relationship between a construction or engineering project and the impact of some aspect or phase of that project. In that model, the direct impacts represent some change in the variables describing the initial condition. The continuing effect of readjustment and adaption to change will vary from group to group. In addition, the direct impacts themselves may result in a reaction that changes the planned project. This often takes the form of public opposition. Moreover, the project is the result of a more general policy and has history in that it is the solution to some pre-existing concern or issue. The historical conditions affect public receptiveness at the point of impact and adaptation. Finally, exogenous variables, random or systematic, add to the difficulty of isolating project-associated change from

39

other changes in the socio-economic environment. Wolf's model, although very simple, is (still) a good reflection of the general flow of interactions in SIA. However, as Carley and Bustelo (1984) have pointed out, it does not try to grapple with the problem of measuring social change.

In 1977, the first edition of *Methodology of Social Impact Assessment* was published, edited by Finsterbusch and Wolf. The second edition appeared in 1981. This volume has become one of the most influential sources of SIA methodology. A flow-chart of elements in SIA is presented and various methodological problems and applications are discussed in detail. *A Guidebook for Technology Assessment and Impact Analysis*, edited by Porter et al. and published in 1980 has become a landmark in the closely related field. This guidebook includes methods for micro-assessments. A micro-assessment is any form of study that provides a quick and rough assessment at a level of effort of about one person-month or less (Porter et al. 1980: 70). The boom in methodological guidelines was continued by Finsterbusch, Llewellyn and Wolf, who edited *Social Impact Assessment Methods* in 1983. In this book, SIA methodology is closely related to the methodology of EIA.

A different approach can be found in the guideline published by OECD in 1985 on *Management of Water Projects* discussed above. The guidebook presents a model of a major multipurpose water reservoir project, spanning a period of 10–15 years. Economic, financial, environmental and social actions are specified. The step-by-step model deals with 9 major steps and more than 40 substeps of impact assessment. A special feature of this guidebook is the presentation of rules for a number of project reports. Five types of reports are described in detail:

1. *Preliminary evaluation report*: corresponds to the case of a completely new project, for which only a minimum of studies has been done, and a minimum of data has been gathered.
2. *Examination of variants report*: corresponds to the stage where the decision to undertake the project has been taken but no technical choice has been made. The problem is to make the choice in the best possible way.
3. *Selection of variants report*: has fundamentally the same purpose as the preceding report. But in this case, the studies are far more in depth and elaborated.

4. *Final ex-ante report*: corresponds to the stage of the feasibility study; it describes the choices which have been made, and their expected consequences; it will be the basis of comparison for further ex-post studies.

5. *Ex-post evaluation report*: has two purposes: first, to examine all possible discrepancies between forecasts and observed trends, and to analyze their sources and consequences; second, to prepare for any decision of changing the plan previously accepted, in order to adapt it to new circumstances.

In this period in the development of SIA, the co-operation between IA, including SIA, and basic social science was established. Ex-post evaluation of forecasts, IAs and related types of futures analysis and exploration developed into a distinct research programme. The major stimulus for this development was the publication in 1978 of Ascher's book on *Forecasting: An Appraisal for Policy-Makers and Planners*. Ascher evaluated a large number of projects in population forecasting, economic forecasting, energy forecasting, transportation forecasting and technological forecasting. He developed a framework for identifying correlates of accuracy. Ascher concluded:

> The findings on the correlates of accuracy are consistent with a simple proposition: The core assumptions underlying a forecast, which represent the forecaster's basic outlook on the context within which the specific forecasted trend develops, are the major determinants of forecast accuracy (Ascher 1978: 199).

The need for appropriate core assumptions makes the problem of *assumption drag* particularly important. Assumption drag is the reliance on old core assumptions. According to Ascher (1978: 202), it has been the source of some of the most drastic errors in forecasting.

2.5 Towards sustainability: 1986 and beyond

In the mid-1980s, the economic recession, after raging worldwide, slowed down and the first signs of an economic recovery became visible.

In West Germany, school-leaver unemployment decreased sharply, an indication of new economic growth. Shortly afterwards, in a number of other Western countries, inter alia the Netherlands, a revival of economic vitality also took place. The decline of economic hardship paved the way for a reconsideration of long-term developments and an evaluation of the quality of life on this planet. A timely contribution to this reconsideration was the report of the World Commission on Environment and Development, an independent group of experts called together by the United Nations (UN). *Our Common Future*, published in 1987, has become a landmark in the discussion on environmental, economic and social concerns. In everyday life, its publication became known as the Brundtland Report, named after its chairperson, Gro Harlem Brundtland, Prime Minister of Norway. In 1983, the Commission was asked to formulate *a global agenda for change*. It was an urgent call by the General Assembly of the United Nations:

(a) to propose long-term environmental strategies for achieving sustainable development by the year 2000 and beyond;

(b) to recommend ways by which concern for the environment would be translated into greater co-operation among developing countries and between countries at different stages of economic and social development and lead to the achievement of common and mutually supportive objectives that take account of the interrelationships between people, resources, environment, and development;

(c) to consider ways and means by which the international community can deal more effectively with environmental concerns;

(d) to help define shared perceptions of long-term environmental issues and the appropriate efforts needed to deal successfully with the problems of protecting and enhancing the environment, a long-term agenda for action during the coming decades and aspirational goals for the world community.

During the time the Commission met, such tragedies as major African famines, the leak at the chemical factory at Bhopal, India, and the nuclear disaster at Chernobyl, USSR, appeared to justify the grave predictions about the human future that were becoming commonplace during the mid-1980s. But at public hearings held on five continents, the Commission also heard from the individual victims of more chronic,

42

widespread disasters: the debt crisis, stagnating aid to and investment in developing countries, falling commodity prices and falling personal incomes. The members of the Commission became convinced that major changes were needed, both in attitudes and in the way our societies are organized.

The questions of population – of population pressure, of population and human rights and the links between these related issues and poverty, environment and development – have proved to be the more difficult concerns. Another such concern was the whole area of international economic relations.

The Commission summarized the outcomes of its analysis as follows:

> Many critical survival issues are related to uneven development, poverty, and population growth. They all place unprecedented pressures on the planet's lands, waters, forests, and other natural resources, not least in the developing countries. The downward spiral of poverty and environmental degradation is a waste of opportunities and of resources. In particular, it is a waste of human resources. These links between poverty, inequality, and environmental degradation formed a major theme in our analysis and recommendations. What is needed now is a new era of economic growth – growth that is forceful and at the same time socially and environmentally sustainable (World Commission on Environment and Development 1987: xii).

Sustainable development, according to the Commission, is "development that meets the needs of the present without compromising the ability of future generations to meet their own needs" (WCED, 1987: 43). It contains within it two key concepts: (1) the concept of *needs*, in particular the needs of the world's poor, to which overriding priority should be given; and (2) the idea of limitations imposed by the state of technology and social organizations on the environment's ability to meet present and future needs.

The Commission stressed the importance of keeping within the limits of the *physical carrying capacities* of the environment. It also emphasized the importance of *social carrying capacities*. Human resource development demands knowledge and skills to help people improve their economic performance. Sustainable development requires changes in values and attitudes towards environment and development, towards society and work at home, on farms and in factories. Education should also be geared towards making people more capable of dealing with problems of overcrowding and excessive population densities. Improvement of social carrying capacities is essential to prevent ruptures in the social fabric, and schooling should enhance the levels of tolerance and empathy required for living in a crowded world (World Commission on Environment and Development 1987: 112).

The Commission presented a strategy for sustainable development that aimed to promote harmony among human beings and between humanity and nature. In the specific context of the developmental and environmental crises of the 1980s, which current national and international political and economic institutions have not and perhaps cannot overcome, the pursuit of sustainable development requires:

(a) a political system that secures effective citizen participation in decision-making;
(b) an economic system that is able to generate surpluses and technical knowledge on a self-reliant and sustained basis;
(c) a social system that provides solutions for the tensions arising from disharmonious development;
(d) a production system that respects the obligations to preserve the ecological base for development;
(e) a technological system that can search continuously for new solutions;
(f) an international system that fosters sustainable patterns of trade and finance;
(g) an administrative system that is flexible and has the capacity for self-correction.

These requirements are goals that should underlie national and international action on development. What matters is the sincerity with which these goals are pursued and the effectiveness with which departures from them are corrected (World Commission on Environment and Development 1987: 65).

As a result of the World Commission Report, the concept of sustainability has entered everyday language all over the world. The Commission has presented reasonable claims and as a consequence, its report has been accepted as a basis for discussion on a relatively broad scale. The proposition of sustainable growth was acceptable to many countries that would have refused to consider an economic future without any growth. The Commission has come forward with a balanced analysis of ecological, economic and social growth and development.

However, a convincing analysis and a suitable terminology are only a first step. The second step was the Earth Summit at Rio de Janeiro in 1992, an attempt to translate the conclusions of the Brundtland Report into political action. The third step was the UN conference on population development, held in 1994 at Cairo.

In 1986 and the years that followed, the movement for public participation in decision-making concerning local, regional and national development continued. Expectations about results became more realistic, methods were improved and legislation became more sophisticated. In these years, a related movement emerged. Organizations discovered that their survival depends on their capacity to cope with turbulence in their political, economic and social environment. *Strategic learning*, also called organizational learning, entered the scene. A multinational oil company, Shell, experimented with this method and published widely about its experiences. Strategic learning always incorporates an IA of current or future actions of the organization at issue. In most cases, strategic learning includes participation of all members of the organization. Strategic learning within an organization can be combined with public participation in shaping its strategy, as political parties have discovered.

The period exhibited a further unfolding of SIA, both as a specific type of assessment and as a component of integrated assessment. As an example, I mention the assessment of tourism impacts. In developed and developing countries alike, the quest for *sustainable tourism* emerged. Large-scale tourism increasingly threatened the natural environment of tropical and subtropical regions. Islands wanted to protect their coral reefs, threatened by amateur divers. Alpine regions also started to protest. They wanted to preserve their meadows, threatened by excessive skiing. On the other hand, economic interests were at stake. Many of the threatened regions depend on the income tourism provides. New projects for stimulating tourism are more likely to be submitted to IA now, looking at physical, economic and social consequences.

From the mid-1980s onwards, SIA has gained in importance in both developed and developing countries. Increasingly, development projects like large dams show not only physical planning but also economic, ecological and social planning. Later on, I shall discuss practical experiences, inter alios, by the World Bank.

Since the mid-1980s, EIA is legally required not only in North America but also in Australia and in most countries in South America, Asia, Africa and Europe. In most cases, the law demands not only an assessment of the consequences of actions for the physical environment but also an assessment of economic and social impacts.

Following the example of the US National Court of Audits, many countries in western Europe, *inter alia* the Netherlands, require that all major government actions have to be accompanied by programme evaluation or similar types of ex-ante and ex-post evaluation. Governments have discovered that they too have to learn (Leeuw, et al. 1994).

In this period, the institutionalization of IA continued substantially. The International Association for Impact Assessment expanded both as a formal organization and as an informal social network offering opportunities for the exchange of information and the dissemination of professional knowledge and know-how. In 1990, the International Association for Public Participation Practitioners (IAP3) was established, to serve as a focal point for networking about public involvement activity and techniques.

The period yielded a volume on methods for social analysis in developing countries. In this book, Finsterbusch, Ingersoll and Llewellyn (1990) describe how to apply the basic methods of fieldwork, surveys and demographic analysis under the constraining conditions researchers are facing in developing countries. It presents low-cost, rapid methods that can quickly provide information to guide decisions and policy-making.

Between 1985 and 1995, two major new textbooks appeared. Taylor, Bryan and Goodrich (1990) described social assessment theory and practice. Their approach has been developed from international practice and training, and focuses on the New Zealand and US experiences. A second edition was published in 1995. During this time, Rabel Burdge (1994a) presented a community guide to SIA, concentrating on experiences in the USA.

A landmark in the history of SIA was the appearance in 1994 of

Guidelines and Principles for Social Impact Assessment, mentioned earlier. The collective author, the US Inter-organizational Committee on Guidelines and Principles for Social Impact Assessment, wrote this monograph with the purpose of outlining a set of guidelines and principles that will assist agencies and private interest groups in fulfilling their obligations under NEPA, related authorities and agency mandates. Their document has informed much discussion of SIA (e.g., Burdge & Vanclay 1995), including this book, and will be addressed later.

Since 1986, achievements in basic social research have substantially enhanced the potentialities of SIA. First, I will take a look at demographic research. Most SIAs include a submodel on population processes based on national demographic forecasts. Keilman (1990) analyzed uncertainty in national population forecasting using ex-post evaluation. He developed a separation model for the analysis of period, duration and jump-off year related to errors of population forecasts. He also presented an explanatory model for ex-post observed forecast errors. The ex-post evaluation of forecasts in the Netherlands shows that errors in age structures exhibit a very regular pattern. The pattern is that of large errors at young and high ages, and only minor errors for age groups between 20 and 75 years.

In the second place, a comparative ex-post evaluation of forecasts in a number of sectors in society demands our attention. Dewulf (1991) explored the limits of forecasting and developed a theory of forecast errors. He tested hypotheses derived from the theory on educational forecasts in the Netherlands and human resource forecasts in the USA and the Netherlands. Dewulf concluded that accuracy of forecasts primarily correlates with the availability and the characteristics of the data, the methods and techniques used, complexity and stability of the system and the forecaster's characteristics. This implies that the accuracy of forecasts can be predicted in quite a reliable and precise way.

In 1976 in the Netherlands, scenarios on the future of the position of women in Dutch society and on the consequences of emancipation policies were published. In 1990, Schoonenboom and Langeveld presented an evaluation of this scenario analysis. They used four evaluation criteria: (1) did the scenario provide a frame of reference for public discussion? (2) did public discussion take place within the margins of this framework? (3) to what extent did empirical developments follow the lines drawn in the exploration of the future? and (4) what were the consequences of government policies related to the emancipation of women? The evaluation showed that the scenarios had indeed provided a framework for public debate. One exception has to be mentioned, however. In 1976, physical violence against women was not a public issue, and therefore this issue was missing in the scenarios. Social reality followed the trend scenario, not one of the contrast scenarios presented in the original analysis. Government policies concerning the emancipation of women showed very limited impacts only.

The book *The Limits to Growth* (Meadows 1972) was followed in 1991 by *Beyond the Limits*. In this sequel to the first report to the Club of Rome, Donella Meadows, D. L. Meadows and J. Randers. present an exploration of the future that again stresses the consequences of exponential growth. In 1991, the world population growth was 1.7 per cent per year. At this rate, the population of the world will double every 40 years, and in less industrialized countries, the urban population will double every 20 years. Even if, from 1995 on, no woman would have more than two children, the world population would still grow at least until the year 2100. *Beyond the Limits* documents approximately the same warnings as *Our Common Future* (World Commission on Environment and Development 1987) and the Cairo conference of 1993 on world population developments.

Since 1985, the database for SIA has further improved. Data archives provide information on variables that can be used to construct social indicators. International organizations like the UN and many national governments publish social indicator reports on a regular basis. Improvements in the monitoring of impacts imply that SIA can rely increasingly on data that have already been collected.

Parallel to the growth of SIA, the analysis of risk is further institutionalized. Both actual risk and risk awareness are assessed. Risk awareness is closely linked to social development, because if people perceive phenomena as real, they perceive their consequences to be real. Public participation in particular has to take risk awareness into consideration. Risk management has become standard procedure in most major organizations.

Last, but not least, I want to pay attention to developments in scenario analysis. Improved data, models and (methods of) data processing have prepared the ground for the emergence of advanced futures explorations using scenarios. My first example is *Head to Head*, looking at the coming competition between Japan, Europe and America. In this book, Thurow (1992) looks at the dismantling of the Berlin Wall in 1989, the implosion of the USSR in 1991 and the emergence of three economic superpowers. A dynamic assessment is presented of the rules of this new three-way competition, the strengths and weaknesses of the players and their opportunities to win the battle.

In the same year, the Netherlands Central Planning Bureau published the outcomes of a long-term scenario study of the world economy 1990–2015. *Scanning the Future* (Central Planning Bureau 1992) starts with the presentation of a prosperity circle, which sets forth three partly competitive, partly complementary perspectives on economic development, originating from the economic schools of thought founded by Adam Smith, John Maynard Keynes and Joseph Schumpeter. This framework provides the organizing principles of the study. Based on this circle, the study tries to assess the current strengths and weaknesses of the major regions of the world economy. Trends are analyzed which will influence the future development of the world economy, including such topics as demography, technology, the environment, world food supply, internationalization and international co-operation.

The core of the study is the way in which the prosperity circle and analyses of comparative strengths and trends are combined, culminating in four scenarios of how the world economy may develop in the next decades. I will discuss these scenarios later on. At this moment, I want to draw attention to only one aspect of this scenario analysis. According to the Netherlands Central Planning Bureau, the most likely scenario, *global shift* could only be avoided if, in about the year 2005, a major event would shock the Europeans into action. In other words, *only a disaster could save Europe*. Provided of course that the disaster keeps within certain limits.

In 1991, The World Bank published its *Environmental Assessment Sourcebook*. This methodological guidebook includes a chapter on *Social and Cultural Issues in Environmental Review*. A state of the art of SIA, focusing on SIA *in the context of appropriate national, state, or provincial environmental policy legislation* was published by Burdge and Vanclay in 1995.

2.6 Summary

The origins of SIA as an art-science are situated in the seventeenth century, introducing demographic and health IA based on scientific analyses. The years between 1800 and 1945 were characterized by industrialization and confrontation. In this period more examples can be found of investigations for the purpose of making a rational choice between alternative actions. The future consequences of health care policies and social security policies were explored, *inter alia*, in France and the UK. Research in the military field led to the improvement of war games, which in turn stimulated simulation of alternative strategies in other parts of society.

Between 1945 and 1965, the international order was fundamentally restructured. Most of the (later) developing countries still struggled for freedom in those years, trying to get rid of colonial ties. In the (later) developed countries, the application of science in politics and in the management of commercial and nonprofit organizations increased. Incidentally, social strategies were pre-tested by simulations. Nevertheless, in many cases, planned social change led to disillusionment, for instance the War on Poverty (WoP) in the USA.

The years 1966–1985 brought a wave of cultural protest and a severe economic crisis. The cultural protest included the emergence of the environmental movement. In 1969, the protests resulted in the passing by the US Congress of the National Environmental Policy Act (NEPA). Early efforts at environmental impact assessment (EIA) proved to be far from satisfactory. In an attempt to provide a comprehensive perspective, the emphasis on the biophysical aspects of development was expanded to include socio-economic aspects as well. This triggered the incorporation of SIAs in EIA. In the early 1970s, simulation models on an international and a national scale entered the scene. Meadows et al. presented a world model on the limits to growth, incorporating a simulation of demographic aspects. The OECD introduced simulations on the consequences of national educational reforms and regional development programmes like the building of large dams and reservoirs. The methodology for IAs was inaugurated.

In 1986 and the years beyond, the quest for sustainability increasingly dominated the scene. The World Commission on Environment and Development Report (1987) demanded sustainable growth, that is development that meets the needs of the present without compromising the ability of future generations to meet their own needs. In this period, strategic learning emerged, incorporating SIA in interventions that were characterized by a participatory approach. In a number of developed countries, SIA became compulsory with regard to government actions, *inter alia* in order to prevent the squandering of taxpayers' money. In developing countries, large projects, *inter alia* for constructing large dams and reservoirs, were more and more prepared by policy-oriented research, including SIA at the request of funding agencies like the World Bank. In this period, the methodology for SIA was further improved, in particular because ex-post evaluations of SIA studies became available.

CHAPTER 3

Methods for the preliminary phase in SIA

3.1 Introduction

Until the early 1980s, social impact assessors had little methodology of their own. They had to use methods developed for simulations (e.g. Julien et al. 1975). In the 1980s, SIA gradually acquired a methodology of its own. Early versions of SIA methodology discussed a number of key issues, but did not focus systematically on major methodological pitfalls (Finsterbusch et al. 1983; Porter et al. 1980). For instance, problem analysis, project design, reporting and ex-post evaluation were dealt with in passing, or not at all. In order to avoid these shortcomings, more and more textbooks adopted a flow-chart approach. The first textbooks following this approach started with a limited application. Over the years, the use of step-by-step models increased. An early example is the textbook by Taylor et al. (1990). Burdge (1994b) also adopts detailed flow-charts from environmental impact assessment (EIA).

A watershed in this development was the report by the Inter-organizational Committee, already discussed in Chapter 2, that stressed that a SIA should contain ten steps. These steps are logically sequential, but often overlap in practice. The scheme of steps reads as follows:

1. *Public involvement*: Develop an effective public involvement plan to involve all potentially affected publics.
2. *Identification of alternatives*: Describe the proposed action or policy change and reasonable alternatives.

3. *Baseline conditions*: Describe the relevant human environment/area of influence and baseline conditions.
4. *Scoping*: After obtaining a technical understanding of the proposal, identify the full range of probable social impacts that will be addressed based on discussion or interviews with numbers of all potentially affected.
5. *Projection of estimated effects*: Investigate the probable impacts. Among other things this step includes straight-line trend analysis, scenarios, expert testimony, computer modelling and calculation of futures foregone.
6. *Predicting responses to impacts*: Determine the significance of the identified social impacts.
7. *Indirect and cumulative impacts*: Estimate subsequent impacts and cumulative impacts.
8. *Changes in alternatives*: Recommend new or changed alternatives and estimate or project their consequences.
9. *Mitigation*: Develop a mitigation plan.
10. *Monitoring*: Develop a monitoring program.

The flow-chart shows a close fit with earlier flow-charts (e.g. OECD 1985). For this reason, the plausibility of the guidelines of the Interorganizational Committee is relatively high. Despite this, it has a few shortcomings. In my opinion, a problem analysis step ought to be separately identified in the flow-chart as the first step. SIA has to start with an analysis of the social problem to identify impacts that actions of the central policy-maker could eliminate or mitigate. If impact assessors accept actions at face value, they might find that they are assessing the future consequences of an intervention that is impractical or morally wrong.

The flow-chart of steps is underpinned by a set of guiding principles. They include:

1. *Involve the diverse public*: Identify and involve all potentially affected groups and individuals.
2. *Analyze impact equity*: clearly identify who will win and who will lose, and emphasize vulnerability and underrepresented groups.
3. *Focus the assessment*: Deal with issues and public concerns that really count, not those that are just easy to deal with.
4. *Identify methods and assumptions and define significance*: Describe how

the SIA is conducted, what assumptions are used and how significance is determined.

5. *Provide feedback on social impacts to project planners*: Identify problems that could be solved with changes to the proposed action or alternatives.

6. *Use SIA practitioners*: Trained social scientists employing social science methods will provide the best results.

7. *Establish monitoring and mitigation programmes*: Manage uncertainty by monitoring and mitigating adverse impacts.

8. *Identify data sources*: Use published scientific literature, secondary data and primary data from the affected area.

9. *Plan for gaps in data*: Evaluate the missing information and develop a strategy for proceeding.

Maybe a tenth principle ought to be added, advocating an ex-post evaluation of the SIA with an eye on the improvement of methods in SIA in general. This has also been suggested by Burdge and Vanclay (1995).

The Inter-organizational Committee has concentrated its guidelines and principles on the SIA section of an environmental impact statement. As we will see in this and the next chapter, the benchmarks proposed by the Committee can be matched with general rules for conducting SIA without many problems.

In this book, I want to elaborate upon the scheme presented by the Inter-organizational Committee. I will develop a step-by-step model that provides methodological guidelines for a large-scale project of SIA. In Chapter 6, I will explain how this set of rules can be transformed into a methodology for instant projects and medium-sized SIA studies. I have divided the guidelines into two parts, the first part dealing with the preliminary phase and the second part dealing with the main phase of a SIA study. The preliminary phase of the study advances up to a point where the research process can still be terminated without excessive negative consequences, social as well as financial. In Chapter 4, methods for the main phase in SIA will be discussed. Figure 3.1 summarizes the steps to be taken in the preliminary phase.

Step 1.0 Problem analysis and communication and involvement strategy
    1.1 Analysis and definition of the problem
    1.2 Design of a communication and involvement strategy
    1.3 Preliminary definition of the research problem
    1.4 Iteration and reporting

Step 2.0 Systems analysis
    2.1 Identification of the system
    2.2 Design of the conceptual model
    2.3 Iteration and reporting

Step 3.0 Baseline analysis and scoping
    3.1 Formulation of research questions for the baseline analysis
    3.2 Scanning and evaluation of current knowledge about the problem
    3.3 Time perspective
    3.4 Further eleboration of the theoretical model
    3.5 Data gathering
    3.6 Data analysis, explanation and interpretation
    3.7 Iteration and reporting

Step 4.0 Trend analysis and monitoring design
    4.1 Identification of trends
    4.2 Design of monitoring
    4.3 Further elaboration of the theoretical model
    4.4 Data gathering
    4.5 Data analysis, explanation and interpretation
    4.6 Iteration and reporting

Step 5.0 Project design
    5.1 Formulation of the research questions for the main phase of the SIA project
    5.2 Design of the main phase of the SIA
    5.3 Formation of the project team
    5.4 Planning of the main phase of the SIA project (financial resources, time)
    5.5 Iteration and reporting

Figure 3.1 Flow-chart of the initial steps in a large-scale SIA project.

3.2 Problem analysis and communications strategy

3.2.1 Analysis of the problem

SIA deals with the consequences of a current or future action, as stated in Chapter 1. An action implies that an actor has defined a problem. I define the problem of an actor as a discrepancy between a desired situation or process and an actual situation or process.

Problem setting is a process involving a number of steps. Majone and Quade (1980: 9–10) characterize this process as:

> Analysis usually starts with something less structured than a problem, namely, a problem situation. This is an awareness that things are not as they should be, but without a clear understanding of the nature of the difficulties and of how they might be solved. Problem setting is the intellectual process by which a problem situation is translated into a specific problem. Typical stages of this process are systems definition, systems diagnosis, and goal setting.

In an SIA study, the practical problem has to be analyzed and defined (step 1.1). The assessor has to gather information on: (a) the desired situations and processes, (b) the actual situations and processes, (c) the perceived discrepancies, (d) the actors who perceive the discrepancies, and (e) the reasons why actors perceive the discrepancies. Generally, more than one actor is involved.

The desired situation or process is closely related to the objectives of the central actor. In general, we are talking about an organization that has a mission statement, strategies, tactics and operational planning. The central actor has to determine, what they (a) would prefer as a future situation or process, (b) would be willing to tolerate as a future situation or process, and (c) would reject as a future situation or process. Because it is unlikely that the ideal development is within reach of the central actor, the area of tolerance marks the boundaries for negotiations and operations.

The desired situation is also related to the target actor. What would they like to happen? What would they be willing to tolerate? What would they refuse to accept? In Figure 3.2, a table is presented that can

Actor	(Other) actor	Objective towards (other actor)
Central actor 1	self	
	2	
	3	
	etc.	
Actor 2	self	
	1	
	3	
	etc.	
Actor 3	self	
	1	
	2	
	etc.	
Ect.	etc.	

Figure 3.2   Actors-to-objectives analysis.

assist the impact assessor in summarizing the analysis so far. The *actors-to-objectives* scheme is also a first step towards the conceptual model to be designed later.

Figure 3.2 illustrates that more than one formulation of a problem may be proposed. Conflicting interests and conflicting historical perspectives may lead to lack of consensus concerning the problem formulation. The impact assessor will have to take seriously the diverging interpretations of the practical problem.

As an evaluator, the impact assessor is in a position to formulate a definition of the problem. In this role, the impact assessor is acting as a social critic. The impact assessor is not supposed to accept the action proposed by the central actor at face value. If the central actor has selected an inferior action, the impact assessor must be able to warn this actor. The impact assessor ought to inform the central actor about suboptimal future actions. This is an essential part of the role of the impact assessor.

In order to get a reliable overview of the definitions of the problem that circulate in the central organization and the target system, it is often wise to assemble a number of discussion groups and to invite them to produce problem formulations. The impact assessor then analyzes the intra- and intergroup consensus concerning the formulation of the problem. A high degree of discrepancy suggests various specific project designs, *inter alia* participatory approaches.

The actual situation or process is dominated by trends from the past, and major events changing the direction and the strength of the trends. In the problem analysis, these trends are not yet included.

The discrepancy between ideal and reality is relevant for the discussion about policy formation. Should the problem be left alone? Does the central actor have enough resources and instruments to reduce the discrepancy? What would be the consequences of intervention? The last question marks the relationship between the problem and IA.

Discussing the problem and putting a description of the problem on paper is by no means an easy task. The problem definition is a preliminary answer to all the questions relevant to the SIA study. We can compare the problem definition with a set of hypotheses.

When a central actor is confronted with a sophisticated definition of the problem, the reaction is often an overbold one. The definition suggests to the central actor that the problem has been sufficiently enlightened already. No wonder! Just as hypotheses are preliminary answers to research questions, a definition of a practical problem can easily be mistaken for the outcomes of a full-scale study of policy-oriented social research (Becker et al. 1981).

Problem analysis and problem solving have a long history in the literature on methodology and epistemology. In SIA, we only work with these parts of the literature if we are confronted with a very complex problem, or if we want to include discipline-oriented research in our project. The classical source of ideas is *Human Problem Solving* by Newell and Simon (1972). Newell and Simon discuss not only practical problems, but also knowledge problems. Lack of knowledge and lack of skill may also require solutions.

If very complex interdisciplinary societal problems have to be defined and solved, the impact assessor is advised to apply *Systems Dynamics*, mapping the problem in a computer model and exploring solutions in a systematic way (De Tombe 1994). In this flow-chart for social impact assessment, I will not describe these approaches in detail.

Major pitfalls in problem analysis are:

(a) arriving at a problem formulation that is too broad for the IA study; the practical problem could not be analyzed within the human and financial resources and the time available for the study;

(b) presenting a problem formulation that is incomplete; an example is provided by analyses that leave out important background variables;

(c) arriving at a problem formulation that is not precise enough, resulting in misunderstanding between policy-makers and research team;

(d) premature problem formulation; in this case, important aspects of the problem situation are discovered (too) late in the study (Becker et al. 1981: 46).

3.2.2 Design of a communication strategy

The impact assessors must establish a flow of information between themselves and both the central actor and the target actor. At the beginning of the study, only a limited amount of information requirements can be specified. Much information has to be gathered later.

Generally, receiving information has to be combined with providing information. If people co-operate in assembling information, they expect to be kept informed themselves. This kind of involvement does not yet imply participation in negotiations of decision-making, however. This raises the question of involvement: which individuals in the central organization will be consulted? Who will actually participate in the assessment process and in decision-making?

The requirement for public participation is not necessarily implicit in all cases, as is made clear in the following example. If a political party of a western democratic country was interested in an assessment of one (or more) of its possible future policies (interventions) before endorsing them, the idea of *public participation* in this assessment would not be appropriate. In this case, the assessment study might be carried out by a commercial research consultancy, and the report would be restricted. On the basis of the assessment they might decide to abandon that policy.

If a future intervention relates to a development process, such as building a large dam, an airport or a new town, public involvement is evidently necessary, and is required by law in more than half of the countries on earth – especially because these processes are partly environmental, partly social. If a future intervention concerns social systems, like the social security system, health care, care for the elderly or related situations, then in a limited number of countries, public involvement in SIA is standard practice, or at least is becoming more and more a normal aspect of public policy-making.

I will return to the subject of public involvement in Chapter 6. In any case, the design and implementation of a communication strategy, either a restricted or a broad one, has to take place at the very beginning of the SIA study. It has to take place simultaneously with the problem analysis.

Pitfalls in designing a communications strategy are:

(a) forgetting about communications when the SIA study has started; concentrating too much on doing research and producing the report; developing only tokenistic communications strategies;

(b) overlooking opportunities for involving potential allies in the central organization, or for involving the public in the target system, thereby missing opportunities for turning the study into a learning process;

(c) introducing public involvement or other kinds of participation in processes that are not suited for this; overtaxing people concerning their ability and motivation to participate;

(d) forgetting that public involvement or other kinds of participation require systematic follow-up.

3.2.3 Preliminary definition of the research problem

Next the research problem to be answered in the SIA study has to be defined in a preliminary way (step 1.3). The preliminary version of the research problem is required before systems analysis can take place. We have to keep in mind that the formulations of the questions to be answered in the baseline analysis represent a summary of knowledge already available regarding the history of the problem the SIA is dealing with. In areas that still constitute blank spots in social science knowledge, research activities are general explorations trying to map the open space. However, most areas already have a long research tradition. Each new piece of knowledge increases our capacity to formulate focused questions in the next study.

In mature problem areas, description is more or less a routine activity. Here, explanation and interpretation should receive the lion's share of attention and time budget. Mature problem areas in policy-oriented research enable social researchers to formulate hypotheses and to put predictions derived from hypotheses to an empirical test.

In exploratory research, no methodological stipulation impedes the social researcher from reformulating the research questions of the study. On the contrary, reformulation has to produce an optimal fit between research questions and empirical data. The research contract only puts limits to the process of reformulation of the questions.

Baseline analyses in SIA in most cases include ex-post evaluations of policy activities that have taken place in the past. How have the policy activities been launched and to what extent were they carried out as planned? Discrepancies between intervention-as-planned and actual intervention are no exception. What have been the effects and side effects of the policy activities? What have been their costs and benefits?

If reports on ex-post evaluations are available, an auditing of these reports has to be incorporated in the set of research questions. The same applies to old ex-ante evaluations. What has been the reliability of their futures explorations and forecasts? How can we explain the degree of reliability they have achieved? The latter analysis is a crucial one. SIA has to take account of the experiences gained with this type of policy-oriented research in the past. What have successful approaches been and can they be continued? What have mistakes been and how can they be avoided in new studies?

3.2.4 Iteration and reporting

Iteration (step 1.4) may seem a superfluous addition to the flow chart, however this aspect is often forgotten. In large SIA studies, five to ten *feedback loops* in problem analysis and the initial part of communication processes are required.

The assessor will also have to report on the problem analysis and the communication strategy (step 1.4. continued). As a rule, two reports will be prepared: one unclassified, the other confidential. The problem definition will often include information that might harm the position of the central actor because in many cases contradictory definitions of the practical problem have been put on paper.

3.3 Systems analysis

3.3.1 Identification of the system

The formulation of the practical problem has already elucidated to some extent the social systems involved. We are confronted in SIA with a central (or focal) system that is the organization of the central (or focal) actor. The central system is surrounded by a network of related social actors. First, the assessor has to identify the boundaries of the system. Next, the principal subsystems need to be identified.

Before this stage, the central actor has announced a plan of action. What are the most likely consequences of this action? Identifying the potential consequences in a preliminary way is called *scoping*.

Following scoping, the impact assessor executes a SWOT analysis for each actor identified in the *actors-to-objectives* scheme (see Fig. 3.2). SWOT stands for strengths, weaknesses, opportunities and threats. The outcomes of the SWOT analysis are summarized in an actors-to-constraints table (see Table 3.3).

In some SIA studies, the SWOT analysis is a research activity that requires little time – a quick overview is that is needed. In other studies, the SWOT analysis is a major component of the study as a whole. If an elaborate SWOT analysis is necessary, a number of parallel sessions will have to be organized to get a preliminary overview. Next, documents will have to be analyzed and interviews held. Following this, the preliminary information is elaborated into a causal model. Hypotheses derived from this model are tested using standard procedures of research methodology. The impact assessor will continue the SWOT

Actors	Strengths	Weaknesses	Opportunities	Threats
Central actor 1				
Actor 2				
Actor 3				
Etc.				

Figure 3.3 SWOT analysis.

analysis until the activities of the principal actors in the model are able to be predicted.

3.3.2 Design of the conceptual model

Next, the impact assessor needs a conceptual model or conceptual map, which is elaborated during a conceptual mapping session. A conceptual mapping session is a brainstorming session with participants selected from the SIA study team and from the *sympathetic audiences*, but not *devil's advocates*, who come later.

The first version of the conceptual model shows logical relationships. The concepts or hypotheses listed on the blackboard are linked by lines that indicate *some* connection. Techniques for this kind of conceptual modelling are provided by Systems Dynamics. An example of this comes from an analysis of the spreading of AIDS (see Fig. 3.4).

The next version of the conceptual model already shows arrows, indicating hunches about causal relationships. In Figure 3.5, an example is given which comes from a social impact study (including a scenario analysis) on the greying of the Netherlands and its consequences for health care policy (Hollander & Becker 1987).

An elucidating example of conceptual mapping is provided by

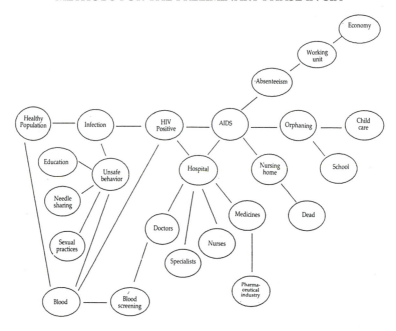

Source: De Tombe 1994: 275 (adjusted).

Figure 3.4 Conceptual model of a baseline analysis on AIDS.

Vennix (1996). He presents a project of group model building using Systems Dynamics. The project was focused on the problem of the Dutch-registered merchant fleet. Before the Second World War the Netherlands played an important role in the maritime transporation of goods all over the world. Since the War, however, the situation has changed drastically. The decrease of the Dutch share in the world merchant fleet has been caused by differences between countries with regard to wages, financial policies and safety requirements. For economic reasons many shipowners resorted to so-called *flags of convenience* (e.g. Liberia and Panama). In the 1970s Dutch government started to protect the Dutch-registered merchant fleet by means of investment premiums and tax incentives. At first the policy seemed a success. In the mid-1980s the Dutch government was forced to introduce new financial aid programmes, however, in order to encourage vessels to

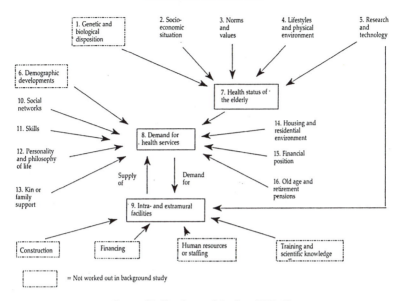

Source: Hollander and Becker 1987: 40.

Figure 3.5 Scheme of clusters of variables from a baseline analysis on health and aging, indicating the direction of relationships.

continue to fly the Dutch flag and to maintain employment in the maritime sector. After 1990 the decline of the Dutch fleet started again. This time the government was not inclined to continue or expand financial support to the Dutch-registered merchant fleet. The Secretary of Finance and the Secretary of Transportation seriously considered ceasing financial aid to the Dutch-registered merchant fleet (Vennix 1996: 12).

In the Department of Transportation, Vennix reports, three groups were involved in the preparation of a policy document on the financial future of the support for the Dutch fleet. The Sea Fleet Policy Unit advocated a continuation of financial aid to the merchant fleet. Another group, responsible for further innovation in the main ports (e.g. Rotterdam and Amsterdam), maintaining safety and gearing activities and transportation modalities to one another, opposed further financial aid to the merchant fleet. A third group, concerned with the advancement of safe and swift shipping traffic in the North Sea, shared this opinion. In the view of the latter two groups the Dutch fleet was *history*. Policy issues related to Dutch ports and the Dutch coast would prove to be much more critical in a rapidly changing world (Vennix 1996: 12).

In 1992 Vennix was invited to conduct a couple of model building sessions because the three groups could not reach a consensual decision. The second and third group saw the *fleet problem* as an isolated phenomenon, largely unrelated to other strategic problems. Vennix succeeded in convincing the three groups that model building might clarify the problem. Much to the surprise of the participants, in three sessions of three hours each, guided by a facilitator, they constructed a model which demonstrated that all three strategic areas were strictly interrelated. A decision taken in any of the three areas would severely affect the other two. Vennix concludes:

> More specifically the model revealed that abandoning the Dutch fleet might in the long run also damage the other two strategic areas (particularly the position of the Dutch harbours), an insight the group had not realized before. The group model-building process thus catalyzed strategic discussions, and consensus was reached during these three sessions to try to maintain support for the Dutch fleet. As a result, a policy document was drafted . . . requesting the financial support for the Dutch fleet be continued. This document was discussed by the Lower and Higher Chambers [of Parliament]. Obviously the arguments in the document were convincing, because it was decided that subsidies for the Dutch merchant fleet would be continued, albeit for a limited period of five years (Vennix, 1996: 13).

Designing a conceptual map requires paying attention to a wide range of aspects of a problem and its setting. In very complete situations it is unlikely that one individual or one working group will be able to produce a valid model, providing an adequate basis for further analysis.

In order to get a valid version of the conceptual model a number of (around three) parallel working groups have to be formed. These groups, having received identical instructions, brainstorm for about two to three hours. The outcomes are presented and discussed in a plenary session, and an integrated conceptual model is designed. If specific areas in the model have to be further elaborated, a new round of brainstorming in parallel working groups is initiated.

A conceptual map is also called a *consistency machine*. Of course, a conceptual map can only be used as a consistency machine if it can be validated. If we want to test a conceptual model with regard to its validity, we assemble a number of discussion groups, for instance, ten, and we number them from 1 to 10. We instruct each of the groups to draw up a conceptual map of the problem and its setting. We analyze the results of the discussion groups, starting with group 1. After having analyzed the results of a number of groups, we will reach a point at which the last three groups have not added new insights. At that point, we consider the conceptual map to be valid.

3.3.3 Iteration and reporting

The assessor has to see to it that the initial problem definition is revised if the outcomes of the systems analysis require it (step 2.3). Experience shows that redefinitions are necessary more often than not.

Finally, the assessor has to report on the outcomes of the systems analysis.

3.4 Baseline analysis

3.4.1 Formulation of research questions for the baseline analysis

As it is impossible to include all *interesting* variables in the baseline analysis, a selection has to be made. Even after a first selection, the scope of the baseline analysis is usually too broad. This leads to a general and focused baseline analysis. The general version provides a global overview only, while the focused version deals with the variables that are closely connected to the current or future action whose consequences are being analyzed.

How do we focus our research questions? By experiment, we alternately omit each question. If the elimination of a specific question does not harm the baseline analysis in a substantial way, that question is eliminated for good from the study.

3.4.2 Time perspective

A specific concern in this analysis is periodization (step 3.2). The assessor is advised to identify major trend deflections relevant to the current or future action. These trend deflections should also be used to distinguish periods of SIA in the past which may assist. The assessor has also to decide at what point in time the baseline analysis should start.

3.4.3 Design of the theoretical model

The theoretical model has to assist the impact assessor in answering *why* questions in the SIA. The theoretical model tries to enlighten causal relationships. That is why it is also called a *causal model*, or *quasi-causal model*. In social research, causal analysis is possible only in a restricted sense, and therefore the term *quasi-* is added as a token reminder of methodological modesty.

Designing the theoretical model starts with an exercise in meta-theorizing. As a starting point, we take the theoretical model sketched in the first chapter. We identify the central actors. Next we identify their objectives. Following this, constraints are identified. Finally, we identify how the central actor ranks behavioural alternatives, taking objectives and constraints into consideration. This process of modelling is repeated for the target actor.

From the meta-level of abstraction, we step down to the level of theoretical hypotheses. Again we include: (a) actor, (b) objectives, (c) constraints, (d) the process of ranking alternatives for action, and (e) the result – the action that had to be explained.

Following this, we translate the theoretical hypotheses into operational hypotheses, and we derive predictions from these hypotheses. Because we can only formulate quasi-causal relationships, hypotheses and predictions cannot be deduced in a strictly formal way.

In the theoretical model, at all levels of abstraction, we do not include all relationships. We restrict the theoretical model to the most important relationships. If later in the analysis we discover that we have overlooked important relationships, iteration is required. In that case, we add the new relationships to the theoretical model, leading to a new confrontation of predictions with (statements about) observations.

Our analysis concerns the consequences (present and future) of actions by a policy-maker. This implies that we have to distinguish between instrumental variables, contextual variables and target variables. A variable is called instrumental if the central actor is able to use it in the course of action. An intervention can be represented in the theoretical model as an instrumental variable or as a set of instrumental variables. Independent variables that are not related to the action are called contextual variables. Macro-constraints are typical examples of contextual variables. The central actor has to accept them as *facts of life*. Target variables represent dependent variables that may show the impact of the action.

Side effects of an action, e.g. unexpected impacts, are also incorporated in the theoretical model. Externalities are an example of side effects of an intervention.

The theoretical model to be used in the baseline analysis looks from a moment in the past $(t-1)$ towards the present $(t=0)$. In the trend analysis and further explorations of the future, the theoretical model will be elaborated to cover also actions up to a moment in the future $(t+1)$.

The theoretical model can be constructed in three ways: (1) as a set of hypotheses in everyday language; (2) as an algorithm; or (3) in semi-mathematical language, e.g. by DYNAMO (Hanneman 1988). Utilizing algorithms, that is formal mathematical language tools (e.g. differential equations, Markov processes, etc.) has a number of advantages, Hanneman (1988) argues. All the information to be conveyed by a statement in mathematical language must be made explicit. Each variable has a defined and shared meaning. The more complex meanings created by stringing symbols and operations together bear determinate relationships to the parts that compose them. Using mathematical language, complex and powerful operations of deduction from systems of statements about dynamic relations can be made.

There are, however, a number of disadvantages to the use of most existing mathematical languages for stating social science theories. First, most social scientists are not very well trained in the uses of mathematical language. While mathematics can provide powerful tools for making statements about dynamics, it is of little practical utility if those who wish to make such statements cannot do so coherently, or if their statements are unintelligible to their audience (Hanneman 1988: 24).

Secondly, some social systems are relatively easy to model (e.g., cohort replacement and population dynamics) and theories formalizing their dynamics can be correspondingly simple. Consequently, most mathematical languages for operationalizing theories of dynamics are more powerful than are needed for these simple problems. But because they are such simple problems, and only a small component of social science research, while they may be some of the most elegant applications of mathematical language in the social sciences, they are viewed by some as arid formalism of trivial problems (Hanneman 1988).

Because of the limitations of mathematical languages for stating theories of dynamics, social scientists have created a number of *intermediate* languages that lie between everyday and mathematical languages. These languages seek to retain much of the rigour of definition and deductive power available from mathematical forms, while at the same time resembling everyday language.

One of these semi-mathematical or intermediate languages is DYNAMO. The role of DYNAMO is to allow the theorist to state ideas about social dynamics in a language that is close to everyday use and to convert these statements into mathematical statements that can be simulated by the computer and understood by experimentation (Hanneman 1988: 48).

There are also alternatives to simulation activities of DYNAMO for the analysis of continuous-state, continuous-time dynamics. By far the most common language for formalizing theories of continuous-state, continuous-time dynamics (i.e. systems in which continuously occurring change in some variables have effects on the rates of change in other variables) is differential equations. Differential equations and their calculus provide powerful tools for concisely describing and making deductions from statements about rates of change in continuous variables (Hanneman 1988: 49).

3.4.4 Data gathering

As soon as the scheme of variables has been decided upon, data gathering can be started (step 3.4). The first step in data gathering is locating existing information stored in data archives, libraries and periodicals specialized in social indicators. Researchers can best employ their social networks to identify individuals who are knowledgeable about the information required by the research question.

Next, additional information will have to be gathered by searching archives. If the owners of the archives are interested in the information themselves, their co-operation may be acquired by negotiation. They may be willing to provide raw data, if they will get analyzed information in return.

In many western countries, researchers can buy names, addresses and core data about individuals to be sampled. A sample constructed this way can facilitate the process of finding respondents.

Traditionally, interviewing takes place face-to-face. However, this type of data gathering is relatively expensive, and in baseline analysis, telephone surveys are replacing face-to-face interviewing (Groves & Kahn 1979), primarily because in telephone interviewing costs and nonresponse are low. Computer-aided telephone interviewing (CATI) leads to protocols that are registered on the computer directly. Quantitative analysis can start right after the interview.

3.4.5 Data analysis, explanation and interpretation

Analysis of data in baseline studies involves looking for, among other things, regularities and trends. This type of analysis is standard practice. Besides this, baseline studies require explanation and interpretation. Explanations of relationships in these data generally take the form of a *postdiction*. This approach literally consists of *predicting the past*. I shall return to this issue.

Explanation has to be supplemented by interpretation (Esser 1993). Now discursive analysis is required of relationships that have not been included in the explanatory study. Also, the outcomes of the explanation itself may have to be supplemented by qualitative comments.

3.4.6 Iteration and reporting

Baseline analyses require many iterations. Here we meet the first pitfall in baseline studies: trying to elucidate the past of the practical problem in a one-shot analysis or in an analysis with a small number of loops only. In this case, the report will show too many loose ends. The second pitfall is trying to provide a complete picture in a single baseline analysis. This leads to an overloaded report that is difficult to read. If both a focused and a broad baseline analysis have been elaborated, the two reports will supplement each other. The third pitfall is omitting to go back regularly to the research question of the SIA study, and as a result forgetting to reformulate the research question as necessary. The fourth pitfall is presenting a baseline analysis without a theoretical explanation, thereby forgoing an opportunity to elucidate the emergence of the practical problem, and there is a risk of lacking insight into the causal relationships governing the fate of interventions in the area concerned.

Generally, both the focused and the broad baseline analysis are made available to the public without restrictions. In a major SIA study, the report of the broad baseline analysis would likely consist of working papers of over 1,000 pages in total.

3.5 Trend analysis and monitoring

3.5.1 Identification of trends

In the preliminary phase of the SIA study, an exploration is required of trends for two practical reasons. First, if the trend analysis leads to an adequate description, explanation and interpretation of the main future developments in the central system and its context, a scenario analysis would be superfluous in the main phase of the SIA study. Secondly, if past trends that are likely to persist can be identified, they can be incorporated in the scenario analysis without making provisions for variations in these trends.

Trend extrapolation is not a simple projection of historical developments based on a naive assumption of continuity. A real effort must be made to determine the economic, social and/or political forces behind the trend, as withdrawal or alterations in these factors can produce discontinuities (Porter & Rossini 1983).

There are two primary trend extrapolation techniques which are applied in baseline analyses: (1) single and compound parameter extrapolation; and (2) envelope and S-shaped curves.

Parameter extrapolation is an indirect way of exploring the course of a future trend. It is the task of the forecaster to identify parameters that accurately portray the context of the trend to be forecast. Martino (1972: 117–18) identifies five characteristics that an appropriate parameter must possess. It must:

1. Be one that can be measured quantitatively in objective and meaningful terms. Therefore, it must be possible to measure the parameter in terms of the characteristics of the device or its operation.
2. Represent a measure of the actual functional capability. A parameter can fail to do this in two ways. First, it may indicate only a single aspect of that capability. For example, in lighting technology both the amount of light produced (output in lumens) and the amount of energy required to produce it (inputs in watts) are important. A device could be unsatisfactory either because of its output or required input. Neither alone is, therefore, representative of functional capacity. Secondly, the parameter must account for the effects of design trade-off. In the design of a jet engine, for example, it is possible to achieve higher thrust levels by sacrificing fuel consumption. The designer can, within limits, trade thrust for fuel consumption. Thus neither measure alone is representative of performance, it is the combination that is important.
3. Serve to represent functional capability for a progression of different technical approaches. It must, therefore, be applicable to each succeeding approach and not peculiar to one. With lighting technology, lumens per watt can be used as a parameter for devices ranging from the paraffin candle to the advanced lighting systems for public spaces.
4. Be one for which sufficient historical data exist to establish the trend. This is the most restrictive of all limitations on parameter selection.
5. Be selected consistently with respect to the level of emergence and impact of each successive technical approach.

An example from SIA forms the relationship between economic prosperity in a country (parameter) and the absence from work for medical reasons (trend).

When an appropriate parameter has been selected and sufficient historical data gathered, the forecaster is ready to examine past behaviour to determine whether a trend exists. This is most easily done by constructing a graphical representation. In such a graph, time t is chosen as the independent variable and plotted on the abscissa (horizontal axis), and the parameter P is the dependent variable plotted on the ordinate (vertical axis) (Porter & Rossini 1983). Whether the extrapolation is done mathematically or graphically, the forecaster should be convinced that factors that could cause discontinuities will not come into play within the time period of the forecast. This conviction has to be based in an explicit way on the theoretical model used in the baseline analysis and the trend analysis.

The examples given thus far use single parameters to represent impacts on the trend to be forecasted. Single parameters, however, often fail to represent a measure of the actual trend. When this occurs, a compound parameter must be developed.

An envelope curve is simply a smooth curve forming a boundary, usually the upper, for the variation of a performance parameter. The performance of many systems grows in an exponential fashion. This growth results from the increase of the performance of a number of different approaches that follow one another sequentially. In the start-up phase of their development, new approaches typically encounter developmental problems that must be overcome before rapid strides in performance can be achieved. Once developmental problems are solved, performance typically increases rapidly, fulfilling the promise that gave rise to the technology. Rapid advance is followed by a slowing of the rate of increase as the last advantage is wrung from the new approach. Typically, during this later phase, innovators are faced with increasingly complex problems whose solution yields only marginal increases in performance until the physical, social and economic limits of the new approach are reached (Porter & Rossini 1983).

Envelope curves are characteristic of sequences of new approaches in a problem area. If the life course of a single new approach is analyzed, as a rule an S-curve can be discerned. Since all forecasting involves uncertainty, a forecast represented by a single curve does not accurately portray the confidence limits that the user can reasonably place upon the forecast. Therefore, it is common practice to use two envelope curves to display this uncertainty. One represents the upper bound and the other the lower. By adopting this representation, the forecaster identifies the region within which the actual development is projected to occur. The range of performance bounded by the envelope curves naturally will broaden as the time frame of the forecast increases, reflecting the growing level of uncertainty (Porter & Rossini 1983).

3.5.2 Design of monitoring

Monitoring means *to observe or watch*. Monitoring can be viewed as an important component of the cyclical process of planning, programme design, implementation of interventions, evaluation and replanning. According to Carley and Bustelo (1984), it can serve one or more of three organizational functions:

1. Monitoring can enlighten us as to the status of critical or changing issues in the policy environment which may be addressed by future action.
2. Monitoring can help us manage our environment by providing feedback in terms of the relative success or failure of previous action in terms of policies and programmes.
3. Monitoring can be used to test compliance with regulations and contractual agreements.

There are a number of types of monitoring which exist as kind of continuum of activity. For SIA, five types are relevant. Carley and Bustelo (1984) describe them as follows:

1. *Inspection.* The simplest form of monitoring is the periodic inspection of some activity to ensure that safe operating procedures are being followed, and that visible environmental degradation is not occurring. For example, an agency of the Canadian government conducts regular on-site, biweekly inspections of drilling activities by energy companies.
2. *Program evaluation monitoring.* Also called productivity measurement or performance auditing. These are attempts, generally by government departments or evaluation teams, to measure the efficiency or effectiveness of policies or programmes in terms of the ratio of organizational inputs to outputs (efficiency), or satisfaction of goals and objectives (effectiveness). Such studies are designed

to: (1) help determine progress towards targets or goals set by public administrators; (2) identify problem areas and help set priorities for efforts at improved productivity and better value for money in government expenditure; and (3) help implement worker incentive schemes. Such monitoring efforts are usually focused on a single set of policies or a particular service delivery programme.

3. *Program evaluation monitoring.* Similar to the above and most common in developing countries where development projects have been funded by international donor agencies, such as The World Bank and others. Also called project audits, these are attempts to determine the relative success or failure of aid projects while they are ongoing or completed, not only in economic terms, but in social and environmental terms as well. Again the focus is on evaluation of efficiency and effectiveness, and on value for money in relatively small or discrete projects. Both programme and project evaluation are part of what is called *evaluation research,* and there is little crossover between these activities and impact monitoring. In many cases, however, similar terminology is used, but with some different meanings.

4. *Monitoring for project impact management.* This is a broader form of monitoring in which a formalized organization or group regularly assesses a wide range of environmental, social and economic impacts from a particular project. This usually occurs during project construction so to ensure a flow of benefits, to control the severity and distribution of anticipated and especially unanticipated negative effects as they occur, and to ensure due compensation where it is required. This type of monitoring is directly linked to mitigation schemes. Organizationally, at its simplest level, it is carried out by project proponents and overseen by an appropriate government agency. More realistically, it is conceived of as high-level monitoring of an entire project management system by responsible agencies in association with independent groups. The intent is to report on the entire project, including objectives; criteria for judging success; the technical and institutional means for reaching these criteria; planning systems; adequacy of inspections and co-ordination; and other tasks. This is an important extension of the IA process. It attempts to overcome

deficiencies in that process, and especially with predictive impact statements. Such statements are static rather than dynamic in nature, and therefore unresponsive to new information and changing conditions. A side benefit of monitoring at this scale may be *ex-ante* testing of predictions in the original SIA.

5. *Cumulative impact monitoring.* This is usually of interest in regions where rapid development is taking place, but the monitoring programme is not confined or limited to project-related direct or indirect impacts. Rather, the focus is on monitoring all critical issues or changing patterns in a region, whether they are related to a project or occur independently. Cumulative monitoring also focuses on the interrelated, and additive effects caused by a variety of industrializing projects and government interventions over time. In other words, it is the cumulative perspective made operational. Such monitoring is characterized by a regional rather than site-specific perspective; attention to overlapping impacts of different projects and policies; and a time perspective stressing the long-term incremental and dynamic nature of social change. It is usually carried out by government to provide a regional overview to citizens, and to provide a co-ordinated and organized flow of information for strategic planning purposes. In addition to documenting non-project-related socio-economic changes, it also serves to co-ordinate the variety of information generated by less strategic types of monitoring. It can begin well before decisions on project acceptability are taken, but more likely it will be a component of a regional or strategic planning process, and therefore be unrelated to the timing or acceptability of particular projects. Although the need for monitoring is well recognized, there are as yet few examples of a cumulative impact monitoring programme.

Experiences with monitoring suggest that no amount of attention to the data collection aspects of monitoring can substitute for beginning the monitoring exercise with a clear conceptual framework and a practical institutional structure. The conceptual framework represents the logical formulation of the goals and means for undertaking the monitoring exercise. The institutional structure is the bureaucratic arrangements made for carrying out the monitoring. Experience teaches us, according to Carley and Bustelo (1974), that the importance of both should not be underestimated.

3.5.3 Data gathering

Both trend analysis and monitoring in most cases rely heavily on official statistics. As a rule, data gathering is supplemented with surveys and panel data. A third approach to trend analysis and monitoring is gathering expert opinions. A sophisticated method of tapping expert opinions is the Delphi method, named after the ancient Greek oracle. Delphi is a technique that interactively iterates the responses of surveyed experts, thereby combining some of the advantages of surveys and panels. The Delphi method can generate systematic thought about future courses of events that are difficult to treat by other means.

Delphi is an expert opinion survey with three special characteristics: anonymity among participants, statistical treatment of responses, and iterative polling with feedback. The procedure is as follows (Sackman 1974: 7–8):

1. Typically a structured, formal, paper-and-pencil questionnaire is administered by mail, in person (e.g. at a conference) or through an interactive, on-line computer console. Participants do not discuss the issues.
2. The questionnaire items may be generated by the study director, participants, or both.
3. The questionnaire is administered for two or more rounds; participants respond to scaled objective items, and sometimes to open-ended responses as well.
4. Each iteration is accompanied by statistical feedback on each item, which usually involves: (a) a measure of central tendency (e.g. the median), and (b) some measure of dispersion (e.g. the interquartile range, that is, the values between which one-half of the responses lie). Sometimes the entire frequency distribution of responses is provided.
5. Respondents in the upper and lower quartiles may be asked to justify their responses; selected verbal feedback may be provided on each iteration (individual responses are kept anonymous).

6. Iteration continues to some point of diminishing returns that is determined by the director; convergence of opinion is sought, but not forced.

There are many variants on the Delphi procedure; for example Mitchell and Ebert (1975) describe a *mini-Delphi* simplified for use by small groups gathered at a conference. Delphi can be used to forecast particular technological or social events. It can be used to determine policy preferences of a particular group. Conditions that make Delphi an attractive alternative to panels or surveys include the following (Linstone & Turoff 1975: 4):

1. The problem is not amenable to analytical techniques, but its solution could benefit from subjective group judgement.
2. The individuals who could potentially contribute most to the problem solution represent groups with extremely diverse expertise and experiences, and who lack a history of effective communication with each other.
3. More individuals are needed than can effectively interact in a face-to-face meeting.
4. Time and cost make frequent group meetings infeasible.
5. The efficiency of a face-to-face meeting can be increased by a supplemental group communications process.
6. Disagreements among individuals are so severe or politically unpalatable that communications must be refereed and/or anonymity assured.
7. Bandwagon effects or the domination by a single individual or group of individuals must be avoided to assure the validity of the results.

The following pitfalls and difficulties are related to the Delphi method, according to Porter and Rossini (1983):

1. It capitalizes on group suggestion to pressure toward consensus, yet it is unclear whether such consensus yields accurate forecasts.
2. The director's control in structuring the process (i.e. selecting items and verbal responses) may suppress other valid perspectives of the issue and yield biased results.

3. Lack of item clarity or common interpretation of scales and feedback responses may lead to invalid results.
4. Participants may become demoralized by the demanding nature of the process (particularly if not compensated for their time).
5. Not exploring disagreements may also cause dissenting participants to withdraw, biasing the results.
6. Delphi practice has tended to be shoddy with respect to the principles of good survey practice.

3.5.4 Analysis, explanation and interpretation

In trend analysis and monitoring, the strongest analytical approach to explanation and interpretation is postdiction. This approach implies, as we saw before, the prediction of past developments as the best approximation of future developments. Postdiction builds a bridge between baseline analysis and futures explorations like trend analysis and *early warnings* by monitoring.

Postdiction starts with periodization of developments that lie in the past. The period covered by the baseline analysis is divided into two or more subperiods. As a rule, a subperiod starts shortly after a major event. Next, the first subperiod (a) is analyzed. Third, the theoretical model is used to *predict* developments in sub-period (b). The postdiction is focused on developments closely related to the practical problem of the SIA. Fourth, postdiction is executed for all periods lying in the past. Fifth, the explanatory model of the baseline analysis is reformulated, learning from the analytical and explanatory experiences gained so far in the postdiction. Sixth, the refined model is used to predict developments in a period (or a series of subperiods) lying in the future.

If the quality of the data permits, postdiction is carried out in a quantitative way. If the data are not suited for quantitative analysis, qualitative analysis is required. As an example, historical analogies can be mentioned (Martino 1975).

Postdictions require not only explanation but interpretation too. This applies in particular to risk and uncertainty involved in the processes to be explored. Risk can be interpreted in terms of probability (high/low) and impact (high/low). In SIA, future processes that show low probability and high impact are highly relevant.

3.5.5 Iteration, pitfalls and reporting

In trend analysis and monitoring, iteration is required right up to the end of the SIA study. Old information has to be included that emerges while the study is under way. New information has to be added that becomes available during the study. A number of pitfalls, *inter alia* concerning Delphi method, has been discussed in this section already. In general, the forecaster has to be aware of the dangers of:

(a) presenting crude projections not based on explanatory models;
(b) revising the explanatory model too late, that is showing the *assumption drag* Ascher (1978) has unmasked;
(c) failing to state the risks and uncertainties included in the exploration of the future;
(d) not presenting an interpretation of the forecasted processes.

In most cases, the outcomes of trend analyses and monitoring are published without restrictions. They may be included in social indicator reports, often presented at regular times.

3.6 Project design

3.6.1 Formulation of the research questions

Taking the problem formulated in step 1.1 as a frame of reference, each component of the main phase of the SIA study has to be covered by a set of research questions. First, descriptive questions (*what* questions). Secondly, questions leading to explanation and interpretation (*why* questions). Thirdly, preliminary answers to the research questions have to formulated. A set of hypotheses helps to focus the research activities even if testing of hypotheses is not one of the objectives of policy-oriented research.

Formulating the research questions requires attention to the explanatory model and to the assumption of the research project. All future processes that do not merit an assumption of continuity will have to be analyzed in the main phase of the project by using scenarios. If an

81

assumption of continuity is not appropriate, we are confronted with risk and uncertainty.

3.6.2 Design of the main phase of the SIA study

Applying strategic learning implies that the SIA study is not only a research project but primarily a development project. In this development project the central actor has to take the lead. In an organization, top management and middle management will have to accomplish the process of strategic learning.

As an example, I take the Nostradamus Project of the Dutch National Bureau of Waters (RWS). The top management of RWS had given a number of bright young managers the task to run the process of strategic learning during a period of two years. The young managers had been promised that after the two years they would get new jobs in the organization at a higher level. As a result of this *contract*, the project was carried out by members of the organization who were able to meet the requirements of the subculture of RWS. This ensured that the project was carried out with enthusiasm.

In a project of strategic learning, consultants are not allowed to dominate the process. RWS safeguarded the project by contracting two consultants for each advisory task. The consultants came from different traditions. As a consequence, the consultants in most cases presented contradictory advice, enabling the project team to make a choice. Often, not only the central actor but also the target actor participates in the project. Acquiring information from experts as a rule takes the form of a Delphi method-project.

3.6.3 Formation of the project team

This set of methodological suggestions is tailored to suit a major SIA study. What are the requirements for the head of the project team? The head of the team must have been involved at least three times in a research project that included SIA in a substantial way. If he or she has less experience, they ought to employ an experienced adviser.

What are the requirements concerning the other members of the research team? They ought to have the experience of some years in policy-oriented social research. The head of the research team ought to check whether the potential team members have shown a co-operative attitude. An SIA study is an unsuitable setting for attempts to resocialize troublemakers. The head of the team has also to check whether the potential team members have shown evidence of having creative minds. Designing scenarios, strategies, implementation settings and the like requires an open mind and experience in designing new solutions to unusual practical problems.

As soon as the team has been brought together, training starts. An excellent way to train a new team is to invite them to evaluate reports of first-class *old* SIA studies. Ask them to criticize the old reports. Next, invite them to design solutions for the weak spots they have discovered in the work of their colleagues. Finally, invite members of the research teams of the *old* studies to react to the *solutions* the newcomers have concocted.

More often than not, members of more than one discipline will have to work together in the research team of the SIA study. How do we invite them to co-operate in a constructive way? There are a lot of solutions to this practical problem. One solution is to invite knowledgeable members of each of the disciplines involved to explain in seminar format when, in their discipline, a hypothesis is considered to be corroborated. Discussions about approaches to test hypotheses provide all participants in the team with an insight into the working of the mind of the others.

This technique to initiate multidisciplinary and interdisciplinary cooperation in scientific research can help to bridge gaps between members of behavioural and social sciences, natural sciences, medical sciences and related empirical disciplines. Bridging gaps between empirical sciences and mathematics or statistics demands different procedures. One way to encourage this type of co-operation is to train empirical scientists to formulate their research questions in an unambiguous way. Next, to formulate preliminary solutions to their mathematical or statistical research problems. If mathematicians or statisticians are confronted with a valid but clumsy solution to a problem in their field, they will usually produce more *elegant* solutions to the problem. At that moment, a viable basis for understanding has been created and a productive process of co-operation can begin.

The head of the research team will have to use the reports of earlier steps in the study to explain the *philosophy* of the study to the members of the team. If the reports do not come up to this expectation, they have to be rewritten.

It is normal for research teams of all kinds, monodisciplinary, multidisciplinary and interdisciplinary to encounter terminological difficulties. There is a simple and quick way to solve this problem. Invite a member of the team to elaborate a taxonomy of key terms and concepts. Invite all readers of the taxonomy to follow the advice of Karl Popper to read definitions of terms from right to left. Why is this illuminating? Definitions consist of a term (a label), a symbol indicating *means*, and a description of an empirical observation or a logical argument. It is relatively easy to acquire consensus about the description of the content matter concerned. The confusion is generally caused by the first part of the definition: the terminological labelling. Why? Because often a phenomenon is defined in a number of disciplines, and each discipline uses its own label. An example can easily be provided. Think about: (a) impact assessment, (b) ex-ante evaluation, (c) analysis of consequences, and so on. Each of these terms has more or less the same meaning.

This section presents suggestions that are not restricted to SIA studies. The suggestions stem from a body of knowledge known as *the management of research projects*.

3.6.4 Planning the main phase of the SIA study

In a project requiring less than about 20 research activities, the head of the team will be able to plan the project with paper and pencil only. In projects that require more than 20 research activities, it is wise to adopt a computerized planning model. Network planning models are available for designing and monitoring research projects. Network planning, *inter alia*, provides insight into the *critical path* of the research project. The critical path indicates at which moment activities must be completed. If the critical path is not followed, the sequence of activities is disturbed and the project is in danger of overstepping limits concerning quality, time and money.

3.6.5 Iteration and reporting

Iteration processes concerning the programming of research projects have to be planned in advance and must not to be left to chance. The head of the research team has to consult the research contract regularly, especially to compare the terms of reference for the project with the actual research process.

Drafting the research contract for the main phase of the project concludes the preliminary phase. This contract is the *report* on this step in the project. The head of the research team has to be knowledgable about research contract protocol. If not, it is wise to consult an expert. In particular, the three main boundary conditions have to be taken into consideration: quality, time and money. If quality and time are strict boundary conditions, financial restrictions have to be lenient or absent. If time and money are strict boundary conditions, quality has to be interpreted in a lenient way. Good advice is the adage that you should never put your name to a research contract which sets strict limits to each of the three main boundary conditions.

CHAPTER 4

Methods for the main phase in SIA

4.1 Introduction

There is not a strict separation between the preliminary phase and the main phase of the SIA study. A lot of activities have to be continued and iteration involves steps belonging to both parts involved. Yet we are dealing with an important threshold in the SIA study. At the end of the preliminary phase, the SIA could be stopped, perhaps only having incurred relatively low costs to date. As soon as the SIA study has entered the main phase, termination may involve major losses of investments.

In an SIA study, the beginning of the main phase usually is a pleasant period. The team is likely to have received positive reactions to the results of the preliminary phase and has received a green light for the real thing, the main body of the study. However, evaluations of this type of project have identified that the transition from the preliminary phase to the major stage is a troublesome time. Many teams self-destruct during this time, basking too long in the sunshine of their early success. SIA teams ought to be aware of this major pitfall.

In Figure 4.1, an overview is presented of the steps that have to be taken in the main phase.

4.2 Scenario design

4.2.1 Choice of types of scenarios

The research team has to select the types of scenarios to be designed (step 1.1). The choice between the American and the French tradition

Step 1.0 Scenario design
    1.1 Choice of the type of scenarios to be designed
    1.2 Design of models
    1.3 Design of scenarios
    1.4 Design of critical incidents
    1.5 Iteration and reporting

Step 2.0 Design of strategies
    2.1 Evaluation of current strategies
    2.2 Design of an integrated set of strategies
    2.3 Iteration and reporting

Step 3.0 Assessment of impacts
    3.1 Scenario-to-strategy simulation
    3.2 Additional simulations
    3.3 Iteration and reporting

Step 4.0 Ranking of strategies
    4.1 Choice of tyep of ranking
    4.2 Ranking process
    4.3 Iteration and reporting

Step 5.0 Migration of negative impacts
    5.1 Redesigning of strategies and reassessment of impacts
    5.2 Revision of ranking of strategies
    5.3 Iteration and reporting

Step 6.0 Reporting
    6.1 Decision about the types of reporting
    6.2 Executive summary
    6.3 Full report
    6.4 Background papers
    6.5 Press release
    6.6 Workshops

Step 7.0 Stimulation of implementation

Step 8.0 Auditing and ex-post evaluation
    8.1 Auditing
    8.2 Ex-post evaluation.

Figure 4.1 Flow-chart of steps in the main phase of a large-scale SIA project.

(see Chapter 2) sets the stage for the whole design process. The American tradition, which takes a turbulent environment of the central actor into consideration, is appropriate whenever cautious strategy formation is demanded. If the central actor has limited powers only, and if actions of many rivals have to be taken into consideration, the American tradition will yield the best results. The French tradition is appropriate if utopian mind stretching is required. In this tradition, the power of the central actor is often slightly exaggerated in order to create space for designing with vision. The French tradition is also appropriate for the design of a more just world. In this case, utopian vision might bring in new allies.

As we saw before, the American tradition tempts participants in the design and utilization process to act overcautiously. The French tradition fosters overboldness. The project co-ordinator is in a position to avoid these extreme reactions. The rules of the game can be stated in such a way that they stimulate boldness (to some extent) in the American tradition, and so that some circumspection is rewarded in the French tradition.

Is it possible to combine both traditions in one and the same scenario project? In combined projects, participants are first invited to design in the French tradition. In a second design process, contextual scenarios are elaborated. In a third exercise, the utopian proposals of the first round are confronted with the pragmatic constraints of the contextual scenarios of the second round. Finally, a balanced report is articulated.

If the American tradition is selected, the research team will have to start with programming a trend scenario. In this trend scenario (or baseline scenario or zero scenario), developments of the past are projected to a future point in time. If no new developments are taken into consideration, we have a *surprise-free* scenario. However, sometimes a number of new developments are included in a trend scenario. If major new policy actions are expected in the near future, it makes sense to include these actions in the trend scenario. An example of this would be legislation that has been accepted by parliament and will become operational in the near future. Next, the research team will have to plan one or more contrast scenarios, that is, scenarios that are in contradiction with the trend scenario.

If the French tradition is preferred, the research team also has to include a trend scenario. In this case, the trend scenario is a *scénario de l'inacceptable*. In other words, the trend scenario is a *doomsday scenario*. The trend scenario is surrounded by normative (or prescriptive) scenarios. A normative scenario is also called a *preferential scenario*, because it envisions a situation in the future that is preferred to the doomsday future.

This section has presented the main types of scenarios. In Chapter 5, more types of scenarios will be discussed.

4.2.2 Design of model

The preliminary choice of the type of scenarios is followed by the design of the model (step 1.2). The research team should try to design a theoretical model that resembles a causal model as far as possible. The model incorporates *prime movers*, or *driving forces*, which, generally, have already been identified by the representatives of the different scientific disciplines co-operating in the scenario project.

As an example, I summarize the explanatory framework used by the Central Planning Bureau (CPB) of the Netherlands in 1992. The CPB emphasized that economic science has failed to provide a clear, undisputed and integrated theory of economic development. Just as history is a discussion without an end, so is the question, What are the driving forces behind economic progress? In spite of this judgement of current practice, a long-term study, *Scanning the Future*, was commissioned in which the main theme was economic development. To undertake such a study, it was necessary to have a clear idea of the major factors that determine economic success, otherwise it would become just an incoherent summary of trends and possibilities. In the report by the CPB, an attempt was made to solve the problem in an eclectic manner by distinguishing between three perspectives on economic development that more or less concur with three schools of economic thought. The three perspectives are competitive in the sense that they hold different views about economic process and the role played by individuals, companies, collective arrangements and government. They can be seen as different ideas about how the world works, or as different brands of political economy. However, they are also complementary in that they place different emphases on the major factors determining economic development. The three perspectives combined present us with a relatively complete picture of the process of economic development. They serve as the *organizing principles* on which the scenario report of the CPB is based (Central Planning Bureau 1992: 40). The three perspectives can be identified as the equilibrium perspective, the co-ordination perspective and the free market perspective.

The *equilibrium perspective* is based on a well-functioning price mechanism which balances supply and demand in the various markets. Economic subjects are rational, well informed and have accurate expectations of the future. The level of prosperity hinges on the production factors available: natural resources, quantity and quality of the labour force, and capital stock, as well as the state of technology. For growth, the level of savings is crucial: the price mechanism translates savings into an expansion of the (tangible and intangible) capital stock. The role of a national government is limited to supplying purely public goods, such as defence, justice and infrastructure, and to correcting prices through levies and subsidies, in case of negative or positive external effects. Free international trade and floating currency exchange rates improve prosperity.

The *co-ordination perspective* stresses that economic subjects have imperfect information and that the future is fundamentally uncertain. This can lead to volatile expectations and unstable behaviour, resulting in cumulative disturbances and a certain short-sightedness among economic subjects. In this view, anti-cyclical policies and various forms of co-operation between government, business and labour may reduce uncertainty and lead to a collective adjustment to new circumstances and expectations. Correction for short-sightedness and striving for stability may give rise to various government regulations in the labour and product markets, to subsidized or free education and to facilities for research and development (R&D) and investment, thus enhancing economic progress. Fixed exchange rates reduce uncertainty and are thus preferred. Trade restrictions are often judged to be in the interest of an individual country, but co-operation between nations, resulting in free trade agreements, may be beneficial to all.

The *free market perspective* emphasizes that in an uncertain world with incomplete information, competitive entrepreneurs with different views on the present and the future play a dominant role in enhancing economic progress as inspirators and organizers of inventions and innovations. Creative destruction, the will to win and the fear of losing drive the dynamics of the market economy. Human nature is viewed as vital, creative and intuitive, provided that individuals are assured of picking the fruits of their labour. This requires a well-developed system of property rights, autonomy in the economic sphere, low taxes and a frugal system of social security. There is a profound distrust of government policies. Government is no better informed than individuals and is not corrected by the market when it makes wrong decisions. Policies may make the future even more unpredictable and cripple the dynamics of the economic process, while the idea that selfish individuals can suddenly become altruistic once they join the government is thought to be absurd. In the field of international trade and exchange rates, the free market is advocated without reservation (Central Planning Bureau 1992: 39).

According to the CPB, economic success may coincide with different emphases on the three perspectives, depending on culture and circumstances. The neglect of one of the three perspectives, however, would prove to be very dangerous. The ultimate challenge is social innovation, meaning the capability and willingness of individuals, companies and governments to continuously change old success formulas and to strike a new balance between the driving forces of economic progress in light of new developments (Central Planning Bureau 1992: 39).

This example clears the way for a general discussion on models in SIA studies using scenario analysis. According to Gibbs:

> Models are selective approximations of a real situation which, because of their simplifications, allow those aspects of the real world which are under examination to appear in a generalized form. Models are basically of three types, iconic, analogue or symbolic. A model is a set of organized assumptions about a system (Gibbs, 1978: 90).

Designing models is an art-science. According to Shannon (1975: 20), the art of modelling consists of 'an ability to analyze a problem, abstract from it its essential features, select and modify basic assumptions that characterize the system, and then enrich and elaborate the model until a useful approximation results'.

4.2.3 Designing the scenarios

As soon as the model is ready, the designing of the scenarios can begin (step 1.3). As a rule, several researchers should co-operate in this activity. If participation of potential users of the scenarios is required, individuals from this social category are invited to take part in the exercise. Preferably two or more groups are instructed to design scenarios, starting from an identical assignment. The assignment specifies the practical problem, the type of scenarios required and the variables to be taken into account. More aspects of the designing process may be specified if necessary. Ideally, the instructions are kept as short as possible. The groups are given a number of hours to design the first versions of the scenarios. A frame game can be used to structure the designing process. Next, the scenarios are discussed in a plenary session. In the third round, each group redesigns its scenarios, taking the critical comments of the plenary session into account. The fourth round again brings a plenary discussion.

In medium- and large-scale scenario projects, the process of designing scenarios may be repeated up to ten or even more rounds. Iteration is necessary in order to arrive at a *saturated* set of scenarios. During the iteration process, various labels for each scenario are proposed. The proposals are documented. At the end, a decision about the labels is required. This is a crucial decision, because later the labels play a vital role in communication with actors crucial for the utilization of the scenarios.

What does a set of scenarios look like? As an example, a summary will be presented of the four scenarios developed by the CPB for the world economy 1990–2015. The scenarios are called Global Shift, European Renaissance, Global Crisis and Balanced Growth.

The *Global Shift* scenario is characterized by the strong dynamics of technological change. In order to benefit from the dynamics, vigorous entrepreneurship, incentives and market competition are essential preconditions. The gale of creative destruction continuously threatens market positions and vested interests. America's business sector, under pressure from Japan and the dynamic Asian economies (DAEs), demonstrates that, during the 1990s, the free market perspective was still a major source of strength for the USA. Immediate trends that constrain growth are tackled by private enterprise, leading to a vitality which spans business practices and attitudes, as well as social activities, such as the sponsorship of basic education. The subsequent recovery in productivity also generates the financial means by which government deficit can be reduced and human and physical capital bottlenecks tackled on a large-scale basis.

Japan and the DAEs tackle their internal and external challenges with great enthusiasm and flexibility, and a strong shift in favour of the free market perspective is achieved. For Japan, the rapid ageing of the population and labour shortages are a special motive for opening up to the world economy and liberalizing their sheltered sectors. This leads to a rapid catching up in those low-productive segments of the economy.

Despite steps taken in the direction of an internal market, Europe appears generally ill-prepared in the light of the innovative and competitive capabilities emanating from the Asian-Pacific region. Economic reforms intended to promote or restore market competition are not realized or are implemented half-heartedly because of effective resistance by pressure groups. This applies particularly to the labour market. The European bias in favour of security, stability and risk aversion behaviour prevails once again. As a result, economic growth recedes and important industrial sectors quickly lose ground. A number of countries will make the shift towards protectionism by awarding subsidies to vital industries and introducing non-tariff barriers, for example. Other countries oppose this, however. The European Community (EU) is once again split. Fortress Europe is in the making. Eurosclerosis has returned to the stage.

In the *European Renaissance* scenario, new entrepreneurship encounters more barriers than in Global Shift. Huge funds are needed for research and development, involving large risks and uncertainties. Increasing returns to scale in finance, production, marketing and R&D continue to be very important. As a result, global competition increasingly leads to the emergence of worldwide oligopolies and strategic alliances. These conglomerates seek support from government in order to reduce the degree of uncertainty. Consequently, strategic technologies, together with industrial and trade policies, become more important. In European Renaissance, the emphasis therefore falls on the co-ordination perspective, while in Global Shift the emphasis is on the free market perspective.

Despite increasingly strained relations with the USA, western Europe develops very favourably in the European Renaissance scenario. The high expectations of the integrated internal market in Europe, as implemented in the Europe '92 agreement, are fulfilled and the European Monetary Union (EMU) is launched. The European process of integration is an important stimulus toward strengthening incentive structures on the West European product and labour markets. A farreaching process to reform of the West European welfare state is set in motion, especially in north-western Europe. In this, attempts are made to combine the European tradition of social equity with an increasing sensitivity to economic incentives.

The *Global Crisis* scenario explores the risks and changes of an unintentional neglect of regional and global challenges. Despite the optimistic beginning of the 1990s, the USA does not really seem to break away from the trends of the 1980s, while in western Europe high expectations about Europe '92 are not met. Although no dramatic setbacks take place, the process of economic decay is slowly but surely settling in to stay.

For Japan, too, the trends of the 1980s continue, but these are more positive. Emerging bottlenecks, such as the ageing population, are taken care of with relative ease. As far as the outside world is concerned, it remains a closed *Japan Inc.* that competes in an *unfair* manner.

The further rise of the Far East, on the one hand, and the economic impotence of Europe and America on the other hand, ensure a continuous deepening of tensions on trade issues during the 1990s. The major regions of the world gradually degenerate into antagonistic protectionist blocs. As a result, market structures are again becoming less competitive. The diffusion of new technology is consequently delayed. Both factors contribute towards further slackening of global economic growth. Moreover, economic antagonism between the three large blocs also mars international talks concerning environmental problems. Everywhere tensions are mounting. The world seems to become more and more trapped in a vicious circle.

In the *Balanced Growth* scenario, the revived and ever stronger striving toward sustainable economic development, combined with continuously strong technological dynamics, constitute the dominating forces. This calls for a new balance between the economic perspectives.

During the 1990s, the weak points of the major industrial countries are corrected. The US government reduces the budget deficit and improves education and infrastructure, while American business changes its attitudes and practices. Western Europe strengthens incentive structures and Japan liberalizes and opens up to the world economy. At the same time, reform processes continue or gain new strength in regions like Latin America, the former Soviet Union, India and China. As a result, during the second half of the 1990s, worldwide economic growth picks up strongly.

These positive developments on a regional level also stimulate an open and co-operative attitude on the international level. There is more growth, primarily due to specialization and dynamic economies of scale, but also because more competitive market structures stimulate innovation. The virtuous circle created by all these developments helps to crack the strong, internal, growth impeding factors in regions like Africa. In the less developed countries (LDCs), the economic breakthrough propels a rapid decline in fertility rates, slowing down population growth. In addition to the free market element, co-ordination is also a factor of great importance in Balanced Growth. This is apparent from international treaties on security, leading to a further reduction of defence spending in the world.

In the four scenarios, information from economic theory, a comparative strength analysis and an analysis of long-term trends have been combined. Balanced Growth is the most optimistic scenario. It shows that an annual growth rate of the world economy of more than 3.5 per cent, which is ecologically sustainable and embraces all the major regions of the world, is still a quite realistic possibility. However, the scenario will not easily be realized, as it demands formidable changes at the regional and global level.

What are the main characteristics of these scenarios? Global Crisis explores the risks and changes of an unintentional neglect of, and a late response to, regional and global challenges. The scenario shows how the world may end up in the throes of a widespread distress that can only be corrected at great cost. Global Shift and European Renaissance explore divergent developments with respect to the two most powerful economic blocs in the world, western Europe and North America. The message is that their economic performance will have profound radiating effects on other regions, especially those located nearby.

In the Netherlands, the set of scenarios has been widely used as a background for the exploration of many subjects which require a long-term view. Further elaboration was necessary in order to meet the special demands of the various decision makers in the country. Structures and processes that might be subjected to planned change by governments of the major countries in the world and by international organizations constituted *given* boundary conditions for decision-makers in a small country like the Netherlands.

4.2.4 Designing critical incidents

Modelling critical incidents (step 1.4) follows more or less the same rules as designing scenarios. Critical incidents are characterized as having low probability but high impact. In the CPB scenarios summarized in the previous section, critical incidents play a major role. The Global Shift scenario is confronted with a critical incident, which is as follows: *after a number of years western Europe reaches the bottom of the vicious spiral. Somewhere in the midst of the next decade a new consensus permits the spiral to be broken by means of unavoidably harsh measures.* In European Renaissance, we read:

> At a certain moment, between 1995 and 2000, a fundamental crisis in confidence emerges with respect to the American economy, for example, during a stock market crash . . . Only after a difficult period in the United States, does a strong recovery begin somewhere during the 2000 to 2005 period. This gives a boost to the world economy as a whole, which also improves opportunities for international talks on global issues, such as the environment where, until 2005, hardly any progress had been made (CPB, 1992: 370).

The Global Crisis scenario is accompanied by the following critical incident:

> At some stage, a disruption takes place which, in view of the fragility of the system, assumes the nature of a system shock. For the Global Crisis scenario, a serious worldwide crisis in the area of world food supply is assumed. The agricultural crisis will be interpreted by many as decisive evidence of the negative effects

of the greenhouse effect or as the consequence of lasting deterioration of agricultural land. For this reason it will be considered an ecoshock. As a result, a deep economic recession is set in motion: Global Crisis. A few years after the acute crisis the world economy begins to show signs of recovery. The fresh memory of the crisis also creates new windows of opportunities with respect to international co-operation. The late response to many challenges does, however, bring with it many extra costs, all of which slow down the process of recovery (CPB, 1992: 371).

As a second example, I summarize a scenario report presenting two critical incidents (Hollander & Becker 1985). In *Growing Old in the Future*, scenarios on health and ageing are developed for 1984–2000 in the Netherlands. I will summarize them briefly. Scenario A presents a projection of current trends. Scenario B deals with increasing growth in the demand for facilities. Scenario C sketches decreasing growth in demand for facilities. The strategies assessed range from (1) maintaining the present course to (2) top care, and (3) towards a reciprocal aid society.

The first critical incident discussed in this scenario report deals with the postponement of senile dementia by five years. It relates to medical and medical-technological developments which could result in a reduction of demand for (health) care facilities. In the simulation, it was assumed that the age-specific admission figures for dementia will move upward by five birth year cohorts. If such a shift were realized by the year 2000, this would mean a reduction of one-quarter in the number of nursing home patients, compared with the situation in the year 2000 without such postponement (Hollander & Becker 1985: 29).

The second critical incident relates to social developments. An extreme lessening of intergenerational solidarity is simulated: care of elders by family members is reduced to zero. This development will result in an increased demand for professional assistance. In 1984, 67 per cent of elders received care from family members of between one and six hours per week, while 19 per cent received more than six hours of care per week from family members. In the report, the consequences of the disappearance of care of parents by children are simulated with a quantified model.

Both critical incidents have been confronted with the three contextual scenarios. As it turned out, the first critical incident would not lead to a substantial decrease of health care costs in the country because people would live longer and die of illnesses more costly than senile dementia, such as cancer.

Most SIA studies need to maintain close communication with the central actor, and often with actors in the target systems. In these cases, it is essential to involve the intended audiences of the SIA report in the process of designing the scenarios. Sometimes members of the intended audiences actually participate in the designing process. In other cases, audiences of the SIA report are invited to *redesign* the scenarios before they are invited to develop strategies and to assess their effects and side effects. The integration of scenario design in the process of *strategic learning* will be discussed later.

In all settings, the communication of scenarios to an audience poses a lot of questions. How can the essence of a scenario be conveyed without losing the flavour of the design? How can we assist the reader in coming to grips with the complexity of the system represented in the scenarios? In Figure 4.2, an approach is presented that summarizes a number of

	Senario 1	Senario 2	Scenario 3
Economic	*		
developments			
Dynamic of politics	*		
and government			
Demographic	*		
developments			
Etc.	*		

*Developments relevant to more than one scenario

Figure 4.2 Scheme to summarize scenarios and key variables.

scenarios. The scheme allows the description of variables that differ between scenarios, and variables that are the same in one or more scenarios. This scheme will be elaborated later to present *inter alia* a summary of a scenario-to-strategy analysis.

In Figure 4.2, only scenarios are described, and critical incidents are excluded. Whenever in a scenario analysis critical incidents are involved, the format of Figure 4.2 can also be used to facilitate an analysis of critical incidents to strategies. In this case, the scenarios are represented in separate schemes. Each scheme represents the analysis of one or more critical incidents and their principal variables.

4.2.5 Iteration and reporting

The designing of scenarios requires numerous iterations. Ten and more loops are quite normal in scenario projects. Writing a report on the outcomes of a scenario design is a demanding task. It is a major pitfall in scenario design. The text has to preserve all the flavour of the design process. The text will have to inspire future readers and prepare them for their own designing activities: reshaping the scenarios, and often also designing scenarios for a similar setting.

In a number of projects, artists and writers have been commissioned to describe the summaries of the scenarios and critical incidents. This has proved problematic, however, as employing a different artist for each scenario leads to sketches that are difficult to use with an integrated frame of reference. If one professional journalist or writer takes responsibility for the final version of all scenarios and critical incidents, the result may be a text that is satisfactory.

4.3 *Design of strategies*

4.3.1 Evaluation of current strategies

The research team will have to start with evaluating current strategies (step 2.1). Here, the positional map developed in the preliminary phase of the study should be applied. In many SIA studies using scenarios, the evaluation of current strategies leads to the conclusion that the central actor has never told the scenario team about a number of important policy options.

4.3.2 Design of an integrated set of strategies

Designing an adequate set of strategies (step 2.2) cannot be accomplished by an approach that is purely logical or empirical. If all possible options have to be taken into consideration, the number of strategies to be specified and analyzed quickly exceeds the number of strategies that can be handled in the study. This implies that a selection has to be made that is partly based on normative and intuitive arguments. Taking all alternative strategies into consideration, for example, by morphological analysis, is a blind alley. Porter et al. (1980: 175) state: "Morphological analysis could, at least in theory, be applied to search the impact field in an exhaustive fashion. The chief limitation to this application would seem to be that of obtaining a clear problem definition and exhaustive identification of parameters."

Designing an integrated set of strategies can best be accomplished by parallel design processes. One approach is to use two or more designers, each having identical instructions, to work on an individual basis. The second option is to use two or more design teams that also receive identical instructions. After two or more hours of separate designing activities, the outcomes of the endeavours are reported in a plenary session. The preliminary sets of strategies are analyzed. If feasible, they are integrated in a limited number of sets of strategies. Following this, the individual designers or the design teams are set to work on improving the preliminary sets of strategies. Iteration will have to be continued until designs are produced that are *saturated*. Elsewhere, testing of designs for the level of saturation have been discussed.

How can designers arrive at saturated sets of strategies? In most areas of policy-making, overviews of strategies (or policy instruments) are available. The designers can use these overviews as checklists and heuristics.

In the area of government interventions, a list of more than 30 types of interventions is available (Osborne & Gaebler 1992). The policy instruments are categorized as sermons, carrots and sticks (van der

Doelen 1992). *Sermons*, using verbal and nonverbal communications techniques and interactional persuasion, include: mass communication campaigns, public relations campaigns and negotiations. Each of these policy instruments is based on exhaustive ex-post evaluation research of applications. As an example, I mention the Harvard Negotiation Project, yielding not only data and theories, but also a methodology for carrying out negotiations (Fisher & Ury 1981).

Carrots represent intervention techniques that offer rewards and state criteria for obtaining those rewards. Examples from the area of government are subvention programmes, and human resources development programmes. Subvention programmes offer financial resources, either total government financing or co-financing by government. Co-financing ranges from almost 100 per cent to almost nil. Participating on the basis of a high percentage empowers government to select and monitor in a strict way. Participation on a low basis restricts government selection and monitoring to marginal interventions.

If human resource development is involved, government selects and fosters human capital. This may apply to personnel outside government employment, for example, teachers in private, government-subsidized educational institutions. It may also imply guidance of government personnel. In public sector human resources management, both selection and control are involved. The state as principal actor may regulate hiring and firing, stimulate in-service training and enforce retirement arrangements (Gilley & Eggland 1989).

Sticks are prominent in direct power plays. In the area of government, the toolbox of sticks includes: legal measures; organizing and reorganizing; privatization; regulation and deregulation. In the 1980s, privatization and deregulation have been applied by governments in the West on a large scale, for example, to fight the economic recession and organizational stagnation. Exhaustive ex-post evaluation has resulted in substantial improvement of intervention methods (Donahue 1989; Kay et al. 1986).

The Inter-organizational Committee on Guidelines and Principles for Social Impact Assessment has published in its 1994 Report suggestions for (a) planning and policy development, (b) implementation and development, (c) operation and maintenance and (d) decommissioning and abandonment of projects. The suggestions make clear that the

Inter-organizational Committee has focused its guidelines mainly on large-scale development projects, such as large dams within the US NEPA context. The guidelines also focus on projects directed by government or private–public partnerships.

4.3.3 Iteration and reporting

Iteration (step 2.3) enters the scene again. This iteration has to be organized in conjunction with activities in the project described later in this chapter.

Writing a report (step 6.5) on strategic design leads to a classified document, at least if the exercise has been restricted to the staff of the focal actor. If public participation has been involved, the report will have to be written in an accessible style.

4.4 Assessment of impacts

4.4.1 Scenario-to-strategy simulation

Next, the research team has to engage in the core activities of IA: evaluating the consequences of current or proposed action (step 4.1). The baseline analysis has to provide information on past action and its impacts. The theoretical model has to add hypotheses on the impact of trends. The theoretical model also has to predict the effects and side effects of interventions. The theory of collective action, for example, provides predictions of the outcomes of social movements.

Identifying the future consequences of a current or proposed action requires a specification of the degree of accuracy of the information on the future to be provided. It also demands an insight into the explanatory model behind the data. We do not have a well-established typology providing an overview of this kind. To overcome this handicap in Figure 4.3 and 4.4 a preliminary typology is presented. Ten types of information are distinguished. Type 10 represents forecasts about processes in a system with little noise, combined with an elaborated theoretical model. We can find this type of predictions in demographic

level 10 hard forecast
    09 soft forecast
    08 hard extrapolation
    07 soft extrapolation
    06 hard exploration
    05 soft exploration
    04 hard speculation
    03 soft spectulation
    02 informed guess
    01 assumption of chaos

Figure 4.3 10-scale of predictions based on the degree of accuracy and the quality of the explanatory model.

	Degree of accuracy	Quality of the explanatory model
level 10 hard forecast	+ + + +	+ + + +
09 soft forecast	+ + +	+ + + +
08 hard extrapolation	+ + +	+ +
07 soft extrapolation	+ +	+ +
06 hard exploration	+ +	+ + +
05 soft exploration	+	+ + +
04 hard speculation	+	+ +
03 soft spectulation	+	+
02 informed guess	+	±
01 assumption of chaos	±	±

Figure 4.4 10-scale of predictions specified by scaling (a) the degree of accuracy and (b) the quality of the explanatory model.

research on developments in cohorts aged 20–40, for instance. Type 9 is about forecasts about processes in systems with more noise. Type 8 provides information based on projections or extrapolations; the information is backed by a weak theoretical model only. Type 7 is about processes with relatively much noise. Types 8 and 7 are temporary "homes" for predictions only, because in most cases researchers will improve the explanatory model as soon as possible. Type 6 presents explorations. This approach is adequate if the developments have not yet been studied elaborately, and we can assume that they show relatively little noise. In type 5 there is a little bit more noise. Types 6 and 5 are already related to an explanatory model. Type 4, hosting speculations, is related to processes with relatively much noise, already combined with a theoretical orientation. Type 3 shows most of the characteristics of the former type but is haunted by more noise. Type 2 presents informed guesses. Type 1 provides examples of processes social researchers assume to be chaotic, that is, unpredictable.

The ten-scale of predictions is designed as a frame of reference, not an ordinary scale. The ten-scale helps to classify predictions with regard to accuracy, and relationship to an explanatory model. This new typology will require a lot of trial and error before it reaches maturity.

Whenever forecasting, projection, etc. are required, computer simulation is worth considering. Computer simulation provides a solution to handling complexity, however, the costs of designing and testing computer simulation models are relatively high. Futures speculation requires simulation exercises that can best be handled by human simulation. Also interactive simulation can be applied, combining human simulation and computer simulation.

Simulating impacts starts with scenario-to-strategy analyses. In Figure 4.5, a scheme is presented illustrating this kind of analysis. The

	Scenario 1 (trend)	Scenario 2 (growth)	Scenario 3 (decline)
Strategy A (business as usual)			
Strategy B (conservative)			
Strategy C (progressive)			

The examples are illustrations only
Handle critical incidents as subscenarios

Figure 4.5 Scheme of cross-impact simulation.

scheme can be used in human simulations using qualitative information. It can be used in conjunction with Figure 4.2. The scheme also provides a guideline for designing cross-impact computer simulations.

At the start of the assessment, the first order impacts of the current or proposed action are identified. As an example, I take the impacts of a new airport. Because IAs are named after the principal first order impact, the simulation in the example will be called an EIA. The new airport will produce noise (caused by aircraft movements) and air pollution. Next, the second order impacts come to the fore. The new airport will increase risk in the area, *inter alia* by increasing the risk of crashes (risk assessment). It will also increase opportunities for employment (demographic and SIA). It will also increase health problems, *inter alia*, because it leads to headaches as a consequence of noise (health and social IA). Third order impacts are more or less indirect consequences. The price of land, houses and office buildings in the area will change (economic IA).

4.4.2 Additional simulations

In most large-scale SIA studies, additional simulations of impacts are required. First, simulating the impact of strategies on target variables. Figure 4.6 illustrates this kind of simulation. Second, critical incidents may demand similar simulations. In this case, the impacts of each critical incident for each strategy are identified.

4.4.3 Iteration and reporting

Assessment of impacts requires iteration of analyses (steps 4.1 and 4.2), particularly because scenarios and strategies will be redesigned a number of times.

Writing a report on IA implies reporting procedures that are standard in policy-oriented social research (step 4.3). If public participation is part of the process, special skills will be required to write the text, design the tables and draw the pictures.

	Strategy A	Strategy B	Strategy C
Target variable X	*		
	**		
Target variable Y	*		
	**		
Etc.	*		
	**		

N.B.
*Planned effects
**Side-effects, either favourable or unfavourable

Figure 4.6 Scheme of simulation of the impact of strategies on target variables.

4.5 Ranking strategies

4.5.1 Choice of type of ranking

Which strategy has to be preferred in which scenario? Which strategy is second best in a specific scenario? Which strategy is to be preferred if a specific critical incidence does occur? Which strategy represents disaster planning in a specific scenario? These questions illustrate that ranking strategies requires serious attention.

The oldest method to rank strategies is cost-benefit analysis (CBA), however the applicability of this method is limited. In order to overcome a number of these limitations, multi-criteria analysis has been developed. We will discuss both ranking methods.

CBA achieved formal recognition in the USA in the 1930s. The US Flood Control Act of 1936 enunciated the principle that a project be declared *feasible* (i.e. desirable) if the benefits, *to whomsoever they may accrue*, are in excess of the estimated costs. But the precise meaning of a *benefit* remained obscure. In the late 1950s, the Harvard University Water Program brought together a team of scientists who developed a reasonably integrated theory of CBA, with costs and benefits being related more clearly to welfare losses and gains, so that the substantial body of welfare theory could be brought to bear on the issue.

CBA does attempt to refer to individuals' preferences and to place them on a comparable basis for measurement, but some unresolvable problems exist. If a motorway reduces the risk of deaths in road accidents, how is a life saved to be valued? If a project totally destroys a species of wildlife, how is such an irreversible loss to be evaluated (Dasgupta & Pearce 1972)? CBA purports to be a way of deciding what society prefers. Where only one option can be chosen from a series of options, CBA should inform the decision-maker as to which option is socially most preferred (Dasgupta and Pearce 1978: 19).

Decision-makers are assumed to have *objective functions* that are to be maximized. These objective functions may be profits, income or net social benefits defined in a way so as to incorporate things other than income. CBA works with an objective function defined in terms of some concept of net benefits. Of course, it is possible that the decision-maker wishes only to achieve some given level of net benefits. If several policies meet that aim, it is conceivable that a decision-maker will be indifferent. In general, however, it would seem odd if decision-makers did not try to rank the alternatives in terms of their objective function, choosing the alternative with the highest value of this function. It is assumed that the decision-maker aims to maximize the difference between social benefits and social costs (Dasgupta & Pearce 1972: 21).

If the costs and benefits of a project like a large dam cannot be expressed in monetary terms, a number of escapes are available. If, for instance, a wildlife resort will have to disappear because a large dam is being built, the costs of the loss of the wildlife resort can be represented by the price of a *shadow project*. The shadow project specifies the costs that have to be made to construct a comparable wildlife resort elsewhere. The shadow project can actually be realized, or compensations can be paid.

In general, CBA relates to large-scale, government-controlled development projects, such as building large dams. In practice, CBA is used also to rank alternative strategies in situations requiring small-scale projects, involving either government activities or private initiative.

Often, not all costs or benefits can be expressed in money terms in an adequate way. In that case, ranking methods have to be applied that also take nonmonetary criteria into account. If criteria other than monetary ones are used, this is known as *multiple criteria analysis*. The field of multiple criteria analysis is supplementing the more advanced techniques in several disciplines (e.g. economics, operations research, management sciences, mathematics, psychology, sociology, organization theory, planning, etc.) (Nijkamp & Spronk 1981).

By taking account of a wide variety of issues inherent in any decision problem and by offering an operational framework for a multidisciplinary approach to practical choice problems, attention can be paid to the specific requirements of decision-makers, decision processes and the practice of decision-making.

In a multiple-criteria analysis, the identification of consequences of current or proposed actions takes place by assigning money values, symbols (pluses, minuses, plus/minuses) and verbal expressions. Ultimately, of course, a unified set of criteria has to be used allowing policymakers to choose between alternative actions in a systematic way. In multiple-criteria analysis, assessors do their utmost to avoid quasi-mathematical representations that might induce oversimplification of the ranking process. An interesting approach to this dilemma is ranking alternatives by allocating different shades of colour.

4.5.2 Ranking process

Ranking according to the rules of CBA can be accomplished by members of the SIA team.

Multiple-criteria analysis often requires a different approach. Here, ranking is effected by inviting two or more groups to allocate weights to alternatives. In this exercise, the teams receive identical instructions, but they must operate independently at first. After the first round, they report their ranking of alternatives and then participate in a plenary discussion. After this discussion, a second and third round of ranking can be staged.

Ranking alternative actions in this way, taking their consequences into account, forces decision-makers to reveal a lot about their preferences. This can lead to tension and conflict among the raters. The SIA team has to anticipate this and be prepared for it. If conflict flares up, the team must be prepared to interrupt the exercise immediately. At a later time, the participants can be invited to comment on the clash.

4.5.3 Iteration and reporting

If decision-makers are involved in the ranking process, communication with the central actor has been taken care of. It depends on the objectives of the SIA study whether or not other actors have to be involved too.

Checking on pitfalls involves attention to naïve ranking by relying too much on quantification, and ensuring that the SIA team has invited the appropriate participants to take scenarios and critical incidents into consideration.

Iteration is standard procedure in ranking alternatives, especially if human players are involved and a human simulation is used in the ranking process.

Does the SIA team have to publish the report on the ranking? If decision-makers will have to reveal most of their preferences, it is likely that they will require that the report be restricted.

4.6 Mitigation of negative impacts

4.6.1 Redesigning of strategies and reassessment of impacts

Mitigation is a relatively new element in IA. In the *Guidebook for Technology Assessment and Impact Analysis* (Porter et al. 1980), the subject is treated in a restricted way only. The *Guidelines and Principles for Social Impact Assessment* (Inter-organizational Committee 1994) designate two steps in their model to mitigation. Their recommendations will be summarized and analyzed here.

An SIA not only forecasts impacts, it should also identify means to mitigate adverse impacts. Mitigation includes *avoiding* the impact by not proceeding with the activity, or modifying the action; *minimizing, rectifying or reducing* the impacts through the design or operation of the project or policy; or *compensating* for the impact by providing substitute facilities, resources, or opportunities (Inter-organizational Committee 1994:15).

Ideally, mitigation measures should be built into the selected alternative, but it is appropriate to identify mitigation measures even if they are not immediately adopted or if they would be the responsibility of another person or government unit.

In the *Guidelines and Principles*, a sequencing strategy to manage social impact is suggested, having been modelled on one used with wetland protection and other natural resource issues. During the first sequence, wetland managers strive to avoid all adverse impacts. In the second sequence, managers strive to minimize any adverse impacts that cannot be avoided. During the third sequence, managers compensate for adverse impacts. Compensation for the loss of a wetland, for example, could be to acquire a different wetland, enhance a degraded site or create a new wetland. The amount of compensation can be based on the type of wetland or resource lost, the severity of the impact and the location of the wetland mitigation site.

This approach to mitigation is analogous to designing a *shadow project* in CBA, and to paying financial compensation for the liquidation of the endangered wildlife reservoir, or to building a new wildlife reservoir elsewhere. Shadow prices and shadow projects have been discussed in a prior section of this chapter.

The first two steps of sequencing advocated in the *Guidelines and Principles* – avoiding and minimizing – can be applied to the project itself, to the host community or the impacted region. For example, the project may be revised to avoid or minimize adverse social impacts (e.g. extend the construction period to minimize in-migration), or the community may be able to take steps to attenuate, if not avoid, any adverse effects. Application of the sequencing concept for the mitigation of adverse social impacts requires that the assessor first rank the level of importance of each significant SIA variable determined during the estimated effects step.

The first step in evaluating potential mitigation for each variable is to determine whether the proponent could modify the project or proposed policy to avoid the adverse effects. For example, a road that displaces communities could be rerouted.

The next step in the sequencing process is to identify ways to minimize adverse social impacts.

Each new alternative or recommended change should be assessed separately. This implies a reassessment of the whole package of current or proposed actions.

4.6.2 Revision of ranking of strategies

Mitigation of negative impacts has to be followed by a new ranking of strategies. The methods used in step 4.4 apply here, but usually on a more modest scale. The SIA team has by now gained experience in ranking strategies in this particular setting.

4.6.3 Iteration and reporting

The number of iterations of this step will depend upon time, funding and the magnitude of the project or policy changes. The report on the mitigation exercise will be made available to interested actors in SIA studies involving public participation.

4.7 Reporting

4.7.1 Decision about types of reporting

During the SIA process, a number of reports must be produced. In the final reporting, most intermediate reports will appear as background papers. Which types of reporting will the team use at the end of the main phase in the SIA study?

In 1979, the OECD reported on the *Interfutures* project in the following way:

(1) an executive summary of two pages;
(2) a report, *Facing the Future*, of 425 pages, including a summary of the scenarios of 12 pages;
(3) background documents of about 2,000 pages in total;
(4) a press release of one page;
(5) workshops and conferences.

This approach represents a communications strategy that has a number of advantages. First, it is geared to the main audiences of the outcomes of the project. Secondly, it not only presents information in print but combines this approach with direct interactions. Conferences imply lectures and discussions, workshops entail gaining hands-on experience with the method of scenario design and IA and the outcomes of a particular enterprise. If the SIA study is integrated in a process of organizational learning, multiple reporting is automatically involved by including workshops that invite participants to design their own scenarios and strategies and to assess impacts themselves.

Communication with the audiences of the project in general, and reporting in particular, are notorious pitfalls. If the team starts to work on the reports when it is tired, an uninspired set of documents will be produced and much of the efforts invested in the SIA study will remain without result.

4.7.2 Executive summary

Policy-makers generally prepare for negotiations and decision-making by reading only the executive summaries of the main research report and the briefing memoranda written by their staff. Their preparation also includes discussions with colleagues in the area of policy-making and members of their staff. Only in exceptional circumstances do they read complete reports or engage in discussions with scientists or impact assessors. Policy-makers may browse through research reports, and they are likely to infer much from their own experience and perspective, often trying to guess at the reliability of the research outcomes. They will also make a guess at the relevance other actors in their social network will attach to the research report. This implies that designing the executive summary is a crucial activity in the SIA study. It is not to be left to unexperienced team members. Nor is it to be reserved for last minute desk clearing activities.

The research team has to keep an eye on the life course of the executive summary. Does it reach the policy-maker in its original phrasing? Frequently, individuals in the chain of communication between researchers and policy-makers try to *translate* the message, often injecting ideas of their own.

4.7.3 Full report

Reports like *Facing the Future* and *Scanning the Future* are examples of very successful final reports of scenario projects incorporating SIA.

What is the secret behind their success? First, they show a structure of chapters, sections and so on that is convincing at first sight. Secondly, they are written in a way that resembles the style of publications explicitly prepared for a large but demanding audience. Their readability is comparable to articles in leading newspapers.

The final report requires a single editor or a team of closely co-operating editors. If a large number of team members have contributed fragments of text, rewriting the draft of the report has to be included in the planning of the reporting.

The draft report has to be confronted with the critical comments of devil's advocates.

4.7.4 Background papers

A list of nonclassified background papers ought to be included in the full report. Background papers enable other scientists to evaluate the SIA study. Background papers also enable other scientists to use the outcomes of the SIA study as stepping stones for new projects.

Preparing the background papers for (limited) publication has to be combined with arranging the archives of the SIA study. The research team or other scientists may want to use the database or background reports as an input to a new baseline analysis.

4.7.5 Press release

Designing a press release is a specific art-science. Only few journalists have the gift and the experience to write an announcement to the press that catches the attention of editors of journals, TV programmes and related channels of mass communication. Putting together a summary for the press requires co-operation with specialists that have demonstrated ability.

4.7.6 Workshops

More and more written reporting is supplemented with organizing workshops and reporting orally and by audio-visual means. In a workshop, participants can be invited to *redesign* the scenarios and the critical incidents, specifying and augmenting what has been written in the report. In a workshop, participants can also be induced to select strategies and to guess at social and related impacts.

In strategic learning, this approach has been refined, by *inter alia* introducing *scenario-to-strategy-workshops*. These workshops will be dealt with in detail in a later chapter.

4.8 Auditing and ex-post evaluation

4.8.1 Auditing

SIA studies related to interventions taking a number of years to be completed require some kind of social auditing. If the intervention is launched as part of government policy, social auditing may be required by law. Social auditing resembles environmental auditing in a number of aspects. For this reason, I summarize the main ideas and practices of environmental auditing. According to Buckley (1995: 283), environmental audit is simply a check on some aspect of environmental management. From the first uses of the term in this context over a decade ago, a number of somewhat different activities have been referred to as environmental audits. Some of these arose, Buckley states, in response to the various requirements of such bodies as the US Environmental Protection Agency and the US Securities and Exchange Commission. Others arose as practitioners attempted to evaluate the success of EIA and related environmental planning tools. Others arose from the internal practices of transnational corporations, as they began to compare environmental aspects of their operations between different operations, sometimes spanning different countries (Buckley 1995: 283).

Social auditing, in many cases, is part of an integrated IA of such development projects as large dams. In settings like these, environmental, economic and social assessments accompany the development project during a period of 10–15 years, and continue to examine its effects and side effects for a number of years after completion.

Legislation introducing a revision of a national social security system or a national penal system also often includes provisions for auditing the consequences of these alterations.

A major pitfall in social auditing is finishing the auditing too soon. It takes many years before a large-scale development process shows its major positive and negative effects. If legal requirements restrict auditing to the first two to three years after the intervention, the outcomes of the auditing will provide information that is seriously incomplete.

Auditing systems have to be designed and institutionalized early in the development process. Auditing is closely related to monitoring. There are significant differences, however. Monitoring implies description, explanation and interpretation as part of social analysis. Auditing also requires description, but its main characteristic is the confrontation of what actually happens with legal and contractual requirements.

4.8.2 Ex-post evaluation of the SIA study

Why should one wish to evaluate an impact statement, Porter et al. ask (1980: 443). Certainly, those preparing the statements do not typically encourage their evaluation by others; people usually prefer not to be critically scrutinized. Evaluation consumes resources, Porter et al. argue, that could be spent on more assessment activities. Furthermore evaluations are difficult to perform. However, they conclude that there are two potential payoffs that make evaluation desirable: (a) the *assessment of assessments*, to help potential users judge the worth of particular TA/EIAs and (b) the improvement of assessments in general, through feedback as to strengths and weaknesses. Such evaluation information can benefit sponsors, users and performers of IAs.

Four important dimensions for the evaluation of impact assessments can be distinguished (Porter et al. 1980: 447):

1. Formative versus summative. Formative evaluation provides feedback to the study while it is in progress. It addresses validity in terms of currently available knowledge and method, as well as internal consistency and completeness. It also considers the potential utility of the study by identifying the prospective users and matching anticipated study outputs to their needs. Summative

evaluation weighs the merits of a study after its completion. They can be used to judge the effectiveness of assessors, particular types of studies, or particular methods.

2. A priori evaluations versus *post hoc* designed evaluations. A priori evaluations are developed as an integral part of the impact assessment study. *Post hoc* ones are constructed after the assessment project has been designed, usually even after their completion.

3. Single versus multiple assessments of assessments. Single-study evaluations are most appropriate to help interested parties to judge the validity of a particular study. Multiple-study evaluations offer a wealth of possibilities for advancing the state of the art of IA.

4. Immediate evaluations versus extended term evaluations. Immediate evaluations provide information to potential users on the validity of a study in terms of scientific propriety, absence of bias, and so on. This can aid users in interpreting the assessment findings. Extended term evaluations can take place long after completion of a study to assess the realism of its projections or its usefulness over time.

An interesting example of ex-post evaluation of (*inter alia*) SIA is provided by Meadows et al. (1982) who have evaluated global modelling in its first decade. The title of their book, *Groping in the Dark*, characterizes the outcomes of the evaluation in an adequate way. The authors, all of them experienced global modellers and social impact assessors, summarize their evaluation as follows:

1. It is better to state your biases, insofar as you are able, than to pretend you do not have any.

2. Computer models of social systems should not be expected to produce precise predictions.

3. Inexact, qualitative understanding can be derived from computer models and can be very useful.

4. Methods should be selected to fit problems (or systems); problems (or systems) should not be distorted to fit methods.

5. The most important forces shaping the future are social and political, and these forces are the least well represented in the models so far.

6. In long-term global models, environmental and resource considerations have been ignored.

7. Models should be tested much more thoroughly for agreement with the real world for sensitivity to uncertainties, and over the full range of possible policies.

8. A substantial fraction of modelling resources should go to documentation.

9. Part of the model documentation should be technically complete, so that any other modelling group could run and explore the model and duplicate all published results.

10. Part of the documentation should be so clear and free from jargon that a nontechnical audience could understand all the model's assumptions and how these assumptions led to the model's conclusions.

11. Modellers should identify their data sources clearly and share their data as much as possible.

12. Users, if there are any clearly identifiable ones, should be involved in the modelling process as directly and frequently as possible.

13. It is necessary to have an international clearing house for presenting, storing, comparing, criticizing and publishing global models.

14. There should be many more global models.

These conclusions are a checklist in disguise of pitfalls related to large-scale modelling of developments and of consequences of intended interventions. At the same time, they elucidate pitfalls in the ex-post evaluation of SIA applying this type of model.

117

CHAPTER 5

Types of SIA

5.1 Introduction

This chapter develops a typology of impact assessment in general and social impact assessment in particular. Both typologies are elaborations of the brief outlines presented in Chapter 1. We will take a closer look at each of the types identified in the typology and the main problems, actions and actors associated with these types. The principal methods associated with each type and the experience gained so far will also be described.

Before embarking on the IA typology and its subtypologies, I will examine typologies in general. A type is *that by which a phenomenon is symbolized*: a typology deals with two or more phenomena (Copi 1978). It is a symbolic representation of phenomena at a relatively high level of abstraction. The counterpart of a typology is a classification. A classification presents categories formulated at a relatively low level of abstraction. A classification serves to sort phenomena according to precisely formulated criteria. A typology in most cases is limited to four or five types. It provides a global overview, but boundaries between types are often quite fuzzy. A classification provides a precise categorization, and sometimes uses more than a hundred categories. In most cases, a classification is too complex to provide a general overview (Copi 1978).

We often use typologies in everyday life, for example, left and right in politics and lower, middle and upper classes in society. Typologies have to meet a number of criteria. First, they must be plausible. They must

118

show a reasonable fit between categories and types. They must also show a reasonable fit between the symbols used and institutionalized terminology. New terms should only be introduced if institutionalized terms are seriously deficient. Secondly, they must be logically consistent. There is an exception to this rule, however. Logically inconsistent typologies are permitted whenever we want to use this inconsistency to draw attention to the typology. An example here is the juridical expression, *summum ius summa iniuria est*, meaning that the pinnacle of justice is often the pinnacle of injustice. Thirdly, typologies must be heuristic. They must stimulate an understanding of the phenomena symbolized in the typology. Fourthly, they must be practical. Good typologies provide a rapid overview of the phenomena they symbolize. A good typology is not too complicated and can be memorized without much trouble.

5.2 Towards a typology of impact assessment

As we saw earlier, we do not yet have a sophisticated, generally accepted typology of IAs. What we do have is a number of preliminary typologies, each of them rather *ad hoc* in their design. In this chapter, I want to proceed more systematically. I have scrutinized the volumes of *Impact Assessment* and its predecessor, the *Impact Assessment Bulletin*, for examples of IA and I have *clustered* my findings according to their first order impacts.

Cluster 1: Environmental impact assessment (EIA). The process of identifying the consequences current or future actions will have on the environment, and is a legal requirement in about half the countries of the world. Although EIA is often combined with other types of IA, it is in practice a field of expertise in its own right. This implies that I have defined EIA here in a narrow sense because I object to any definition of EIA that tends to treat it as being identical to IA in general (Ortolano & Shepherd 1995: 3 *passim*).

Since it was institutionalization in the USA by the NEPA in 1969, thousands of environmental impact statements have been produced and, as required by law, each of them has been published. These procedures have not lead to any standardization of EIA methodology, however. There are a number of checklists and guidelines, but these serve simply as frames of reference. The assessment exercise in EIA involves the identification, prediction and evaluation of impacts on the environment. The identification of probable impacts worthy of study is aided by the scoping process (Ortolano & Shepherd 1995: 6). Technical specialists, individuals from agencies and nongovernmental organizations and citizens potentially affected by a project give their opinions on the types of impacts likely to be important. This process of scoping is enriched if the technical specialists know the impacts to be expected in the type of project under study. It should be noted here that this kind of scoping is restricted to EIA. The second half of the EIA is concerned with predictions. The methods used for impact prediction are not restricted to EIA but come from research methodology used in the natural and social sciences. Thirdly, EIA requires an evaluation of predicted impacts on the environment. There are algorithms and computer programs available for assisting environmental impact assessors in evaluating these impacts (Ortolano and Shepherd 1995: 7).

The most common positive outcomes of EIA are measures suggested to mitigate (or offset) the adverse effects of a proposed plan. Ortolano and Shepherd conclude that mitigation may involve one or more of the following:

(a) minimizing adverse effects by scaling down or redesigning a project;
(b) repairing, rehabilitating or restoring those parts of the environment that are adversely affected by the project;
(c) creating or acquiring environments similar to those adversely affected by an action. The latter sometimes takes the form of a *shadow project*. Here the loss of an environmentally valuable area is compensated by creating a similar area elsewhere.

I have located ecological IA in this cluster as well as defining it as "a formal process of defining, quantifying and evaluating the potential impacts of defined actions on an ecosystem" (Treweek 1995: 172). In this kind of IA, biodiversity is often the main dependent variable.

I will now add climate impact assessment to this cluster. This is defined as "a sequential set of activities designed to identify, analyze, and evaluate the impacts of climatic variability and climatic change on natural systems, human activities, and human health and well-being,

120

[and] to estimate the uncertainties surrounding these impacts" (Taplin & Braaf 1995: 249).

Cluster 2: Technology assessment (TA). By TA I follow the definition provided by Coates (1976): ". . . the systematic study of the effects that may occur when a technology is introduced, extended, or modified". However Coates makes a specification *with emphasis on the impacts that are unintended, indirect, or delayed* which I do not accept here because, in IA in the 1990s, the intended effects of current or future action are generally included in the definition. Contrary to standard practice, the term technology assessment does not refer to a major first-order impact of the current or proposed action being analyzed.

In the words of a workshop organized by the United Nations (UN) and the Office of Technology Assessment in 1991, technology assessment:

> ultimately comprises a systems approach to the management of technology reaching beyond technology and industrial aspects into society and environmental domains. Initially, it deals with assessment of effects, consequences, and risks of a technology but it also has a forecasting function in that it looks into the projection of opportunities and skill development as an input to strategic planning. In this respect, it also has a component for monitoring and for scrutinizing the information gathered. Ultimately, technology assessment is also a policy and consensus building process (cited in Porter 1995: 69).

In his review of the state of the art of IA, Porter (1995) indicates that TA remains a cluster of various expertises in its own right primarily because the technology and its context have to be analyzed and its likely development over the time horizon of interest anticipated. The description and forecasting of technology emphasize the functional capabilities of changing technology and its direct applications. Societal context description and forecasting seek to ascertain the key influences on technology's development and subsequently impact identification, analysis and evaluation are required. These progress through asking such questions as what might result? how much is likely? and so what? In principle, Porter continues, these steps consider each potential impact and how it affects the parties concerned. Porter concludes that extending the notion of all impacts through a cascade of indirect impacts conveys the challenge of IA.

Cluster 3: Economic impact assessment. This may be defined as "estimating changes in employment, income, and levels of business activity (typically measured by gross receipts or added value) that may result from a proposed project or program" (Leistritz 1995: 129). As with all types of IA, economic IA involves projecting levels of activity that might be expected to prevail in the study area with the project and then making the same assessment without the project. The difference between the two projections gives an indication of the project's impact (Leistritz 1995: 129).

Economic IA models are related to economic base theory, also called export base theory. In these models, the economy of an area is divided into two types of economic units. First, the basic sector, defined as those firms which mostly sell goods and services to markets outside the area. Second, the nonbasic sector, defined as those firms which supply goods and services mainly to customers within the area. A key concept in economic base theory is that the level of nonbasic activity in an area is uniquely determined by the level of basic activity, and any change in the level of basic activity will bring about a predictable change in the level of nonbasic activity. This relationship is known as the multiplier effect. Economic base theory considers external demand for the products of the basic sector as the principal force determining change in the level of economic activity in an area. The basis for the multiplier effect is the interdependence of the basic and the nonbasic sectors in an economic area. The magnitude of the multiplier effect is determined by the proportion of a given unit of additional income that is spent locally. High multiplier values are associated with high levels of local spending, which in turn imply a diversified, relatively self-sufficient economy. Larger regions tend to have higher multiplier values (Leistritz 1995: 130).

Two kinds of models can be applied when estimating the magnitude of secondary economic effects for a specific project in a given area: an export-base model, focusing on employment or income multipliers, and an input-output model. Input-output models are being increasingly used because this technique provides more detailed impact estimates than other approaches and can better reflect differences in expenditure patterns amongst projects. This technique is being increasingly used because there are now databases and data management systems available that enable the development of input-output models tailored to local conditions although based largely or sometimes entirely on secondary data sources (Leistritz 1995: 131).

I also include fiscal IA in this cluster. Investigating the fiscal impacts of new projects or programmes (Leistritz 1995: 133), the purpose of fiscal IA is to project the likely changes in costs and revenues of governmental units that might occur as a result of a development project. Fiscal IA focuses exclusively on public sector costs and revenues associated with a project or programme.

Cluster 4: Social impact assessment (SIA). In Chapter 1, I defined SIA as *the process of identifying the future consequences of a current or proposed action for individuals, organizations, institutions and society as a whole.* As we saw in Chapter 2, SIA started as a kind of pretesting of actions related to old-age pensions (annuities) and the health of individuals in society. Gradually this kind of pretesting unfolded, covering more and more aspects of social life. In Chapter 2, I argued that I expected that ultimately each major component of society would have a type of SIA. SIA would become standard practice. This process of unfolding has been accelerated by the emergence in the USA of NEPA and other legal requirements for environmental IAs, which, in most cases, included SIA. The combination with EIA has lead to the widespread diffusion of SIA in the USA. As soon as EIA was required by law in other countries, SIA followed EIA.

However, the growth and diffusion of SIA has also occurred in situations that are only loosely connected with EIA. An example of this is demographic IA, that is, identifying the future consequences of current or proposed actions on human fertility, household formation and other kinds of individual behaviour in cohorts (Becker 1995). In North America and western Europe, national governments have explored the consequences of policies to stimulate or curb fertility, immigration and other developments in the population. My second example relates to the consequences of regional development, such as urban and rural building activities on landscapes. Aesthetic IA has been used to identify consequences of these activities on the perception of the landscape by inhabitants of the region (Roebig 1983). Further examples include tourist IA (the impact of tourists on the culture of host communities) and assessment of impacts on labour markets. SIA can be initiated by government (legal IA), private firms and NGOs.

123

SIA is gradually covering a large number of impact activities. As a consequence, a typology is needed to assist understanding of SIA and communication about this type of impact study. I propose a typology covering three types, taking the level of analysis as the basis for distinguishing between types:

(1] SIA at the level of micro-systems, for example, demographic IA;
(2) SIA at the level of meso-systems, for example, organizational IA;
(3) SIA at the level of macro-systems, for example, legal IA.

In addition, SIA can be seen as being applied to purely social issues, but more commonly, SIA is part of integrated IA.

This cluster also contains a type of SIA known as *strategic learning* or *organizational learning*. Strategic learning has been described in Chapters 3 and 4.

In the context of this cluster, SIA consists of what has become institutionalized as oriented basic research and its related activities. These activities have been summarized, for example, by the Inter-organizational Committee on Guidelines and Principles for Social Impact Assessment (1994). I will discuss SIA in more detail below.

Cluster 5: Integrated impact assessment. In this type of assessment, two or more types of IA are applied in a co-ordinated way. As we saw in Chapter 2, a major pioneering project in integrated IA was *Limits to Growth* by Meadows (1972) and his team. Subsequently there has been integrated IA related to meso- and macro-projects in many countries throughout the world. In Chapter 2, large dam and reservoir projects were discussed. These required not only environmental and economic IA but SIA as well. Multiple criteria analysis is an example of a method appropriate for many integrated impact analysis studies (Nijkamp 1986).

Cluster 6: Auxiliary approaches. In social impact studies, we often find methods that play an auxiliary role, that is, they are not major components but are nevertheless important, and in some ways they can be regarded as being independent and somewhat separate from the main activity of SIA. An example of this is a survey of expert opinions which might be carried out by a Delphi procedure and which might be included in the main phase of a social impact study. Each method that plays an auxiliary role in a social impact study could be used in other studies as the main approach. I pointed out in Chapter 4 that a Delphi survey could also be carried out as a separate study, not related to a SIA.

An auxiliary approach in SIA that requires special attention is the stimulation of public involvement, which can increase the democratic quality of a development project. It can also enhance the feasibility of a project if it stimulates the co-operation of the stakeholders. Methods for stimulating public involvement will be discussed in the next chapter. We have to bear in mind, however, that stimulating public involvement is sometimes a project's major objective and SIA is only an auxiliary process within public involvement. The nationwide debate on energy in the Netherlands in the early 1980s is an example of such a situation.

Risk assessment can also be seen as an auxiliary approach in SIA particularly if risk awareness is to be measured. The analysis of risk as one of the main features of SIA will be discussed in the next chapter. Like public involvement, risk assessment can be the principal objective in policy-oriented social research, and here SIA plays the role of auxiliary subproject.

I also include environmental auditing and related activities (Buckley 1995: 283) as an auxiliary method. An environmental audit is a check performed on aspects of environmental management and involves checking the performance of environmental monitoring equipment, corporate compliance with environmental legislation and the accuracy of environmental impact predictions. Some of these activities can be seen as a response to the requirements of the US Environmental Protection Agency, and others arise as practitioners try to evaluate the accuracy of environmental IA. Some are, in fact, the result of the internal management practices of transnational corporations as they begin to compare the environmental aspects of their operations in different nations (Buckley 1995: 283).

Finally, environmental management systems (EMS) also require our attention. In an EMS, monitoring of environmental processes is combined with actions to keep negative impacts on the environment as low as possible, or as low as required by explicit standards. In an EMS, policy-oriented research is combined with interventions. We find EMSs, for instance, in reservoir projects that are completed as far as the building and resettlement processes are concerned. The EMS has to guide the day-by-day decision-making in the system.

5.3 Micro-level SIA

On this level, individual behaviour – including individual life courses – is a dependent variable. In Chapter 1, I introduced the notion of micro-simulations using person-period files as dependent variables. Other types of simulations using individual level data can also be applied.

In many cases, micro-level SIA consists of demographic impact assessment (DIA) which can be defined as *the process of identifying the future consequences of a current or proposed action that may have an impact on demographic processes, or on issues related to demographic processes*. Demography as a scientific discipline was once restricted to the analysis of fertility, family formation, mortality and other events in the life course of individuals. Since the 1970s, however, demographers have expanded their field of study, and today they also consider such aspects as education, employment, income, housing and retirement. The broad definition of demography implies that the boundaries between demography and related social sciences, for example, sociology, cultural anthropology and political science, have become less strict (Becker 1995: 141).

Opportunities for demographic analyses have increased over the years. Since the early 1960s, demographic trends in western Europe and North America have been regularly analyzed, and gradually demographic trends throughout the world are being subject to periodic analysis. At first these statistics had a major drawback: they tended only to provide transversal data. Transversal data are restricted to snapshots of isolated situations in a process. In most DIAs, longitudinal data are required, especially cohort-related data on the life courses of individuals. The increase in panel research since the 1970s has reduced this original drawback.

DIAs are a regular feature in world models. An early contribution was made by Forrester (1971), who explored the consequences of current and future actions related to population growth, food production and pollution. Meadows and his team (1972) further developed Forrester's model. Their computer simulation of the world system is an analysis of the consequences of elaborating Malthus's model. Like Malthus, however, Meadows et al. underrated the impact of technological innovation on the dependent variable in their model. Later social world models all contain demographic submodels. This is illustrated by the Brundtland

Report (World Commission on Environment and Development 1987), described in Chapter 4, which tried to demonstrate that sustainable development was feasible only if population growth was curbed, environmental devastation stopped and sustainable technology introduced.

Our next example introduces a DIA study where an explanatory model has been applied. The project was designed to assess the impact of the economic recession of 1975–85 on the life courses of individuals born between 1955 and 1970 in four western countries (Sanders & Becker 1994). The project was also set up to assess the impact of educational and labour market policy between 1955 and 1970 and to assess the consequences of current and future educational and labour market policy. The project focused on the question of how nonlinear increases in the age of transition from the educational system to the labour market could be explained. The utilitarian individualistic model summarized in Chapter 1 was used as a meta-theory. On this basis, two theories were applied to explanatory problem: the theory of individualization and the theory of generations.

Individualization theory focuses on the modernization that has taken place within Western society since the end of the eighteenth century, when rationalization, secularization, urbanization and industrialization began to develop rapidly. As a result of these developments, individualization theory predicted that individuals in modern society would follow life courses that would differ more and more from standardized life courses. Individual diversity would increase in a linear way (Becker 1992; Ester et al. 1993). If research data were to show a new standardization of life courses, individualization theory would not be able to explain this new standardization and would not be supported.

The theory of generations argues that individuals have a formative period that begins when they are about 10 and lasts until they are about 25 years old. If individuals experience major events (wars, economic recessions, cultural shifts) during their formative period, these events will mark their life courses. Generations theory proposes three hypotheses. First, the hypothesis of differential cohort socialization. This hypothesis leads to the prediction that value orientations acquired during the formative period will last a relatively long time, at least longer than value orientations acquired at other periods in the life course. The second hypothesis is that of relative scarcity. This hypothesis leads to

127

the prediction that economic and social constraints experienced in the formative period will be felt for a relatively long time, at least far longer than constraints felt at other periods in the life course. Third is the hypothesis of reinforcement. This hypothesis predicts that value orientations acquired during the formative period will only last if they are reinforced during later periods of the life course. If reinforcement does not take place, life-long socialization will institutionalize new value orientations. In the research, the economic recession of 1975–85 was taken as a major event. From the theory of generations, predictions were derived concerning differences between cohorts related to the age at transition from school to work and social independence.

In the study, the theory of generations leads to better predictions of the age of transition from the educational system to the labour market, and from social dependency to social independence, than the theory of individualization. Data from Great Britain, the USA, Western Germany and the Netherlands were used, and interpretation of the outcomes of the study points to the impact of cohort differences on career opportunities and opportunities for arriving at an optimal family life. The outcomes have also been used to assess the impact of social security policies on the members of the cohorts that emerged between 1955 and 1970.

5.4 Meso-level SIA

At this level, the dependent variables are organizations and institutions. In Chapter 2, a number of examples of meso-level SIA were discussed, for example, the analyses of the consequences of future regional development projects. In this section, I will discuss a number of examples from another section of society, namely pretesting proposed actions within the context of the hospital system in a number of western countries.

Concern for cure and care has gradually increased since the early 1980s. The World Health Organization (WHO) has analyzed developments in health status and the use of health resources in Europe, warning that the population is ageing and thus likely to make greater demands on services. Given these trends, the resources of health care systems have to be redistributed to provide cure and care for new categories of individuals in need (WHO 1986). In the late 1970s, as we have seen in Chapter 2, WHO launched the Health for All by the Year 2000 programme. In the 1980s, medical sociology used sociological methods and theories, such as the epidemiological analysis of statistics of health and diseases, to advance medical objectives. Medical sociology also applied a sociological critique to medicine itself, examining the social relations and power structure involved in doctor–patient relationships as well as the social divisions in health and health care (*inter alia* Turner 1987).

In many western countries, cure and care were analyzed in order to design health policies capable of coping with the opportunities and threats that lay ahead. A much-praised example of the latter was *Time to Care*, a report issued by the Swedish Secretariat for Future Studies (Lagergren et al. 1984). The report was praised because it sketched the outlines of a caring society in which citizens use their spare time to increase cure and care for those in need.

A completely different response to the challenge facing health care can be seen in the American hospital system. The privatized nature of health care in the USA, poses special problems. In order to understand those problems, it is necessary to comprehend the nature of health care in the USA, to undertake a sort of baseline analysis. Stevens (1989), for example, has identified six characteristics of the US hospital system:

1. Segmentation and diversity of hospital ownership. As major expressions of charitable, social and economic interests, American hospitals affirm the pluralism in American society and its division into diverse and competing ethnic, racial and religious groups. Voluntary hospitals have a particularly strong tradition in the north-east, while profit-making hospitals have long been the most firmly established in the south and west. Hospitals became *standardized* in the years between the two world wars through voluntary acceptance of physician-established accreditation requirements. In some ways, US hospitals are more highly (and centrally) regulated than those in Britain, even though the latter has a government-run National Health Service.

2. Social stratification. American hospitals have long served as vehicles for defining social class and race and for interpreting

American attitudes to poverty: in the USA, poverty means failure. The distinction between hospitals has been buttressed by the stratification of patients within the hospitals themselves according to their ability to pay. In the large cities, there has been an exquisite social patterning of patients across the hospital system and within individual hospitals.

3. The money standard of success infuses all aspects of hospital operation. American hospitals have been successful in attracting paying patients largely because of the pay ethos. Hospitals present themselves as having something valuable to sell: surgery, glamour, expertise and healthy babies.

4. Focus on acute care and technology and surgery in particular. The American hospital has been, and is, a projection of a medical profession whose archetypes are science, daring and entrepreneurship.

5. Built-in tension between hospitals and the medical profession. To American physicians the hospital is an extension of private practice. The average American hospital is an *open-staff* institution. This means that it expects to provide all qualified practitioners with hospital privilege, subject to the rules and regulations of the institution.

6. The strong yet largely informal influence of medical schools in the hospital system. The most powerful hospitals in terms of the prestige structures of medicine and of hospital administration continue to be teaching institutions.

In his book *The New Hospital*, Coile (1986) also presents a baseline analysis that has much in common with Stevens's historical account of American hospitals. Coile went a step further than Stevens, however. Taking the year 2001 as his time horizon, he designed a set of four possible scenarios.

Scenario 1: High technology. Technological advances have eradicated many diseases. Genetic engineering has virtually eliminated birth defects. Improved tranquillizers have reduced mental health problems and eliminated state mental hospitals. The computer has replaced the physician as the primary diagnostician and therapist, with nurse practitioners and other paraprofessionals providing much of the hands-on care. The price for technological solutions has been heavy, however, and more than 20 per cent of the gross national product is required for health. Although there are complaints by some who claim technology has eroded the citizen's abilities to take care of their own health, most are willing to pay the price for its benefits. This scenario presupposes an economic boom.

Scenario 2: Conglomerates. Continuing economic stagnation and decline are the conditions that bring about real competition in the market place of health care. The number of hospital failures is smaller than expected but many fall prey to takeovers by one of the mega-systems that come to dominate the health care scene. By the year 2001, four multinational corporations have emerged. In this scenario public hospitals have disappeared, either closed or sold off by financially beleaguered governments. Consumers get what they can pay for. Technology, such as organ transplants, is available but expensive. In this competitive market, customers have to take care of their own interests. The market system has reinforced wider public recognition of the importance of lifestyles and modest gains in life expectancy have resulted.

Scenario 3: Reregulation. In the third scenario, government has intervened on the public's behalf to provide health care services. The mixed regulatory strategies of employing both cost controls and competition were inadequate to ensure there would be no breakdown in the health care system and in the economy in general. Physicians have become salaried employees, bargaining in guilds and unions with their public employers. Even before the year 2000, the government had started to intervene directly in individual health decisions. Risk and cost-benefit analysis was required for costly therapies, with centralized rationing and control. Those with antisocial or criminal tendencies were monitored and controlled and cost control has been achieved by direct government action. While problems of queuing and shortages persist, the public in general has adapted to the national health system by the year 2001.

Scenario 4: Wellness. In the fourth scenario, a cultural transformation toward voluntary simplicity has had a pervasive influence in reforming health attitudes. The wellness movement symbolizes the gains of this new social ethic. Recognizing the physical and environmental aetiology of disease, a shift was made away from a disease-oriented medical system to health enhancement. Employers, recognizing the contributions of workplace stress and health hazards, have taken responsibility for eliminating them. Hospitals have shrunk dramatically in numbers and importance except for a few regional repair centres. Health education, fitness and mental health programmes receive most of the nation's health investment. A new respect for the environment has dramatically enhanced the quality of life. The wellness system has successfully encouraged people to take effective responsibility for their own health.

My third example is *The Hospital in the Twenty-first Century*, by Dominique Jolly (1988). This book focuses on developments in the Parisian hospital system and considers hospitals with teaching obligations as well as those without. Demographic variables are explored up to the year 2030, other variables up to 2005. Jolly designed three scenarios. Her first scenario represents *Muddling Through*. Economic prosperity in France increases slightly. Budgets of hospitals increase but only slowly and evidently budgets are not sufficient to meet all the demands for hospital care. Government intervention grows considerably and bureaucratic procedures become more and more suffocating. In this scenario, hospitals take a passive attitude towards problems arising in their urban and regional environments. Private clinics prosper and they attract a lot of wealthy patients. As a result, the state-owned Parisian hospitals become financially drained. Jolly introduces two subscenarios. In the first subscenario, high-tech prospers in parts of the hospital system leaving the rest in the shadow of a downward spiral of deficits and diminishing quality. The second subscenario shows an ultimate decline of both high-tech and the rest of the hospital system.

Jolly's second scenario is called *The Charismatic Hospital*. The economic situation in France has continued to decline. Hospitals are confronted with drastic retrenchments. The Parisian hospital system reacts by continuing its activities as far as it can pay for them out of the money made available by government and the funds earned from wealthy patients. The charismatic hospital reactivates procedures that were in use before 1940. Whenever the hospital has excess capacity, it uses this capacity for the cure and care of the poor. The spare hours of the medical and auxiliary staff and each bed that is temporarily free is used for humanitarian purposes. Of course, only a few people in need can get help: the rest go on suffering. This scenario grants the Parisian hospital system and its staff a clean conscience. The blame for the bankrupt hospital system is placed on circumstances and on the individuals politically responsible.

The third scenario introduces *The Professional Hospital*. Economic prosperity in the country is about the same as in the first scenario. In the hospital system, a professional approach is introduced into the medical sector, residential care and the administration. Administration is cut drastically. Costs are reduced by as much as 30 per cent depending on the sector involved. All staff members are mobilized in an effort to meet the highest standards of excellence.

The two scenario reports have much in common. In the first place, they do not present a theoretical framework, perhaps because the authors do not want to lose the attention of their prime audience: medical practitioners. But if we search for an implicit theoretical model, we do not find much that suggests theoretical sophistication. This implies that causal relationships and social technology have not been handled systematically. Stevens's baseline analysis is also devoid of any theoretical framework and application of insights related to social technology.

In the second place, each of the two sets of scenarios contains a scenario that represents a more or less ideal solution. Coile evidently prefers his second scenario: the introduction of many conglomerates into the hospital system. Jolly prefers the third scenario, the professional hospital. The two sets of scenarios differ with regard to the degree of preference give to a specific scenario. The fourth scenario, characterized by wellness, also meets some approval in Coile's report. Jolly emphasizes her preference rather explicitly.

The three reports were published in the 1980s. Actual developments in the USA and France have more or less followed the trend scenario. Both Stevens and Jolly have been able to explore the consequences of *business as usual* quite adequately. Coile foresaw the emergence of rigorous competition in the western hospital system and the emergence of more conglomerates. His second scenario, notionally set in 1995, materialized under relatively favourable economic conditions. In the second half of the 1990s, the conglomerates have not yet replaced all other types of hospitals.

5.5 Macro-level SIA

In earlier chapters, we have already discussed some examples of macro-level SIA with reference to compulsory education and the age of children in Great Britain. In this section, further examples will be presented in order to provide a balanced overview of this type of SIA. We have to keep in mind that most macro-level SIA studies are legal IAs because they explore the consequences of current or future legal actions. We have also to remember that macro-level SIA in most cases requires public participation either on a compulsory or a voluntary basis.

A typical example of macro-level SIA is gender IA (Gianotten et al. 1994; Jiggins 1995). This is a method for analyzing the potential effects of new government policies and other activities on gender relations. Various policy reports have been analyzed with respect to such issues as chronic illness, labour and social security, outdoor recreation and family policies. In the Netherlands, the instrument was first applied to an education proposal (Verloo & Roggeband 1996).

In the Netherlands, policies relating to women have been the subject of assessment from 1974 onwards, and the issue has remained on the political agenda. The formal problem definition was formulated in the 1980s. The basic problem is no longer defined as the unequal character of participation in the public and private spheres, but as *the structurally unequal power relations between women and men*. According to Verloo and Roggeband (1996), power relations between women and men are not of a special kind. Power is seen as directly related to gender because gender is a primary way of distributing and using resources, such as money, time, positions, goods, relations and information. Power is indirectly related to gender in the operation of rules. The unequal distribution of resources legitimizes distinct gender norms and distinct gender norms act as a legitimation of the unequal distribution of resources.

A gender IA has to analyze the effects of an intervention on the gendered division of labour and on the organization of intimacy, and, in doing so, should pay attention to effects produced by a particular distribution of resources through the operation of (gendered) rules (Verloo & Roggeband 1996). The implicit goals of emancipation policy in the Netherlands are equality, autonomy and multiformity. There is consensus about the necessity for removing discrimination but, because of the different starting points of men and women, unequal treatment is sometimes advocated in order to bring about an equal outcome. Elements of the equality criterion include: opportunities which are really equal, equality of all people before the law and equal treatment in similar circumstances. However, equality should not mean that women and men become the same or that women have to change to conform to a male norm. Autonomy is defined as the possibility that women have to set conditions and priorities and to decide for themselves how they can have a say in their social and personal lives. Multiformity – that is a society with many differences that are not hierarchical – is advocated on the level of society as a whole.

Verloo and Roggeband (1996) have designed a procedure for gender IA. It consists of five steps: (1) a description of current gender relations; (2) a description of probable developments without a new policy; (3) a description and analysis of the new policy plan; (4) a description of potential effects on gender relations; and (5) finally an evaluation of the positive and negative potential effects on gender relations. This procedure comes very close to the approach advocated in Chapters 3 and 4.

The first gender IA in the Netherlands was commissioned by the Ministry of Education, Culture and Sciences in 1994. The Department asked for an assessment of a policy proposal on the reorganization of junior secondary education and prevocational education. The gender IA was commissioned in addition to the SIA that is always made before deciding on a policy proposal in this area. The gender IA was sent to parliament as an appendix to the final government proposal and led to a major reconsideration of the proposed policies (Verloo & Roggeband 1996).

My second example of macro-level SIA is the *Corona Group*, active in the Netherlands in the early 1980s. The group consisted of economists and sociologists from the University of Utrecht and trade union members and was established at the time of a debate in the Dutch parliament about a major revision of the social security system. The group rented a number of rooms in the Hotel Corona, a few hundred metres away from the parliament building – and inherited the hotel's name.

The Corona Group announced to the public, press, members of parliament, government officials and everyone else concerned that it was prepared – during the parliamentary debate – to assess proposals for amendments to the bill as well as to related questions. The group was specialized in the Dutch social security system, and its computer model of the system was run on personal computers in the hotel. The structure of the computer model had been published prior to the campaign.

The revision of the social security system was a highly complicated matter. Only a limited number of experts were able to assess the impact of the new system on the income of individuals and households in the Netherlands. Because impacts differed widely between different categories of individuals, information on these impacts was of crucial importance to the parliamentary debate and the ultimate decision to be taken about the bill. The debate centred on such questions as, Will one-parent households with two or three children under the age of 12 be worse off under the new law? and if so, how much less will they receive per month?

The Corona Group's campaign quickly became a success. Special interest groups and the press raised many questions. Members of parliament from the opposition parties wanting to get their hypotheses tested were frequent visitors to the Corona Hotel. However, the political parties represented in the cabinet stayed away.

This example is drawn from an area of social criticism that has only a loose relationship with institutionalized political, parliamentary and governmental authority. It illustrates the structure and the potential impact of macro-level SIA.

5.6 SIA in integrated IA studies

The project-based application of SIA, where SIA is integrated with other forms of IA to assess the impacts of large dams, irrigation projects, industrial plants and public works, such as highways and airports, etc., is very common in the literature, partly because of the NEPA conceptualization of much of that literature. In most cases, the actions to be assessed have been initiated by government and most cases involve public participation on either a voluntary or a compulsory basis.

To illustrate this type of SIA, I have used the assessment of the impact of a rise in sea level will have on society and the effect of improved coastal defence. An increasing body of evidence suggests that a substantial rise in sea level can be expected in the coming decades, and estimates for the next century range from a 0.2 to a 1.0 m increase. Because a large part of the world's population lives in low-lying areas close to the sea, such a rise will have an important impact on society (Wind 1987).

The impact of a rise in sea level has an automatic and direct relevance to coastal lowlands. The direct impacts are:

(a) loss of land by inundation of river deltas (such as those of the Ganges and Brahmaputra, Yangtze, Mekong and Nile rivers), erosion and the flooding of coastal areas;
(b) increased storm damage to dykes, dams, coastal structures; changes in morphology and ecology;
(c) increased salt water intrusion into rivers and saline seepage.

The land area that may be influenced by a rise in sea level is somewhere in the order of 5 million km^2, which is about 3 per cent of the world's total land area and one-third its cropping area. Large parts of the areas susceptible to inundation are densely populated, and include many large cities with populations totalling some 1 billion people. In the ISOS project (Impact of Sea Level Rise on Society), three case studies have been selected. First, the Netherlands, an example of a highly industrialized country with a well-organized coastal defence system and a long tradition of battling against the sea. Second, Bangladesh, a low-lying country with limited economic prospects and where a rise in sea level could have potentially devastating effects. Third, the Maldive Islands, a region of that is perhaps not at the forefront of international interest but which nevertheless faces tremendous social, cultural and environmental impacts if there is a rise in sea level.

In estimating the economic damage that might be caused by a rise in sea level and in making decisions about engineering works for coastal defence, the overall economic conditions of a region are critical. It is assumed that the economic growth rate and the social discount rate can be specified under different economic scenarios. Considering different scenarios will enable us to gain a basic idea about the sensitivity of the results to varying economic conditions.

There is an interaction between social conditions and the impact of a rise in sea level. On the one hand, particularly if no coastal defence is possible, the social impact in the form of abandoned coastal areas and the migration of population could be very severe. Whether or not this is considered acceptable depends on the values and norms of the society. On the other hand, the way in which a society responds to the threat of a rise in sea level depends very much on its social structure. This is very difficult to model in quantitative terms and perhaps a contextual scenario is better for taking these conditions into account, for example, in the form of a delay between the moment that the need for action is identified and the moment that the action is actually taken, whatever its form.

Geological records indicate that the natural environment has a great ability to adapt to changing conditions, and that rises in sea level of 1 m per century have occurred in the past without any species or organisms becoming extinct. We can assume that in many cases, areas of natural interest will be able to adapt to a rising sea level in various ways. The rate of adaptation will depend on the type of vegetation. Grassland takes some decades to adjust, while forests may need hundreds of years. Where protected coasts are involved, the consequences of an inland migration of wetlands being obstructed by dykes or sea walls may mean that certain types of natural environment are reduced in size or disappear completely. The inland environment behind the dykes may be affected by changes in wetness or increases in salinity, particularly if drainage facilities are not adjusted.

The way in which a society responds to a rise in sea level and its impact is determined by a multitude of conditions. Many other problems compete with rises in sea level for the attention of politicians and decision-makers, and experience shows that only a sudden event or disaster will trigger countermeasures even when the problem was already well known. An example is the 1953 flood in the Netherlands, which brought a protection programme into action.

Whatever the circumstances, the choice the decision-maker has to take is between positive defensive action, planned retreat, or abandonment. Each choice can be elaborated in various ways. In the ISOS project, a simulation was conducted, creating the opportunity for a systematic comparison of alternative policies and programmes of action. Each can be evaluated on the basis of its financial, technical, social and environmental consequences and compared with a set of acceptable impacts. A point of particular interest is the time available for taking action given the uncertainty in various context scenarios and the delay inherent in the political, social and technological system. Planned retreat, for example, appears to require much more lead time than the fortification of coastal defences, which in turn requires more lead time than abandonment.

The first case to be considered is the Maldives. The Republic of the Maldives consists of a group of more than 1,200 islands, about 670 km south-west of Sri Lanka. A population of 182,000 people is dispersed over some 200 islands, although nearly 50,000 people live in the capital island, Male. The islands lie little more than 2 or 3 m above sea level and any rise in sea level will mean a loss of land. Since the natural growth rate of coral varies between 1 mm and several centimetres a year, one may expect that the physical elevation of the islands can keep pace with rises in sea level. However, where people have occupied entire islands, as is the case on Male, the natural growth of the coral has been drastically reduced. Artificial measures have to be applied in order to protect the island and its inhabitants from drowning. Given the high porosity of coral and coral sand, the construction of dykes may not be enough to solve the problem, because the continuous flow of water underground will mean that immense amounts of energy will be required for land drainage. A number of strategies have been designed and potential impacts have been simulated. One example is to bring soil from some of the uninhabited islands to build up the soil on the populated islands.

The second case is Bangladesh, a country that lies in the transition zone between the Indian subcontinent and the rest of South-east Asia. With a total population of about 100 million people, 85 per cent of whom live in rural areas, Bangladesh is the most densely populated agrarian country in the world. In the case study, Bangladesh is divided into three segments and each segment has a particular vulnerability to rises in sea level. Segment A is to the west of the main active delta and includes an extensive zone of tidal plains that have been partially protected by dykes. Segment B is the central river delta area, characterized by continuous erosion and increases by a process of deposition. As a result of this, farmers often lose their land and are forced to settle down in other areas. Segment C is formed by a narrow coastal zone near Chittagong, a town which will be seriously affected if there is a substantial rise in sea level. A number of strategies have been developed and pretested for their potential impact. These include the building up of sections of land that could be used as a safe haven during floods (Rahman 1993).

The third case is the Netherlands. Its low-lying position along the border of the North Sea makes the Netherlands very susceptible to any rise in sea level. At the moment, its coastline is protected by a system of dykes and dunes which offer security against the type of storm surge that is estimated to occur with a frequency of once every 10,000 years. This degree of safety was secured by the completion of the Delta Plan in 1986, a massive infrastructure of dykes and barriers in the south-west of the country. A 1 m rise in sea level will reduce this safety margin to 10 per cent of the present factor, that is, the coast will be protected against storm surges which occur with a frequency of once in every 1,000 years. The maintenance of this system is of fundamental importance in view of the size of the low-lying area protected by the coastal defence system, the large numbers of people living there and the tremendous economic importance of the area. A major category of potential measures involves changes in the location of activities and the redefinitions of land use. Measures range from a general retreat and the abandonment of the threatened areas to the sea to a subtle and complicated rearrangement of activities such that highly flood-sensitive activities are removed to less flood-prone areas. It might be sensible, for instance, to move residential areas and capital-intensive industries further inland, while locating national parks and extensive agriculture further seawards. What complicates most of these possible measures is the considerable time lag involved, the resistance of social groups and organizations to change and the political complications of land-use changes that involve different administrative jurisdictions across provincial and even national boundaries.

Potential measures have been assessed in a simulated confrontation with two contextual scenarios. The first scenario describes an upward spiral. A high growth of technology is stated as an assumption. Integrating markets shows a favourable development; migration towards the Netherlands remains within limits and does not give rise to any major difficulties, and the political powers are willing to bear the costs of improving the coastal defence. The second scenario is known as the downward spiral: technological growth is generally slow, or one or more components lag behind; the integration of markets slows down; economic differences trigger mass migration; tensions between segments of the population increase. In periods of military or civil war, the Netherlands will be very vulnerable in this scenario. Dykes are difficult to protect against bombs, and such threats require a set of precautions, *inter alia*, the building of dams and islands near the North Sea shore to protect the area behind the dykes and dunes and to facilitate the evacuation of the population in case of flooding (Becker 1987a).

5.7 Summary

This chapter first develops a typology of IA. This typology consists of a number of clusters. Cluster 1 contains environmental IA. Cluster 2 contains technology assessment. Cluster 3 brings economic IA. Cluster 4 brings SIA. Custer 5 presents auxiliary approaches, like Delphi procedures and risk assessment.

Next this chapter presents a typology of SIA, and a number of examples. First, micro-level SIA is described. In SIA on a micro-level, individual behaviour, including individual life courses, is a dependent variable. In many cases, micro-level SIA consists of demographic impact assessment (DIA), which can be defined as the process of identifying the future consequences of a current or proposed action that may have an impact on demographic processes or on issues related to demographic processes.

Secondly, meso-level SIA is introduced. In SIA at the meso-level, the dependent variables are organizations and institutions. In the chapter examples from SIA concerning hospital systems are presented.

Thirdly, macro-level SIA is discussed. Most macro-level SIA studies are legal IAs. Examples from gender IA are presented.

Fourth, SIA in integrated impact studies demands our attention. Now we are dealing with the project-based application of SIA, where SIA is integrated with other forms of IA to assess the impacts of large dams, irrigation projects, industrial plants and public works, such as highways and airports. Examples are presented from the ISOS project.

CHAPTER 6

Major problems of SIA

6.1 Introduction

In preceding chapters, I have concentrated on methods and types of SIA studies without elaborating on the problems involved in carrying out this kind of policy-oriented research. I have restricted the discussion of problematic issues to presenting an overview of pitfalls. Chapter 6 focuses on the major problems confronting the social impact assessor.

First, the social impact assessor has to determine what magnitude their SIA study ought to be. Of course the central actors, especially if they finance the study, will play an important role in this decision. But ultimately the impact assessor will have to decide whether or not the assessment can be accomplished with the resources in time and money available for the study. The determination of the size of the study is discussed in section 6.2.

Secondly, the impact assessor has to cope with the *systems noise* active in the system that is to be studied. How will the assessor cope with risk and uncertainty? and how will risk management be organized? This issue is discussed in section 6.3.

Thirdly, the impact assessor has to establish the study in its social setting. The study has to acquire an organizational setting. It has to build social relationships with the central actor. It also has to build social relationships with the target actor, in particular with regard to public involvement. Following this, relationships with basic research have to be examined. Next, the study has to establish a relationship with the normative debate concerning IA. How will ethical rules be handled?

Finally, the study has to establish relationships with IA as a social system. The setting of the SIA study will be discussed in section 6.4.

6.2 Determining the size of an SIA study

6.2.1 Introduction

From a perspective of research methods, it makes a lot of difference, as will be argued below, whether we are dealing with an instant, a medium-sized or a large project. We also have to distinguish between research projects and action-research projects. The former provides answers to research questions. The latter implies a combination of research and social intervention. In this section, the categories of SIA will be discussed, again, taking a typology as a frame of reference. In Figure 6.1, the relationship between the typology of SIA studies presented in Chapter 5 and the typology of Chapter 6, mainly related to the size of projects, is summarized.

Figure 6.1 illustrates that I have already collapsed six categories into four categories, because instant, medium-sized and large projects could be specified for both research and action research. In Figure 6.1, I have provided a rough indication of the frequency of appearance of each

	Type 1: micro	Type 2: meso	Type 3: macro
1. Instant projects	+++	++	++
2. Medium-sized projects	++	+++	+
3. Large scale projects	++	++	+++
4. Action research	++	++	+

N.B.
+++ = very frequent
++   = frequent
+   = infrequent

Figure 6.1 Types and sizes of SIA projects.

category in SIA. The indication ranges from very frequent to frequent and infrequent.

6.2.2 Instant SIA studies

Such a study requires, roughly speaking, from 15 minutes up to one month. It demands up to one person year of effort. These limits in time and person power are specified in an arbitrary way. There is enough experience with instant SIA studies to make them an interesting option. We find instant studies, *inter alia*, in disaster relief co-ordination and in analyses during political negotiations. As an example, I mention negotiations concerning the annual budget by the Dutch cabinet in the 1990s. The cabinet ministers discuss the budget proposals, and whenever they want to alter a budget item, the proposal is written on a slip of paper and handed to a number of budgetary experts sitting in an adjacent room. The budgetary analysts specify the consequences of the proposal, *inter alia*, for other items on the budget. The consequences to be expected are added to the text on the slip of paper and the information goes back to the negotiations room. Now the negotiating ministers can take the consequences to be expected into consideration before making a decision.

In most cases, an instant SIA, as in the Dutch example, is launched in a setting wherein a lot of preparation has been done already. Imagine an organization that has an up-to-date problem analysis, systems analysis, baseline analysis, set of scenarios and strategies available. Imagine that this organization is suddenly confronted with a major event in its context or its internal structure. A proposal for a merger, a reorganization or a new move from a competitor. The organization, the central actor in the explanatory model discussed in Chapter 1, wants to prepare a new strategy in a very short period of time. Relying on what has been prepared, and provided experienced staff are available, the central actor will be able to work out a solution to the new problem that has all the advantages of a sophisticated SIA study. In other words, we are not talking about a quick-and-dirty approach, but a planned and controlled approach.

Organizations frequently confronted with situations that require instant SIA will see to it that they have experienced staff at their disposal. The capability of their staff can be enhanced by having a task force of external experts. A task force in this case consists of hundreds of experts that can be consulted by telephone, fax or E-mail on the spur of the moment. A lot of task forces like this are active already in EIA, to give an example from another area. The national headquarters of fire brigades or disaster relief co-ordination organizations can consult experts whenever dangerous chemicals are on fire, for example. In the Netherlands, 400 experts in all kinds of chemicals are members of the task force of the fire brigade; disaster relief co-ordination is integrated in the fire brigade.

I shall give some additional examples. In the preceding chapter, I already discussed the activities of the Corona Group. This group of economists and sociologists provided instant assessments of proposals in the Dutch Parliament concerning legal arrangements for social security. Based on more than ten years of research in this area, computer programs for IA and an experienced team of social scientists, this enterprise turned into a success. I also mentioned gender IA. Instant studies in assessing discriminatory impact of proposals for new laws has been standard procedure for a couple of decades, *inter alia*, in the USA. Also in the USA, discrimination against minorities in proposals for new laws is assessed by a standing task force.

In instant assessments, the pretesting of current or proposed actions is restricted in most cases to a problem analysis, a scenario-to-strategy analysis and an analysis of consequences. Experienced impact assessors with an adequate background information at their disposal can produce a SIA in about 15 minutes, for instance, during negotiations. If more time is available, for instance, two weeks, one full-time equivalent is enough to work out a SIA, provided the groundwork has been done. A team of 25 instant assessors is indeed able to explore potential impacts of a current or proposed action in such a short time. However, without adequate preparation, the situation alters. No kind of IA requires so much preparation as an instant IA!

If adequate preparation is lacking and time is scarce, *ad hoc* assessments cannot be avoided. In most cases, an experienced impact assessor will produce a better assessment than a lay person. Sometimes a small team will produce the best *ad hoc* assessment possible under the circumstances. As an example, I mention a team consisting of one person that is an expert on the current or proposed action to be assessed plus another person that is an experienced impact assessor. Another example is a small committee consisting of field experts and impact assessors. In all cases, it is necessary, of course, for the committee to apply sophisticated procedures to assess potential impacts in a systematic way. One method to do this, for example, is by a frame game.

A major pitfall in instant SIA studies is inadequate preparation, for instance, with regard to the problem formulation and the baseline analysis. Also, inadequate training of impact assessors is a substantial threat. This pitfall can be avoided by simulating the instant procedures beforehand. A third serious pitfall is inadequate reporting.

6.2.3 Medium-sized SIA Studies

These require one to three person years, and it will take one to three years to complete the project. This kind of SIA is frequently used when the time pressure for the IA is not too heavy and the acquisition of data is a relatively easy task, for instance, when the data for the analysis come from a data archive, or when the data can be gathered by a not-too-large survey. Interviewing by telephone has increased substantially the potential for medium-sized SIA studies in western countries. Examples of this type of SIA study have been provided in Chapter 2, *inter alia*, the simulation of increase in the age for compulsory education in the UK.

A serious pitfall in this type of IA is underestimating the requirements with regard to project management. Members of the team will depart, they will have to be replaced, the newcomers will have to be trained.

6.2.4 Large-size SIA studies

Here we are talking about projects with more than three full-time equivalent staff that take more than three years to complete. In Chapters 3 and 4, the methodological aspects have already been discussed in detail. Now I will focus on some more pitfalls.

In a project that takes more than three years to complete, the initial problem will more often than not change before the project is ready. Sometimes the economic situation becomes less favourable and retrenchments are enforced. In other cases, the political power structure shifts. These risks imply that the planning of the project has to include a scenario analysis that takes a change of the societal context into consideration. The co-ordinators of the SIA study will have to be able to reshuffle their human and financial resources when circumstances require it.

Large-size SIAs are often confronted with the outcomes of public participation that has taken place in the past. This introduces the question, How long is a democratic decision binding? After how many years are we free to override a majority decision of a region or an organization? In practice, in most cases the time between two national elections is taken as a benchmark. If national elections are held every four years, it is reasonable to reconsider decisions taken by other groups after the same period.

In large-size projects, the central actor will change, for instance, when individuals are replaced or reorganizations change the scene. Does the impact assessor have to go back to the original contract in order to safeguard the terms of reference? In practice, project co-ordinators first try to find out whether the restructured central actor still retains the old preferences. Maybe the time is ripe for new negotiations, and maybe better terms can be obtained.

Large-size projects show a number of critical transitions. The transition from the preliminary to the main phase is notorious for its pitfalls. If the preliminary phase of the project has been successful and the central actor is satisfied with the results, many teams just lean back and enjoy the situation. They get overbold, and in the main phase they take on more responsibilities than strictly necessary. As a result, the main phase turns into a failure, or at least becomes difficult.

Another critical transition is the step from research to reporting. Teams often forget that it takes a lot of time to write adequate reports, that is, executive summaries, short versions and the full report. If the members of the team are tired and worn out, even excellent results will be reported in a suboptimal way.

6.2.5 SIA in action research programmes

In the 1930s, social research discovered that research itself can change a situation. The classical example is the Hawthorne Project. It turned out

147

in this project that the presence of the researchers and their research activities had a substantial impact on the productivity of the workers studied. In research, these observations have led to the development of methodological solutions, *inter alia*, unobtrusive measurement.

There has been another development too. Social scientists have developed approaches that combine research and action. They go under the name of action research. One of these solutions is strategic (or organizational) learning, already touched upon in Chapter 4. The main idea behind strategic learning is that organizations have to respond in a flexible way to changes in their environment.

An organization that has been prepared for strategic learning will have a staff unit that reacts to early warnings concerning the environment of the organization. For instance, a new government retrenchment, the new marketing strategy of a competitor or a new campaign by a rival political party. Now the staff unit organizes scenario-to-strategy workshops, obtaining participation by top and middle management, maybe lower management and rank-and-file employees, too. These workshops redesign scenarios and strategies, rank strategies, elaborate the least regret strategy, *inter alia*, by assessing the impact of this strategy and report to the top of the organization. Reports of workshops are analyzed, and, step-by-step, a new general strategy for the organization is developed.

In strategic learning, experts play the role of consultants. They are not allowed to adopt management roles. Wealthy organizations sometimes engage two experts for each field of relevant expertise, choosing experts that are known to have different views on the problem to be analyzed. In this way, the members of the workshops can choose between two contradictory expert reports.

6.3 Coping with risk and uncertainty in the SIA study

Already in the seventeenth century, as we saw in Chapter 1, death risks were calculated in order to set the price for annuities. Since that time, risk has been calculated in a large number of fields. Using modern terminology, we can state that it has been an auxiliary activity in health IA, EIA and a number of related types of assessments.

6.3.1 Risk and uncertainty

Risk, or statistical uncertainty, is an event with known probability. Uncertainty, or indeterminacy is an event with unknown probability. Concerning practical problems knowledge about risk is relevant only if it is accompanied by information about impact. This generates four types of risk:

1. low probability, high impact
2. low probability, low impact
3. high probability, high impact
4. high probability, low impact.

For practical affairs, type 1 is especially relevant. Flooding in areas normally kept dry by dykes illustrates this type. In the Netherlands, the law regulating coastal defence against the sea specifies that the dykes and dunes must be strong enough to counter high water with a probability of occurring once in every 1,000 years (as discussed before). Risk assessment tells us not only the probability of having to be evacuated because dykes and dunes are not strong enough, but also the probability of getting cancer or other diseases that are lethal in most cases.

6.3.2 Risk assessment

Both risk and uncertainty are a kind of systems noise, as discussed in Chapter 2. In both cases there always is an opportunity that progress in scientific research will reduce systems noise. With an eye to this opportunity a distinction is made between white and black noise. White noise is "unpredictability" that will be eliminated by new research outcomes. Black noise will always remain unpredictable. Of course we can identify white noise only after its transformation into (relative) predicability.

Carpenter (1995: 195) states that risk assessment addresses four questions:

1. What can go wrong to cause adverse consequences?
2. What is the probability or frequency of occurrence of adverse consequences?

3. What is the range and distribution of the severity of adverse consequences?
4. What can be done, at what cost, to manage and reduce unacceptable risks and damages?

He defines *hazard* as a danger, peril or source of harm.

The linkage between risk assessment, risk management and SIA can be illustrated by taking the phases in SIA as a frame of reference.

In the preliminary phase of SIA, hazardous events and their risk or uncertainty have to be identified. How do they fit into the social system hosting the central actor and its practical problem? In baseline analysis and trendline analysis, hazards have to be included in the scoping process.

In the main phase, scenario analysis has to be supplemented with an analysis of the consequences of *scenarios of exposure* to the hazards specified. Two procedures are available: The Fault Tree procedure begins with an accident and determines with *reverse analysis*, the equipment failures or events that could lead to it. The Event Tree procedure begins with a component failure and follows a *forward analysis* to determine if a major accident could result (Carpenter 1995: 199).

Next the risk has to be specified and mitigation strategies (risk management) have to be designed. Following this, the consequences of the risk management actions have to be assessed and, if necessary, to be revised.

Both the preliminary and the main phase require attention to public involvement. Risk is a matter of statistics. Risk awareness is a phenomenon that asks for psychological and sociological analysis, however. Risk awareness as a rule demands public consultation, sometimes public participation.

6.3.3 Risk management

As soon as risk has been assessed, the central actor will try to mitigate this risk. In most cases a monitoring system will be established, issuing early warnings if unfavourable developments are to be expected at a specific point in time. In disaster relief risk management requires a standing organization that can be mobilized as soon as a disaster has happened. In the case of risk related to fire, the standing organization is a fire brigade. Sometimes the risk to be coped with is the occurrence of criminal acts, such as theft, burglary of physical violence against human beings. In this case risk management consists of police forces or private security services.

6.4 Establishing the SIA study in its social setting

6.4.1 Organizational setting of SIA

The central actor has to design and implement a policy for the organizational setting of SIA. It has to ensure that the organization will get this type of policy-oriented social research according to specifications of quality, costs and time. If the organization needs SIA over a long period of time, institutionalization has to be taken care of.

To a certain extent, using scientific expertise is a general problem not restricted to SIA. There are specific aspects involved, however. SIA is an art-science and it is relatively new. As a consequence, contracting experts has to take place on a sellers' market in most cases. The following specific aspects of the process require our attention.

SIA Staff units. The first option available to the central actor is to entrust SIA to one or more members of staff in a specific unit established for SIA. This has a number of advantages. Scientists employed by the organization have been able to assemble expert knowledge on the organization, its actions and its target system. They are at home in the subculture and the language of the own organization. They will have acquired a position in social networks within the central organization and in networks linking this organization to its target system. Employees are familiar with the dynamics of the central actor organization, being able to provide early warnings and to stimulate the implementation of the output of SIA studies. Scientists employed by the central actor organization have their drawbacks, however. If they have been very long in the organization, they may have become *blind* to the organization's shortcomings. In that case, they cannot play the role of social critic in an adequate way. If they have worked in a specific position for a long time, they may have lost contact with developments in their own discipline. The danger of increasing social isolation is in particularly strong if the staff unit has a high, isolated position in the organizational hierarchy. These negative aspects of staff units can be countered, however. The staff unit can be made to co-operate with a line unit on a relatively low level in the hierarchy. This organizational setting stimulates practical attitudes in staff employees. On the other hand, it endangers the objectivity of the staff unit. In large organizations, this drawback is curbed by appointing a *contact director* (or contact manager) to stimulate co-operation with the top of the organization as well. The organizational solutions are not the only way out. Another option is taking measures in the area of human resource management. Staff employees can be made to circulate between positions. They can also be given sabbatical leaves.

Consultants and related external units. A second major option is employing consultants on a temporary basis. If consultants work for a number of organisations, it is likely that they will keep an open mind. If consultants do their work in an unsatisfactory way, their contract will not be renewed. On the other hand, consultants often leave when a major project is finished. This implies that their experience in this project is lost to the central actor. External consultancies can be contracted by the central actor according to demand in a specific period and according to the expertise required. This implies that in the course of time, consultancy firms with converging expertise can be contracted. The same arguments apply to contracting university departments. The central actor may be interested in a co-operation with basic science in order to profit from scientific innovations. Many academics at universities are also experienced consultants. University departments can also be contracted because the contribution of their graduate students is requested and is a valuable resource. Also talent scouting stimulates co-operation. Experts often belong to specific traditions in their scientific discipline. In other cases, their methods or their theoretical perspectives are rather restricted. In a medium-sized project of strategic learning, the central actor should employ two consultants for every kind of expertise they are interested in. This construction ensures that the central actor will be able to make up its own mind after being confronted with converging advice.

Mixed organizational settings. Many organizations, in particular large ones, prefer to combine an internal and an external input of expertise.

They will institutionalize a relatively small staff unit, primarily as a link between top and middle management of the central actor organization, on the one hand, and external experts on the other hand. The staff unit will, *inter alia*, supervise external contracts. If co-operation is limited to expertise, a mixed *task force* can be an adequate construction. If co-operation in the area of expertise and project management is required, a *steering committee* can be established. In one medium-sized project of strategic learning, the central actor engaged a number of managers from its own organization who had recently retired. These highly experienced former managers were invited to comment on scenarios developed for use in the organization. Their contribution has been highly appreciated by external consultants, staff employees and managers.

6.4.2 Relationships with the central actor

In a SIA study the central actor is a potential key problem, as many impact assessors will have discovered. The assessor has to manage the relationship with the central actor with care. Sometimes handling this relationship even requires a specific project. I shall sketch the main aspects of the relationship that demand attention.

If information about the actor system is scarce, the impact assessor is advised to carry out a systems analysis. In a baseline analysis the history of the actor system has to be studied, focusing on past problems and their solutions. Also a futures exploration has to be carried out, focusing on potential changes in the system. The impact assessor has to find out what the consequences would be of changes in the managerial team of the actor system. The impact assessor has also to explore what a merger or a reorganization of the actor system would mean for the SIA study.

Next the goals of the central actor have to be summarized, just like in the flow-chart presented in Chapter 3. If hidden agendas play a role, they have to be discovered. Also the constraints facing the central actor require attention. An example can illustrate this. During a health policy assessment study a shift in national health policy took place: the doves were replaced by hawks. As a consequence the SIA study had to be drastically reorganized.

Following this the terminology in use in the actor system has to be documented and analyzed. The impact assessor has to elaborate a taxonomy, analyzing the relationships between terms and definitions. An SIA study of hospital system is dominated by medical terminology, an assessment of social aspects of a reservoir project is dominated by the terminology of engineers and economists. More examples of specific terminologies could be given. In most cases an impact assessor cannot afford terminological confusion.

Furthermore the impact assessor is advised to take a close look at the assumptions the central actor is fostering. As an example of assumptions, I refer to the theoretical frameworks discussed in Chapter 3 in relation to scenarios. Closely related to the set of assumptions of a central actor is the line of argumentation that is followed. If, for instance, the central actor has a natural science background, they will argue in most cases according to the model of a laboratory experiment.

Finally, the utilization of the outcomes of the SIA study have to be reflected upon. How will the impact assessor stimulate the use of the outcomes of the study? The responsibility of an impact assessor does not end at the moment the report is presented.

Closely related to the analysis of the central actor system, the impact assessor has to reflect upon the normative frame of reference. What does the impact assessor prefer? What is rejected? What should or could be tolerated? A reflection upon these three core questions has to take place before conflicts with the central actor arise. During an acute conflict there is little time for a relaxed moral reflection. I will return to the normative debate about IA later in this chapter.

6.4.3 Public involvement

Public involvement in decision-making in the West got a major stimulant as a result of modernization, which had gathered strength in the early nineteenth century. Industrialization and urbanization triggered secularization and individualization. The level of education increased. Gradually western countries introduced a wide participation of the population in general elections. Citizen in western countries started to expect a share in decision-making in political affairs. Meanwhile governments interfered more and more in society. Economic developments in larger parts of the world became more and more interdependent. As a consequence of growing interdependence, economic booms and busts were experienced more severely by the citizens of all western countries. The process of increasing government interference and increasing economic interdependence was quickened by the First World War, the economic crisis of the 1930s, and the Second World War. Communication was intensified. Gradually the Global Village appeared.

Public participation at a grassroots level got its modern face through processes of planned change during the economic crisis of the 1930s, *inter alia*, as an outcome of the activities of the Tennessee Valley Authority. The mass media gradually served more and more to advertise the mistakes of government (Roberts 1995: 222). The *Cultural Revolution* of students and other youngsters in the late 1960s and early 1970s increased the speed of the trend towards public involvement. The US National Environmental Policy Act of 1969 (NEPA) further increased the impetus of the democratization movement.

The discussion of these developments requires a number of definitions. *Public involvement* is a process for involving the public in the decision-making of an organization. This can be brought about through either consultation or participation. *Consultation* includes education, information sharing and negotiation, the goal being better decision-making by the organization consulting the public. *Participation* actually brings the public into the decision-making process (Roberts 1995).

Public involvement has focused primarily on consulting the public, with no options for greater involvement. The process has relied heavily on education and information sharing. However, a number of organizations have experimented with public participation in the form of joint planning and delegated authority, where the public actually controls and directs the process and the ultimate results (Roberts 1995: 224).

Public involvement tries to bridge the gap between participatory and representative democracy by allowing individuals some opportunity to influence decisions normally decided by higher authorities. Representative democracy still has to specify the limits of participatory democracy, however. If participatory democracy operates without limits set by parliament, the interests of small groups and regions may interfere with the interests of the nation as a whole. Quite often national interests have to override interests of smaller units. If national (or international) interests are at stake, protests voiced as *not in my back yard* have to be silenced by anti-NIMBY laws. Otherwise highways cannot be built any more, refugee camps will be forbidden by most communities and, in general, national redistribution of privileges and other resources will become impossible. This does not imply that the increase of public participation has come to an end. The relationship between participation and democracy constitutes an ongoing dilemma (Burdge & Vanclay 1995; Roberts 1995: 223).

If public involvement is considered, the situation has to be analyzed before any further steps can be taken. Who is the public in this particular case? Often there is no single *public*. Instead there is a number of publics, some of them visible from the beginning, others emerging during the involvement process. Stakeholders will step into and drop out of the process at their own discretion. Some will join a visible and vocal minority, while others will become part of the silent majority.

An organization involving the public has to ascertain which participants are experienced in public involvement and are informed about the issues. Who are hostile or apathetic? Is the public united or divided? Are ethnic, cultural, or geographical controversies at stake? Roberts states:

> It is a good rule of thumb to expect that the public will be concerned when something new, something large, or something different is proposed in or near their community. Concerns will even be greater if the project or activity is located close to their place of residence. Even relatively common activities which an organisation does not see as a problem itself can cause concern amongst the public when it has not been informed and personal concerns have not been addressed (Roberts 1995: 229).

As soon as the central actor has analyzed the situation and has decided to launch a public involvement process, a number of steps have to be taken.

Step 1: Scoping. Scoping consists of determining the scope of issues to be addressed and for identifying issues related to the proposed action (Burdge & Robertson 1994: 178). The concept has been introduced during the implementation of NEPA. Scoping requires the identification of key people and organizations. They need to be consulted informally. Their assistance is essential for identifying major issues and other concerned parties. They have to help reduce misinformation, rumour and gossip. Also they can be engaged in gathering relevant information on economic, environmental and social developments. Key people and organizations have to be given a clear set of rules. They must be told what to expect. All parties must agree on the mandate and terms of reference. Consensus is welcome, but it is not required. Parties can agree to disagree on certain points.

Step 2: Planning of the public involvement. During this step, the process of involvement has to be determined. The roles of the central actor, the impact assessor as change agent and the key people have to be charted. The major decision points have to be identified. Also the information to be shared has to be defined. Some information will be available to all participants and some will remain classified. If the secret part of the exchange of information is specified in advance, the risk of conflict is considerably reduced. The planning of the involvement process includes the specification and dissemination of the terms of reference. Public involvement is always confronted with constraints that have been introduced by law. Public involvement will also be restricted by the objectives and the limits set by the parties that co-operate in the process. What would each of the parties prefer to happen? what are they prepared to tolerate? and what are they unwilling to accept? These boundary conditions have already been discussed in an earlier chapter. Quite often, the public will have to be paid for its effort. If government establishes advisory committees, stakeholder groups and the like, the costs of participation will normally have to be reimbursed by government.

Step 3: Implementation of the public involvement. Next the process of public involvement has to be put into practice. Roberts states that if the organization has planned all the steps, agreed on the strategy and approaches and has informally involved the public in obtaining their support of the approach, then the likelihood of success is high (Roberts 1995: 234). A process of public involvement is a learning process, however. During the process, a lot of unexpected events will require sidestepping the plan. Coping with risk and uncertainty during public involvement requires monitoring of the process. At set points, the accomplishments of the parties will have to be evaluated. This involves formative evaluation, providing guidelines for improving the process.

Step 4: Follow-up. After the final decision relating to a project, a vital phase in the public involvement strategy starts. As a rule, the key individuals and organizations will be satisfied only partially. It is vitally important to explain to them in detail the reasons for the discrepancy between the initial ideals and the harsh reality that finally emerged. This explanation prevents unnecessary conflicts and paves the road for further public participation. At the end of the process, frequently central actors and their change agents do not have enough resources left to implement an adequate follow-up. This shortcoming will put the whole process in an unfavourable light. It is vital to prevent this kind of late failure.

A number of pitfalls concerning public participation have already been identified in passing. I will now list some further dangers. First, change agents may discern too late that trouble arises. Some early warnings are: participants start adding new issues; they switch from criticizing project-specific issues to criticizing general issues; the leaders become more radical and channels of communication shut down (Roberts 1995). Secondly: public overload. The growing trend toward requiring public involvement in decision-making, both in the public and the private sector, may result in a temporary overload. If competing requests for a democratic input to decision-making are discovered too late, even the best process of public involvement will fail. During the process the agenda of all requests for public involvement has to be monitored. Thirdly, information overload. Participants are often confronted with far more written and oral material than they can cope with. The central agent and its change agents will have to monitor the flow of communication directed at individuals and organizations. Information has to summarized. It has also to be offered in an appropriate format. Drawings and photographs often convey ideas much better than the printed word.

What will be the future of public involvement? Roberts sketches the road ahead as follows:

> We are witnessing a slow change in the role that the public plays in the decisions that affect them toward greater involvement in decisions of all sorts. Governments are moving rapidly toward greater public participation in the development of public policy both for reasons of necessity and because they are being pressured to do so. In the private sector, whether for reasons of strategic success, reduced implementation costs, or developing a positive corporate image, public involvement has an expanding role in the future of corporate decisions. However, the greatest

guarantee of a continuing growth of public involvement is the public itself. Having once been allowed in to participate in decision making, it is difficult to stand on the sidelines next time. If the public is not invited to participate, people will demand it. (Roberts 1995: 243).

6.4.4 Relationship with basic research

In this discussion of the relationship between SIA and basic research, I first have to define my terms. Basic research can be defined as "experimental or theoretical work undertaken primarily to acquire new knowledge of the underlying foundations or phenomena and observable facts, without any particular application or use in view" (OECD 1981). Scientists undertaking basic research can usually set their own goals and to a large extent organize their own work. However, in some instances basic research may be oriented or directed towards some broad fields of general interest, and in this case it is called *oriented basic research* (OECD 1981: 54). Applied research is also original investigation undertaken in order to acquire new knowledge. It is, however, directed primarily towards a specific practical aim or objective (OECD 1981: 54). Applied research is undertaken either to find possible uses for the findings of basic research or to find new methods or ways of achieving some specific and predetermined objectives. It involves the use of available knowledge and its extension in order to solve particular problems. The results of applied research are intended primarily to be valid for a single or limited number of operations, methods or systems. If its objective is to enlighten decision-makers, it is called *policy-oriented research*.

6.4.4a) *The core model of social science analysis*
As we saw in Chapter 1, the core model of social science analysis consists of the goals of an actor, the constraints confronting this actor, the ranking of behavioural alternatives and finally the behavioural act itself. This core model figures in explanation and interpretation. It can be elaborated in many ways, *inter alia*, by specifying the constraints. We can use framing, that is, pay special attention to the social setting of the behavioural act. We can specify resources as a powerful kind of constraints.

159

An application of this core model can be found in research dealing with behaviour on a micro-level. As an example I take game theory, that is, a branch of mathematics that is concerned with decisions in interdependent situations. Three kinds of game theory have to be distinguished. Normative game theory analyzes the strategic behaviour of super-rational actors. Prescriptive game theory is aimed at advising people how to improve their decisions. Descriptive game theory tries to describe and explain how people actually behave in interdependent situations. Now imagine a situation in which actor A wants to interact with actor B, but actor B has no reason to trust actor A. The two actors have not interacted in the past. Now actor A can try to win the confidence of actor B by offering collateral as a security against breach of promises. Processes of trust and commitment have been studied on a micro-level in laboratory experiments (e.g. Snijders 1996). They have also been studied on a meso-level, for example in the interactions of business firms regarding the acquisition of computer software and hardware. In both laboratory experiments and field observations, collateral has been used to measure trust. The outcomes of these game theoretical analyses are relevant to SIA because they can elucidate the consequences of using collateral to enhance trust.

6.4.4b) *Oriented basic research*
On a large scale the core model has been elaborated in oriented basic research. Game theory, for instance, has been used to elucidate negotiations. In the Harvard Negotiations Project (Fisher & Ury 1981), behaviour in negotiations has been studied in a way that constitutes oriented basic research. Following this, the outcomes of research have been used to formulate strategies to win negotiations. I will discuss a number of applications now. Parties in negotiations can engage a mediator who will try to bring them together. Parties can also engage three or five arbiters, who will try to come to an agreement or a kind of verdict. Sometimes, when an agreement is achieved, parties continue negotiations in order to achieve a post-settlement settlement, that is, a solution with still better outcomes for each of the parties. Mediators are used in the USA and a number of other countries to facilitate nego-tiations in conflicts about wages, environmental protection and a host of other controversies.

In the late 1960s and early 1970s, a wave of political unrest, radicalization and polarization swept over western Europe. This wave became most visible in an increase in political action, such as demonstrations and boycotts, and the rise of new social movements, such as the women's and the ecological movements. These shifts in political behaviour are the most visible aspects of the process of political change. Equally relevant are accompanying changes in political orientations among the populations of advanced industrial societies since the 1960s. The postwar generations show an increased emphasis on nonmaterial and emancipatory goals, because they are shifting away from tradition, respect for authority and material wellbeing towards self-fulfilment, independence and emancipation. These shifts that were triggered by the *Cultural Revolution* of the late 1960s and early 1970s, *inter alia*, change beliefs in government. There has emerged a general withdrawal of confidence from many elements of the political and economic system. As a consequence, we see a change in the position of governments to deal with problems in society. Grassroots activities and social movement participation undermine traditional government procedures. Belief in government decreases, not only because the content of values changes, but also because there is an ongoing process of fragmentation or pluralization as new values are added to existing orientations (Van Deth & Scarbrough 1995). These processes of cultural and political change are highly relevant to SIA, inter alia, because shifts in belief in government have consequences for current and future government actions.

My next example of oriented basic research deals with the diffusion of innovations, briefly mentioned already in Chapter 2. Rogers (1995) analyzed the process by which an innovation is communicated through certain channels over time among the members of a social system. He sees diffusion as part of a larger process which begins with a perceived problem or need, continues with R&D on a possible solution, followed by a decision by a change agent that this innovation should be diffused, and then its diffusion. Rogers analyzed 2,297 empirical diffusion research reports and tried to formulate generalizations on the basis of these reports. He started by taking a close look at the generation of these innovations. How does the innovation–development process take place? Next he dealt with the innovation-decision process. He specified the stages that exist in this process and summarized his findings in ten generalizations. For instance: earlier knowers of an innovation have more exposure to interpersonal channels of communications. In the third place, he looked at the attributes of innovations and their rate of adoption. For instance, earlier adopters have more social participation than late adopters. Ultimately he analyzed the consequences of innovations: desirable versus undesirable, direct versus indirect, anticipated versus unanticipated. In total, 84 generalizations were formulated, and information was provided with regard to supporting and nonsupporting empirical evidence. Rogers's research on the diffusion of innovations is of strategic importance to SIA because it provides explanations for success and failure of actions initiated by central actors. Rogers has been criticized, as we saw in Chapter 2, for underrating the impact of public participation, as well as failing to appreciate fully the social and cultural basis of decision-making (e.g. Vanclay & Lawrence 1995).

6.4.4c) *Contributions to SIA*

Oriented basic research contributes considerably to the improvement of policy-oriented research, primarily by ex-post evaluation of old projects. In this kind of oriented basic research, old publications in the field of policy-oriented social research are analyzed and their conclusions compared with empirical data concerning developments that took place after the publication of the original report. Ex-post evaluation of policy-oriented social research requires theories to explain the degree of reliability and validity found in the old reports. The theories enable us to formulate expectations regarding the goodness-of-fit between predicted and actual developments. The theories are a basis for explaining mistakes made by the policy researchers in the original projects. Some mistakes can be explained by shortcomings of the researchers, while others are a consequence of incomplete data, outdated assumptions or pressure from policy-makers or the press.

In reviewing old problem analyses, the study of the Cuban missile crisis by Allison (1971) is a classical example. Allison's major theme is that there may be no one best way of approaching a problem. In the case of the missile crisis, the rational actor model proved to be too vague because it focused too much on macro-structure and gross detail. Models of bureaucratic politics and organizational process provide a more adequate explanation of problem analyses. The lesson behind these conclusions is that problem analysis requires a combination of models on a relatively high level of abstraction (rational choice,

responsibilities of government. If government does not specify what it wants from suppliers, or does not evaluate what it has received, it should not expect to get what it needs. Many municipal services, for instance, are readily definable and easy to measure and evaluate. The second lesson concerns the burden of process. The privatization movement is propelled in part by the longing of public officials to escape bureaucratic complexities, substituting the supposed simplicity of arm's-length contracts. Perhaps the most common error in thinking about privatization, Donahue continued, was to concentrate on potential efficiency gains without considering how to realize this potential. The third lesson concerns the cardinal importance of competition. Organizations (including public ones) that must match the pace set by ambitious rivals are virtually always more efficient than organizations (including private ones) that are secure against challenge. Other evaluations of privatization concern developments in the UK (Kay et al. 1986) and other western countries (Leeuw et al. 1994). In general, the conclusions of Donahue are confirmed by the other evaluators. In any case, these lessons enable social impact assessors to evaluate current or future privatization processes in a more efficient way than before. SIA practitioners are also now provided with new insights that will enable them to design more efficient ways of privatization.

6.4.5 Relationships with normative debates

Morality is a quality of human behaviour related to what has to be done and how it has to be done, in other words, obligations and ethical rules. First, I want to discuss IA, including SIA, as a moral obligation. As a frame of reference I take utilitarianism. This is the moral theory that judges the goodness of outcomes – and therefore the rightness of actions insofar as they affect outcomes – by the degree to which they secure the greatest benefit to all concerned. Utilitarian moral theory has two major elements (Hardin 1988: xvi). One is the concern with consequences in the form of human welfare. The other is the nature of human welfare, the value theory of utilitarianism. The first component is called consequentialism. Because IA is about the consequences of current or future actions, consequentialism is evidently relevant for a moral reflection about IA.

Consequentialism has its limits. A complete account of everything involved in our significant decisions is not possible. If we tried to take all aspects of the situation into consideration, all our decisions would creep to a standstill. March and Simon (1958) escape this dilemma by noting that often we do not maximize but satisfy, by stopping calculating and considering when we find a merely adequate choice or action. When, in principle, one cannot know what is the best choice, one can nevertheless be sure that sitting and calculating is not the best choice. But, one may ask, how do we know that another ten minutes of calculation would not have produced a better choice? Nobody knows precisely! Only a reasonable approximation can be achieved.

6.4.5a) *Utilitarian moral theory*
Utilitarianism has two different roles. On the one hand, as a theory of personal morality, and, on the other hand, as a theory of public choice. This is evident in the work of John Rawls, in particular his book *A Theory of Justice* (1971). It is also evident in normative game theory, discussed above. An act-utilitarian is someone who decides which of available alternative actions to undertake by first deciding which will produce the greatest utility overall. Now we all know that it will often be difficult to determine overall utility because causal theories are deficient, the time for decision is short, and so forth. Moreover we may see things too much from our own vantage point and maybe therefore tend to take actions that serve our own interests more than they serve the more general good. The answer to these problems is some form of rule-utilitarianism, in which we follow well-established moral rules (do not lie, do not break promises, etc.) instead of trying to calculate the overall good of our actions in each specific case.

Utilitarianism can best be seen as a programme, not as a definite theory (Hardin 1988: 205). Many of its issues are closely linked to the framework of game theory. A lot of its problems are far from being solved, as can be illustrated by paternalism, which can often be interpreted as being both right (concern for the other's welfare) and wrong (robbing the other of freedom). Also, the problem of transaction costs proves difficult to solve. A transition from the present situation on the roads of Europe to a system of everybody having to drive on the same side of the road would save numerous lives, but would cost a huge amount of money. Would that money yield the same profit for human welfare as alternative investments, for instance, in cancer research?

In the first place, utilitarianism obliges all actors, individual as well as corporate, to analyze the consequences of their current or future actions. As Hardin puts it: "The fundamentally moral impulse of utilitarianism is the concern with consequences for people in general. Hence, the core of utilitarianism is its consequentialism, its universality, and some kind of value that is value to individual." (1988: 19).

In the second place, utilitarianism obliges corporate actors to assess the consequences of their actions before they decide to launch the actions. Sometimes IA is prescribed by law, for example, in the case of EIA. In other situations, there are overall legal requirements for IA, as in the Netherlands regarding all actions by governmental organizations. In general, consequentialism includes the moral obligation to engage scientific research whenever it can contribute to the moral quality of the decision.

6.4.5b) *Moral obligations in SIA*

These have been elaborated by Finsterbusch (1995) in a paper called *In Praise of SIA*, in which he presents a moral evaluation of SIA. According to Finsterbusch, there are seven major ethical bases for evaluating public policies, and SIA has a positive value in all seven ethical paradigms.

The first is utilitarianism, which judges the policy that produces the greatest good for the greatest number as the best. This translates into the largest excess of benefits over costs. Since a SIA is needed to determine the full set of benefits and costs, it contributes to the information basis for good policy choices, according to the utilitarian paradigm.

The second moral basis is the libertarian view that elevates individuals and their rights (mainly freedom) above all other values. This translates into limiting the state almost entirely to defence and law enforcement. In its most extreme form, libertarianism would find most government actions unacceptable because they step on individual rights. In its pure form, libertarianism has also little use for SIA. In its less extreme form, however, it would find SIA useful. When government actions are taken, the SIA would estimate which impacts it has on individuals and their rights and could help minimize and compensate for the negative impacts. In this way, it would serve a major concern of libertarianism.

The third ethical basis for evaluating public policies Finsterbusch lists is Rawls's (1971) *Theory of Justice*, which requires that policies treat all members of the contractual society equally. When policies must involve inequality, as they do in the real world, they are *just* if they benefit everyone equally and if all members have an equal chance to get the better positions. If in fact some must bear more costs than benefits, the policy may still be just if the more advantaged groups rather than the less advantaged groups are the ones to bear these costs. The justice paradigm justifies SIAs because they provide the information whereby one can monitor the justice criteria.

The fourth ethical basis for evaluating policies is the Marxian condemnation of exploitation. Marx argued that social institutions are created by the powerful and are structured to serve the interests of the powerful, so they consistently produce biased results. Marxism calls for the eradication of all exploitation and bias. This requires radical reform and sometimes even a revolution. SIA is not an instrument for the revolution of social institutions to equalize power and results. However, by bringing to light information on the distribution of costs and benefits of government actions, it tends to reduce the generation of inequality by government actions, because governments produce the most inequality when they act in relative secrecy.

The fifth ethical basis for evaluating policies is functionalism in which policies are judged positively if they improve the functioning of the target system and the larger system of which it is a part. SIA enhances system functioning by enabling better performance and increasing the legitimacy of the system.

The sixth ethical basis for evaluating policies is a truly democratic decision-making process. The previous five criteria emphasize good outcomes and this criterion emphasizes a good process (which may or may not produce the best outcome). Truly democratic decision-making requires knowledge to be equally shared among the parties affected by policy decisions. An SIA that clearly reveals who gets adversely or beneficially impacted would serve this need.

The seventh and final ethical basis for evaluating policies, according to Finsterbusch, is ethical pluralism. This view does not accept the arguments of the proponents of the other views that emphasize one criterion over others, instead, it assumes that the weights for the various relevant criteria vary from case to case, so they must be traded off against each other anew in each situation. The pluralist paradigm has a greater requirement for SIA than the other ethical paradigms. There are two major methods for trading off values against each other: through a fair political process, or through a technically rational procedure. An SIA that fully identifies the distribution of all significant impacts (both benefits and costs) on various groups is essential to both processes for the assigning weights for impacts.

Finsterbusch concludes that SIA is required in all ethically grounded decision-making processes, and should therefore be widely used in all public decisions regarding projects and programmes.

There is one ethical basis for claiming that certain SIAs should not be conducted. This is the case when the costs exceed the benefits of the SIA. Another situation that might result in higher costs than benefits is when the SIA research process itself produces significant unintended negative consequences. Social impact assessors should minimize the chances of this.

Finsterbusch focuses on government activities. If we look at actions of business firms or nonprofit organizations, the same arguments can be applied. Shareholders, stakeholders and related beneficiaries of non-governmental organizations have the same rights to fair treatment as citizens of the state. In a number of countries, SIAs are already required by law. The Netherlands is an example of this. In the near future, many other countries will follow. This expansion of the demand for SIA will put social impact assessors in a delicate position. They will have to refuse demands for their services if they are not ready for these services or if they lack the human resources necessary to meet the demand in an adequate way.

6.4.5c) *Towards a code of ethics*
The International Association for Impact Assessment (IAIA) has formulated a code of ethics concerning EIA:

1. The member shall carry out his or her professional activities, as far as possible, in accordance with emerging principles of sustainable development and the highest standards of environmental protection.
2. The member shall conduct professional activities, as far as possible in accordance with emerging principles of sustainable development and the highest standards of environmental protection.

3. The member shall at all times place the integrity of the natural environment and the health, safety and welfare of the human community above any commitment to sectional or private interests.

4. The member shall be personally accountable for the validity of all data collected, analysis performed, or plans developed by the member, and for the scrutiny of all data collected, analysis performed, or plans developed under the member's direction.

5. The member shall actively discourage misrepresentation or misuse of work the member has performed or that which was performed under the member's direction.

6. The member shall ensure the incorporation of environmental protection and social or socio-economic impact considerations from the earliest stages of project design or policy development.

7. The member shall not conduct professional activities in a manner involving dishonesty, fraud, deceit, misrepresentation or bias.

8. The member shall not advertise or present the member's services in a manner that may bring discredit to the profession.

It is worth looking at the codes of conduct of related professional associations to get an idea of other issues that confront the social sciences. The *Ethical Principles of Psychologists and Code of Conduct* of the American Psychological Association (1992), for example, reflect more than 40 years of practical experience. I shall reproduce a number of their articles that SIA professional ought to reflect on:

- Psychologists design, conduct and report research in accordance with recognized standards of scientific competence and ethical research (6.006.a).
- Psychologists conduct research competently and with due concern for the dignity and welfare of the participants (6.07.a).
- Psychologists obtain informed consent from research participants prior to filming or recording them in any form, unless the research involves simply naturalistic observations in public places and it is not anticipated that the recording will be used in a manner that could cause personal identification or harm (6.13).

Informed consent is one of the hot issues in social science research ethics. How much should we tell people we are interviewing or involving in an experiment? Are social scientists allowed to contact organizations by telephone, disguise themselves as customers and confront employees of the organization with racist proposals? This type of field experiment leads to a valid exposure of racial discrimination. In this way valuable information is gathered that can lead to the design of new actions against racial discrimination. But is it within the limits of professional codes of conduct to deceive the employees of the organizations? One argument in favour of this kind of field experiments is that getting involved in a field experiment is a normal risk of working in organizations that have a lot of contact by telephone with customers.

In the recent past, IA has had a number of ethical controversies, and as an illustration I will describe one of them. At the Shanghai conference of IAIA in 1993, I chaired a session in which a discussion was started with regard to an assessment of the impacts of a large-scale estuary project, the Three Gorges Project in China. The controversy focused on the question of whether the impact assessors involved were free to exclude from their report the consequences of the estuary for the income of people outside the catchment area. It turned out to be impossible to give a satisfactory answer to the question because generally accepted standards for carrying out an IA are not yet available.

6.4.6 Relationships with IA as a social system

Social impact assessors depend in many ways on a number of scientific communities. First, science as a social system is involved. Academic research and related research outside universities is responsible for enhancing knowledge, including oriented basic knowledge relevant to SIA. Universities are furthermore responsible for educating future impact assessors. The social system of science is also responsible for disseminating knowledge.

Secondly, *invisible colleges* have to be mentioned. An invisible college is an informal social network which provides its *members* with opportunities for knowledge and information exchange as well as professional support and ideas sharing. This occurs through electronic discussion groups, Internet home pages, as well as through the circulation of preprints.[1]

Thirdly, the boards of funding agencies, such as national science foundations, editorial boards of scientific journals and editors of companies publishing the outcomes of scientific research, have to be mentioned. In this case, we are talking about the gatekeepers of resources and communication in science.

The first type of scientific communities is improving its activities in a considerable way. There is a growing production of state-of-the-art publications, for example, *Environmental and Social Impact Assessment*, the volume edited by Frank Vanclay and Dan Bronstein (1995). Since 1989, Frank Vanclay has produced a regularly updated computerized database of SIA literature. I also mention the *Handbook of Contemporary Developments in World Sociology* edited by Mohan (1994). Most disciplines publish annual reviews or state-of-the-art reports in a specific journal or in yearbooks. As examples, I mention the journals *Current Sociology*, the *Annual Review of Sociology* and the *Yearbook of Sociology*. Special attention has to be paid to the Social Sciences Research Methodology (SRM) index developed at the Erasmus University, Rotterdam, the Netherlands, providing information on CD-ROM about publications on research methodology, including IA.

The second type of scientific communities is also taking its responsibilities seriously. A growing number of informal social networks of scientists is discovering the advantages of E-mail and Internet for an exchange of scientific information.

The third type of scientific community is still a misty affair. There is no institutionalized system yet that evaluates funding agencies. Also editorial boards of scientific journals and publishers of scientific books are still operating without external control.

Scientists that are a member of a professional association can use the power of the association to ensure that professional standards and rules of conduct are enforced. Scientists operating on their own do not have enough power to enforce compliance with professional ethics that concern their own work. This implies that being a member of a professional association is a moral requirement.

In IA, the IAIA is the obvious choice as far as a professional association is concerned. Many impact assessors are also a member of similar organizations, operating *inter alia* in risk assessment.

6.5 Summary

The discussion of major problems in SIA starts with the determination of the size of the study. An instant SIA study requires, roughly speaking, from 15 minutes up to one month. It demands up to one person year of effort. There is enough experience with instant SIA to make them an interesting option. Organizations confronted frequently with situations that require instant SIA will see to it that they have experienced staff at their disposal. They will also see to it that they have a problem analysis, a baseline analysis and a set of scenarios prepared in advance. A medium-sized SIA study will require one to three person years and will take one to three years to complete the project. In the case of large-sized SIA studies, we are talking about projects with more than three person years staff that take more than three years to complete. Strategic learning, combining research with action, requires a medium-sized or a large-sized project.

Coping with risk and uncertainty in the SIA study requires risk assessment. Both subjective and objective risk demand the attention of the social impact assessor. Mitigating risk demands risk management.

The central actor has to design and implement a policy for the organizational setting of SIA. If the organizations need SIA over a long period of time, institutionalization has to be taken care of. An option available to the central actor is to entrust SIA to one or more members of staff in a specific unit established for SIA. Another option is employing consultants on a temporary basis. Many organizations, in particular large ones, prefer to combine an internal and an external input of expertise.

If public involvement is required, either consultation or participation will have to be established. A number of threats are involved. Change agents may discern too late that trouble arises. The public may be overloaded with invitations to co-operate in consultation or to participate in decision-making.

For its progress SIA is heavily dependent on oriented basic research. The SIA community has to monitor developments in this kind of research. As soon as progress has been achieved in data acquisition, statistical analysis and theory formation, the new knowledge has to be transfered to the practitioners in the field.

SIA has also to be discussed as a moral obligation. Consequentialism advocates the assessment of the consequences of interventions. It also advocates taking responsibility for the consequences of the interventions. The normative debate leads, *inter alia*, to the design and institutionalization of a code of ethics.

Note

1. The IAIA, for example, although being a formal entity, also plays a considerable role as an informal college. Its Web Page and links to other environmental Web sites are used by many IA professionals and environmental agencies. Under the direction of Frank Vanclay, IAIA also facilitates many electronic listserver discussion groups dealing with different aspects of IA. Details about these discussion groups are available on the IAIA Home Page: http://IAIA.ext.NoDak.edu/IAIA/Warning, this address is case sensitive!

CHAPTER 7

Experiences with SIA in Europe and North America

7.1 Introduction

In the last decades, developments in SIA in Europe and North America has been by a process of trial and error, with gradual progress in research methodology and slow improvements in application. As we saw in Chapter 2, in the early 1980s these processes changed both in content and in speed. I will elaborate on four key developments now.

First, the economic recession has taken its toll. Business corporations have been forced to reduce their staffing levels and restructure their procedures and organizational arrangements. In the struggle for survival, many firms started to train their employees in decision-making, negotiating, planning and social relationships. They employed social scientists to assist in these training programmes. Many social scientists started private research and consultancy firms, and earned their living on a contract basis. A relatively small number of social scientists entered the employment of business firms.

Second, the ecological crisis put its mark on western society. Environmental arguments had to be taken into consideration. In the late 1980s, the debate about sustainability increased the awareness of the limits to growth. Demographic developments like the increase in population worldwide and western discontinuities like the baby boom and the baby bust cycles demanded attention for the carrying capacity of the natural environment and limits to economic resources. Legal requirements led to environmental impact assessment (EIA). In many cases, EIA had to be combined with SIA.

Third, the restructuring of governments plays a major role. The economic recession forced western governments to launch retrenchments and reorganizations. The increasing complexity of society and changes in value orientations in the political area led to political conflicts and parliamentary scandals. The dual pressure from the economic and the political realm forced western governments to change their procedures and organizations. Governments decided to deregulate, privatize and decentralize. At first, the new regimes had good intentions, and gradually many of these decisions were implemented. It became obvious that deregulation, privatization and decentralization could be pretested in policy-oriented social science research. As a consequence, governments had to employ social scientists to carry out the pretesting. Governments also had to employ social scientists to train their employees in innovative management techniques. Governments had to learn how to handle public protest and the public participation that was demanded, and they discovered that social scientists could provide knowledge and methods to deal with these problems. Governments increasingly employed the social sciences to improve and to legitimize their decisions. Criticism by parliament and press on financial and procedural activities of government triggered legislation that prescribed policy-oriented social research, in particular SIA.

Fourth, the late flowering of the social sciences has to be taken into account. In the 1960s and 1970s, the social sciences lost a lot of goodwill because they could not meet the expectations they had evoked. In the early 1980s, the social sciences succeeded in making considerable progress, both in basic and policy-oriented research. These achievements did not lead to a substantial change in the opinions policy-makers, public and press had about these sciences. Nevertheless, the economic recession, the ecological crisis and the restructuring of government each generated an increase in the demand for the services of the social sciences. Social scientists were increasingly employed to analyze problems, pretest actions, explore future developments and assist in reorganizations. The demand overruled the reputation.

As an illustration of the impact of these four developments, I take health care policies in the West since the early 1980s. Before that time, the medical establishment showed little interest in co-operation with social scientists. In 1979, the World Health Organization (WHO) launched the programme called *Health for All by the Year 2000*. Futures research,

176

management, and planning of health care play an important role in this· programme. Three countries, Finland, Sweden and the Netherlands, have agreed to carry out trial projects with the scenario method. On the basis of the results of these trial projects, further steps have been taken to enlarge on the scenario method in the interests of this WHO programme. Anybody who would have predicted a large-scale application of scenarios, social impact analysis and planning of change in western health care policy would have been ridiculed in the past!

In this chapter, I will first take a close look at changes in methods and theory in the social sciences as far as they are relevant to SIA (section 7.2). Next, I will discuss experiences in SIA in the West, focusing on micro-, meso-, and macro-assessments. I will present examples coming from best research practice and discuss their methodological and theoretical merits and weaknesses.

7.2 Method and theory in SIA in the West

The four developments discussed in the preceding paragraph led, in the early 1980s, to a change of the social climate in the scientific disciplines concerned. As an example I take sociology. In this discipline, we see in those years a growing emphasis on step-by-step attempts to improve methods and theories. Debates about stagnation and crisis in the discipline recede into the margin of the discipline. State-of-the-art reports document achievements in most components of the discipline. Progress in sociology since the early 1980s did not result in substantial improvements in the reputation of the discipline, however (Becker & Leeuw 1995; Bryant 1995; Bryant & Becker 1990). Other disciplines in the social sciences show similar developments in this period. This applies to cultural anthropology, demography, social and institutional economics and political science (Mohan & Wilke 1994).

Improvements can be discerned in problem analysis. Here the Cultural Revolution has had a favourable impact. Since the social criticism practised in the 1960s and 1970s, problem analysis now pays more attention to the interests of the principal actors afflicted by a social problem and its mitigation or abolition. Social scientists have elaborated a methodology for social criticism, as we saw in Chapter 6. Nowadays, actors in the target system are incorporated in SIA more carefully than before. Public participation in analyzing and tackling social problems has gained importance. Also, data acquisition shows major improvements. In the West, interviewing by telephone has grown into a widely applied, sophisticated approach, although many drawbacks still have to be reduced. Data archives, housing raw data of thousands of old research projects, provide an empirical basis for micro-simulations. Gathering expert opinions by Delphi projects has grown into a frequently used approach.

Third, systems analysis demands our attention. This analytical approach has provided a terminology and a format for discussions within and between natural and social sciences, *inter alia*, by introducing concepts like open and closed systems, systems boundaries and systems noise (also called unpredictability). Systems analysis has developed techniques for conceptual mapping, thereby improving problem analysis. Systems analysis has also elaborated languages to deal with complexity, to facilitate computer simulations and to bridge the gap with artificial intelligence. SIA is closely related to systems analysis because it uses this approach to represent the activities of central and target actors and to assess the impacts of current and future actions (Vennix 1996).

Fourth, explanation and interpretation in social sciences research have gradually been improved from the early 1980s onwards. Because SIA has to explore future developments, it depends on the availability of valid theoretical models. In the late 1990s, the social sciences can provide an integrated system of explanation and interpretation using meta-theories, theories and research hypotheses. In most areas in social research, a set of theories and research hypotheses is available (see *inter alios* Mohan & Wilke 1994).

Sixth, a distinct methodology for the simulation of the consequences of current and future actions has been elaborated. We saw in Chapters 3 and 4, that this methodology already shows a considerable degree of sophistication. We also saw that many components of the methodology are still lacking scientific rigour and that many improvements are required. The methodology for SIA is not an exclusive box of tools, however. The social sciences, both basic and applied, have a common methodology, and subfields like SIA select a number of methods according to their specific requirements. The subfields test these methods, redesign them and, in general, contribute to their improvement.

Seventh, basic social science is concerned. With regard to SIA, special attention has to be paid to the ex post evaluation of IAs. SIA, like all types of IA, depends on evaluations of its projects after the hour of truth has passed. The outcomes of these evaluations are vital inputs to redesigning SIA methods. When legal requirements for SIA exist, large numbers of SIAs are undertaken, and basic science gets a substantial input to the process of improving SIA methods.

7.3 Micro-analyses

Micro-analysis is a type of SIA, as I defined it in a preceding chapter, that has the behaviour of individual actors as its main dependent variable. In most cases, large numbers of individual actors are concerned, in particular, if demographic processes are analyzed. Demographical studies often deal with future consequences of a current or proposed action. An excellent illustration is provided by *Future Demographic Trends in Europe and North America*, edited by Lutz (1991). I will discuss a number of contributions to this volume, all showing relevant experiences in SIA.

Mortality trends in western countries are analyzed by Valkonen (1991). Mortality is influenced by socio-cultural, economic and medical developments, furthermore by critical incidents like wars and catastrophes. Socio-cultural, economic and medical developments can be changed by interventions, *inter alia*, by improving lifestyles, income distribution and health care facilities. Mortality tends to show slow and relatively even changes, but in the long run uncertainties concerning the future average life expectancy are not less than those concerning fertility and migration. Gains in life expectancy can be achieved by eliminating such social determinants of premature death as smoking, excessive animal fat consumption, hypertension and alcohol consumption. Eliminating or diminishing these causes of death is curbed by the biological limit to life expectancy. There are unavoidable biological restrictions to life expectancy. Taking avoidable premature deaths into consideration, four issues appear to be of crucial importance: female mortality, male mortality, high-mortality countries and critical incidents, such as medical breakthroughs and catastrophes.

In all industrialized western countries, females have higher life expectancy than males. The decline of female mortality is likely to continue, even in those countries where female life expectancy already is the highest. How far can this continue and is there a fixed or changing limit to longevity? If a limit exists, is it closer to 80, 90, or 100 years? and how long will it take to reach this limit? Secondly, what will be the future of excess male mortality? In general, the difference between female and male life expectancy has increased in industrialized western countries. Research has not yet shown to what extent excess mortality and the increasing gap between female and male life expectancies are determined by biological factors, or to what extent by socio-cultural factors – the latter being partially susceptible to interventions. Thirdly, differences in mortality between countries demand our attention. There is no explanation so far for the persisting gap in mortality between eastern and western Europe. The gap has been widening (Valkonen 1991). Fourthly, unanticipated factors have to be looked at. There will be breakthroughs in medicine, already foreshadowed by breakthroughs in oriented basic research, to prevent or cure cancer, heart disease and other major causes of death (Hollander & Becker 1987). On the other hand, an unexpected increase of mortality may be caused by wars, ecological or economic catastrophes, or epidemics (like AIDS).

Existing biotechnology has considerable potential for increasing life expectancy, resulting in a further decrease in mortality (Manton 1991). With the present mortality levels reached in industrialized western countries, further decreases in mortality will lead to a significant aging of the population, because the gains in survival will be achieved mainly at older ages and not, as in the past, in infancy and childhood. The greying of the population will have considerable consequences for the size and the composition of the labour force and the costs of social security, including health care. The aging of the population is studied in DIA, especially with respect to the future age of retirement. The volunteer activities of a healthy active mobile young elderly population also ought to be considered in any assessment of the social impacts of aging and retirement.

Occupational impacts on mortality declines have been analyzed by Andersen (1991) for the Nordic countries. He undertook a comparative study on differences in mortality among occupational groups in Denmark, Finland, Iceland, Norway and Sweden. He focused on the potential for a reduction in overall mortality by decreasing mortality of the high-risk groups to the level of the lowest-risk group, that is, teachers. The reasons why some occupational groups have low mortality while other groups have high mortality are very complex. First, occupation groups face varying occupational health hazards. Secondly, there may be a selection effect – only physically healthy people will seek, acquire and later retain a physically demanding job, a phenomenon commonly known as the *healthy worker effect.* Sometimes there is socio-economic selection – children of educated parents are more likely to have had a healthy upbringing and to choose high-status jobs. Thirdly, working conditions are important. For instance, occupational studies have shown that shift work is unhealthy. However, general lifestyle (living standards, drinking, smoking habits, etc.) is equally or even more important than an individual's working conditions. Lifestyle and working conditions are connected.

Demographic and health IA come together in explorations of the impact of AIDS on future mortality. Heilig (1991), for example, has evaluated these relationships. According to his analysis, three successive epidemics have to be distinguished. The first, the most vigorous, took place among homosexual and bisexual men in highly developed countries and among heterosexual urban populations with high-risk behaviour, such as promiscuity and prostitution. Behavioural changes to avoid high-risk behaviour (changed sexual practices) or to block transmission of the virus (using condoms) often came too late in these groups to stop the spread of the virus. The second wave of the epidemic took place among intravenous (IV) drug users, the transmission of the virus occurring through contact with infected blood (needle sharing) and sexual activity. While the first epidemic in developed countries was male (90 per cent), the second is feminized. Among HIV-infected IV drug users, some 50 per cent are females. Heterosexual transmission of the virus to the partners of IV drug users or bisexual men is the most rapidly growing kind of infection in the USA. This heterosexual transmission could trigger a third wave of the HIV epidemic in some developed countries that would affect highly sexually active categories of the population, especially in urban areas. Heilig also discusses the potential impact of AIDS prevention campaigns in Europe, North America, Africa, the Caribbean and some Asian countries. This discussion continues in the next chapter.

In the West, fertility has already been declining for some time. The decline is not a recent response to the Pill, or to the legalization of abortion, or to the modern women's movement (Westhoff 1991). These developments have certainly accelerated the process, however. Höhn (1991: 252) states:

> modernization has strengthened the welfare state and, in Europe and the West, unintentionally weakened the family. The . . . indirect policies of a modern state are antinatalistic. I therefore believe that any pronatalist policy fights a hopeless battle against political and social forces that are not only implemented by governments, but also desired by the majority of the population. These political and social forces are based on the ideals and aims of our time: more freedom, equality, and personal independence; more leisure and consumption; more economic growth and social justice. Apparently, singles and childless couples, perhaps families with one to two children, can profit most from the blessings of the welfare state.

Höhn reports that in Germany a number of measures have been taken that can be called population-relevant policies of adaptation. The most important one is a proposed reform of pensions, where the percentage of contributions, a prolongation of age at retirement and the recognition of *baby years* in the pensions of mothers are taken into consideration. As a reaction to further demographic aging, a comprehensive reform of health care costs has been initiated. Höhn advocates nursing insurance, perhaps compulsory, to compensate for declining voluntary nursing by members of the family. She also draws attention to the fact that taxation still discriminates against families. An equalization of the living standards of families and childless couples is desired, she concludes.

In most industrialized countries, the low fertility rate has caused concern to some sections of the public. However, most scientists warn against dramatizing the demographic situation, and some environmentalists even welcome the expected decline of population.

There are fears that the demographic *implosion* will bring high economic, social and political risks. In Germany, there has been a discussion on this topic as part of a consideration of that country's immigration policy. Steinmann (1991) in evaluating Germany's immigration history, advocates that Germany should pursue a policy of selective immigration. The costs and benefits from immigration for the receiving countries depend on the education and the skills of the immigrants. Recruitment policies should attach more importance to this aspect in the future than they have in the past. Immigrants are needed, but they cannot replace children. Immigration bears tremendous social risks if the proportion of foreigners exceeds certain limits. Higher fertility is the only way to reduce the long-run dependence on immigration.

Similar conclusions are drawn by Beaujot (1991) concerning immigration policy and socio-demographic change in Canada. Beaujot simulates the consequences of four basic alternatives. The first alternative would be to continue with the policy of annual (or short-term) determination of immigration levels, based in turn largely on economic consideration. The main advantage of this approach is that it allows immigration to adjust to changing circumstances. A second alternative would be to reduce immigration to a minimum, admitting persons only on the basis of family reunion. Such an alternative would probably have considerable public support, but it would not allow Canada to follow strategies needed to use immigration as a means of facing future economic, social and demographic challenges. A third alternative would be to hold immigration constant at a figure around the postwar average of 150,000 admissions per year. Such a strategy would more clearly establish immigration as a demographic policy with a long-term horizon, and would enable the institutions associated with recruitment and settlement to have a more secure planning horizon. It would also probably prompt the nation to recognize the need to sustain fertility, if population decline is to be avoided. A fourth alternative would be to move to a substantially higher level. Beaujot suggests the figure of 250,000 arrivals per year, or some 1 per cent of the receiving population. More immigration would probably be good for Canada on economic grounds: greater supply of labour, more demand for goods and services, more competition and therefore productivity. A higher figure would also permit Canada to admit more refugees, and therefore it would have positive humanitarian implications. An openness to the cultures of the world, Beaujot argues, may be taken up as a socio-cultural and demographic challenge that would bring Canada into the modern international world, where European-based societies are a declining component. Beaujot concludes:

The determination of an appropriate immigration level, and its composition, is clearly a political question. Research can provide some indication regarding the past impacts, but it is for the political community to decide what it wants for its future, and how immigration is to figure in that social vision. Basic to this vision is whether to intervene in population decline or to adapt the society's institutions to a declining population. (Beaujot 1991: 377).

On the basis of a 1988 survey, Keilman evaluated the methodological aspects of national population projections in 31 developed countries. His international comparison included demographic characteristics of future populations (Keilman 1990). A demographic projection is a simulation showing what would happen if certain assumptions regarding fertility, mortality and migration were born out. About half of the countries used a cohort-component approach, involving a model without behavioural equations. Assumptions about the (future) behaviour of the population are expressed by trends in exogenous demographic trends, that is, the death probabilities and the numbers of migrants. Keilman concluded that the techniques used were relatively simple, especially when compared with techniques that are available in the literature on analytical demography.

One possible reason for the underutilization of advanced analytical techniques is the restrictions imposed on analysis by the data. In most cases, only transversal data are available. As soon as longitudinal data are acquired, for example, data on life course events for large numbers of individuals, analyses will become less simple. As an example, I mention the construction of person-period files, summarizing data on changes in individual life courses. Based on person-period files, *inter alia*, event history analysis can be applied (Courgeau & Lelièvre 1992). Event history analysis attempts to place changes in the time and space of individuals' lives, taking the social context into account. The point of event history analysis is to see how an event – of a family, economic or other nature – which is experienced by individuals will change the probability of other events happening to them over their lifetime. In this kind of analysis, we try to discover, for example, how marriage might influence a professional career, spatial mobility and other occurrences, such as the birth of children or a break with original family ties. We are dealing with a method of analysis which uses a dynamic rather than a static approach, not in a deterministic way, but basically probabilistic (Courgeau & Lelièvre 1992).

An example of an event history analysis in the area of SIA is a study of the transition to adulthood (Iedema et al. 1996) that analyzes social injustice in the life course of members of the lost generation in the Netherlands. These individuals had to postpone their transition to the labour market and to social independence because they had to shoulder more than a fair share of the economic hardships caused by the economic recession. Continuation of current action would lead to cumulative social injustice to these individuals. Current action would oblige members of the lost generation to contribute relatively much to the costs of the greying of the nation.

Other examples of micro-analyses in SIA in most cases also come from the area of government. Micro-analyses in SIA in the area of business of nonprofit organizations do exist, but their outcomes are not published in most cases. Private enterprises use micro-analyses to simulate developments regarding their actual customers and potential customers. Churches simulate changes regarding their actual and potential members. Political parties simulate developments in their membership and in the electorate. The methods used in these areas do not differ much from the methods used in government micro-analyses, however. Given the increase in competition in many sectors of society, and progress in data acquisition and analytical methods, micro-level SIA is likely to become more important in the next few decades. Hopefully, private companies and NGOs will be willing to publish, maybe not their models, but at least their experiences with SIA in the field of micro-level analyses.

7.4 Meso-analyses in SIA

In preceding chapters, some examples have already been presented of meso-level SIA. In this section, I want to add some more examples dealing with issues not discussed yet. My first example is about a multiple-criteria decision support model and geographic information system (GIS) for sustainable development planning of Greek islands (Van Herwijnen et al. 1993). It presents an evaluation of various scenarios for sustainable development on the Greek island of Alonnisos, part of the Sporades, using the new information technology of GIS. In this tourism impact assessment, six development alternatives have been applied:

D-1. *Steady growth*: A steady growth development path, based on extrapolation of present trends without any specific policy constraints on land or marine use. Tourist numbers continue to rise and tourists are allowed to visit the Marine Park area in the Sporades. This alternative may act as a zero or reference alternative.

D-2. *Marine Park*: A steady growth development path as alternative D-1, but now with a strict control on the tourist flows to the Marine Park. The fishing activity is held at a safe (sustainable) level, the waste management and sewage treatment activities are maximized, and tourism in the park area is restricted.

D-3. *Strong growth*: A steady growth development path with a controlled tourist flow to the Marine Park as in alternative D-2, but with a higher potential growth rate of tourism.

D-4. *Limited tourism growth*: A steady growth development path with a controlled tourism to the Marine Park (see alternative D-2), but with a strict limit to the growth of tourism on the islands as well as the Marine Park.

D-5. *Sustainable fishing*: A steady growth development path with a controlled tourism flow to the Marine Park as an alternative D-2. The fishing in this alternative is limited to such levels that the stocks of fish are not reduced.

D-6. *Agricultural incentive*: A steady growth development path with controlled tourism flows to the Marine Park as in alternative D-2. Employment in agriculture, especially cultivation of land, is strongly stimulated.

Following the articulation of alternatives, an effect table was elaborated comprising for all development options, the foreseeable effects on a set of relevant policy criteria. The alternatives described above have effects on two criteria, that is, the socio-economic and ecological development of Alonnisos. Next, policy weights have been formulated for each of the effects. Furthermore, the alternatives have been ranked according to the weights attached to the effects. Summarizing the results, Van Herwijnen et al. (1993) conclude that it seems plausible that the Marine Park is the best alternative, except when the ecological development is deemed far more important for the Sporades Islands than the socio-economic development. In that case, the *limited tourism* appears to be the best.

I have not described the actual weighing process, nor the sensitivity analysis or the GIS procedures because they can be studied in the original article. This example of tourism IA has strong ties with economic and environmental IA. Ultimately we are dealing with an SIA, however, because policy choices in this case are very much influenced by the various actors involved and their conflicting interests, as the authors of the article emphasize.

Also, aesthetic impact assessment (AIA) represents SIA on a meso-level. An effective means of determining AIAs is required to maintain the quality of our visual environment. Sometimes AIA enables us to enhance this quality. Roebig (1983) warns that many visual simulations rate low on accuracy, most mislead regarding true visual impacts, and most fail to establish credibility or lead to problems of comprehension among people evaluating the projects. In order to avoid these problems, he merged an on-site simulation and photomontage technique with an AIA methodology, thus allowing planners to combine high simulation accuracy with a comprehensive visual impact assessment and project planning. The details of the method were worked out for an industrial project, a coal export terminal in the New York Harbour at Staten Island. Storage silos for coal, conveyor belts and the coal vessels themselves would block the view of the waterfront for inhabitants of the area. Once the location and project design were finalized, an on-site simulation was carried out to determine the visual impact of the project. Ten helium-filled weather balloons were flown to mark the corners of all major structures, including the position of boats being loaded. Once these balloons were in place, Roebig took photographs from important vantage points to allow simulation from a number of views. Such photographs were incorporated in the draft and final assessment, allowing people in the community to assess for themselves the visual change, make comments and suggest changes to minimize the impact.

7.5 Macro-level SIA

My first example of good research practice in macro-level SIA is a study by Commoner (1994) on the relations among population, economic development and environmental quality in developed countries. These countries show relatively stable populations, well-developed systems of production and highly unsatisfactory levels of environmental pollution. For these countries, the crucial policy question is to determine how best to improve their own environment and to reduce their contribution to global environmental degradation. Commoner presents data on a clear-cut example of environmental improvement in a series of developed countries, the reduction in the annual emissions of a major air pollutant, carbon monoxide, between 1970 and 1987. This improvement was accomplished in the face of small increases in population and much larger increases in affluence by changing the technology of vehicular traffic to reduce the carbon monoxide output per vehicle-kilometre.

The same data are used by Commoner to test the efficacy of a policy that is designed to reduce this environmental impact by reducing population or affluence rather than the technology factor. This can be done by setting the technology factor, carbon monoxide emissions per vehicle-kilometre at 1.0, representing no change between 1970 and 1987, and then computing the reduction in either population or the affluence factor that will result in a substantial decrease in net emissions, as illustrated in the following results.

In Spain, which achieved the largest reduction in carbon monoxide emissions (-75.5 per cent), in order to achieve this same result by reducing only the population factor (i.e. with the affluence factor changing as observed but with the technology factor set at 1.0, signifying zero change), the population would need to be reduced by 88 per cent between 1970 and 1987. If the observed reduction in emission were to be achieved solely through the affluence factor, there would need to be a 79 per cent reduction in vehicle-kilometre per capita.

In a more typical developed country, the Netherlands, where a 53.9 per cent reduction in carbon monoxide emissions occurred, to achieve this same result it would be necessary to reduce the population by 69 per cent, or the vehicle-kilometre per capita by 54 per cent, between 1970 and 1987.

In the USA, where largely by introducing a control device, the catalytic converter, carbon monoxide emissions were reduced by 41.8 per cent, to accomplish the same result without improving the technology factor, the population would need to be reduced by 60 per cent, or the vehicle-kilometre per capita by 51 per cent, between 1970 and 1987.

The current study, Commoner concluded, showed that the most effective strategy for reducing the severe environmental impact of the present system of production is to replace them with ecologically sound ones in which the pollution generated per unit of goods produced is greatly reduced. Such technologies exist. Some examples are electric vehicles that do not produce the serious air pollutants generated by internal combustion engines; photovoltaic cells that produce electricity directly from sunlight, avoiding the pollutants generated by conventional power plants; and organic farming that eliminates the environmentally hazardous agricultural chemicals now so widely used. The effort to improve environmental quality, the relevant decisions and the precepts that should guide them ought to be directed towards the transformation of production – in industry, agriculture, energy, transportation and commerce generally. This means that the nearly universal social commitment to environmental improvement must be translated into social decisions about the design of the systems of production (Commoner 1994: 77).

7.6 Settings of SIA in the West

In which settings have the three types of SIA been applied in the West? As we saw in preceding chapters, *inter alia*, 3 and 4, and in this chapter so far, in Europe, SIA has evolved as a specific kind of policy analysis. In SIA *per se*, the future consequences of a current or proposed action on social phenomena like individuals, organizations, social networks and social macro-systems have been identified without reference to the environment or to technology. A striking example is health IA. In the USA in the early 1970s, SIA had evolved as a component of EIA. Later on in the USA, there also grew up an SIA that had no ties with EIA. I describe these developments in a neutral way, not advocating a change. I certainly do not want to be understood as implying that SIA ought to be integrated in EIA, TA or economic IA. It depends on the objective and the research problem of the social impact assessor whether or not an integration of the SIA study in a larger impact study would make sense.

In the USA, in most cases SIA is taken as a project, or a component of a project. As an example, I take a reservoir project that requires that attention be paid to the social consequences of the intervention to the lives of the villagers living in the valley to be inundated. The restriction to a project often leads to very restricted IAs, leaving out social consequences that transgress the boundaries of the development project. For this reason, in the USA a change from project assessments to policy assessments, also called strategic assessments, is advocated. In most cases, a policy assessment provides the best setting for SIA. A broad approach facilitates an assessment study that includes effects to be expected in the long run in a wide circle around the development project and in all relevant sectors of social life.

7.7 Summary

In the early 1980s in Europe and North America, developments in social impact assessment changed both in speed and in content. The economic recession forced government agencies and business firms to become aware of their political, economic and social environment. They employed social scientists to assist in training programmes, for example, in strategic learning. They invited social scientists to analyze problems, pretest actions, explore future developments and assist in reorganizations. Many social scientists started private research and consultancy firms.

The social sciences in those years show a growing emphasis on step-by-step attempts to improve methods and theories. Improvements can be discerned in problem analysis. Systems analysis has elaborated languages to deal with complexity, to facilitate computer simulations and to bridge the gap with artificial intelligence. Explanation and interpretation in social sciences research have gradually been improved from the early 1980s onwards. In the late 1990s, the social sciences can now provide an integrated system of explanation and interpretation using meta-theories, theories and research hypotheses.

Micro-analyses in SIA have prospered, in particular in DIA, primarily because population problems have become more and more pressing. Demographic data on individual life courses were available on a large scale. Analytical models and explanatory theories were available too. Meso-analyses and macro-level SIA followed a similar trend.

In Europe, SIA has evolved as a specific kind of policy analysis. A striking example is health IA. In the USA in the 1980s there also grew up SIA that had no ties with EIA. It depends on the objective and the research problem of the social impact assessor whether or not an integration of the SIA study in a larger impact study would make sense. In the USA, restriction to a project often leads to very restricted IAs, leaving out social consequences that trangress the boundaries of the development project. For this reason, in the USA a change from project assessment to policy assessment, also called strategic assessment, is advocated.

CHAPTER 8

SIA in a number of developing countries

8.1 Introduction

This chapter focuses on SIA in developing countries. For our purposes, developing countries can be regarded as those countries in Latin America, Africa, eastern Europe, the Pacific islands (other than New Zealand) and Asia, with the exception of Japan. The conduct of social research in developing countries demands attention for a number of specific methodological issues. These issues will be dealt with in section 8.2. Following this, we will look at SIA in developing countries on a meso- and macro-level (sections 8.3 and 8.4). SIA on a micro-level is still very restricted in developing countries and therefore I will not deal with it in a separate section. Finally the settings of SIA in developing countries are discussed (section 8.5).

Following the approach used in Chapter 7, I will focus on the best available examples of good research practice, describing these examples and giving my comments. This will provide the social impact assessor with guidelines for carrying out SIA in developing countries. A number of state-of-the-art reports on SIA in developing countries can be found in the literature (Cernea 1991; Derman and Whiteford 1985; Finsterbusch et al. 1990).

8.2 Methodological aspects

Social analysis in developing countries requires the utilization of both general and specific research methods. We assume that the impact assessor has access to standard textbooks on social science research methodology. What additional information is necessary? Before we try to answer this question, a preliminary issue demands our attention. It would be a mistake to draw too sharp a distinction between methods of research used in the developed and in the developing world. A simple dichotomy between these *worlds* would conceal the very wide variation within each group, particularly among developing countries, where some are much more industrialized than others. Singapore, for example, is very different from neighbouring Indonesia, which is generally less urbanized and much poorer (Bulmer 1983: 3).

Major issues in the use of social science methods to provide social data for policy-making are:

- How can social science methods produce data which can be trusted by those who use the data, in other words, accurate in terms of reliability and validity?
- Do the procedures and techniques used give an adequate picture of the state of the society (or one aspect of it) at the time of the study?
- Is the evidence provided consistent and meaningful?
- Does it represent the true state of affairs at the local level and do its measures really measure what they claim to measure?
- Is the evidence provided as objective and free from bias as possible?
- How well does the evidence stand up if the exercise is repeated and the results of a second enquiry under the same conditions are compared with the first?
- Is it possible to conduct high-quality research that avoids political controversy and avoids ethical difficulties?

These questions provide the basis for a critical examination of the means by which social data is collected in developing countries and an analysis of the social conditions of its production (Bulmer 1983: 4). Drawing on the literature on social research in developing countries, dealing with social analysis in general and SIA in particular (e.g. Bulmer 1983; Chambers 1991; Ingersoll 1990), the principal approaches in policy-oriented research will be appraised.

8.2.1 Administrative data

Development officials often lack adequate data on basic issues like the size and the composition of the population and indicators of development, such as agricultural production. Particularly serious defects are likely in official statistics collected as a by-product of administration. Governmental statistical offices have developed slowly in Third World countries because there were competing priorities for funding. More basic economic needs had to be met first.

Skilled labour for gathering administrative data is scarce in developing countries. Trained statisticians are particularly likely to be scarce at the middle and senior levels. There are, however, variations in the ability of trained labour. In a few developing countries, for example India and Korea, such skills are more plentiful than in, say, Indonesia, Mali or Brazil (Bulmer 1983: 5).

Reliance on administrative sources for data can lead to misleading information. In many cases, officials rely on administrative estimates of human resources, crops and the like. In many developing countries, despite affirmations of interest, traditional administrators do not really believe in the value of social science data in formulating and implementing public policy. Even where there is a real demand, many administrators do not know what to do with quality data. Most have not been trained in social science methodology, most do not have the intellectual background to make real sense of the usual tables and most do not have the time available for serious study of the results (Bulmer 1983: 5). As a consequence, the demand for data gathered from other sources is high. Also the demand for training of administrators is considerable.

8.2.2 Population census

A population census is a complete instantaneous enumeration of the population of a country carried out by the government. These are usually undertaken once in a fixed time period, which varies between countries but is usually between five and ten years. A census is an extremely costly operation. It requires large numbers of census workers, who must be recruited and trained. Covering the whole country at the same time demands a large organizational effort. Usually census gathering has the force of law behind it.

In a population census, considerable problems of data quality may arise. Large parts of the population may be illiterate. The quality of the available pool of people to be census workers may be low. Supervision of field staff in a large national census is also difficult to regulate properly. As a consequence, censuses take place infrequently. The data they provide become rapidly out of date for policy-making purposes. Consequently, it is rather likely that censuses will gradually disappear in developing countries, and in a number of developed countries, *inter alia* the Netherlands, censuses have been already abolished.

8.2.3 Social surveys

These provide a feasible and relatively economical alternative to censuses. One of the principal characteristics of survey procedures is probability sampling. Because only a fraction of the population is sampled, a survey is much less expensive than a census. Fewer staff and a smaller organization are required. An Indian census in the early 1980s, for example, employed nearly 1 million census workers to gather data in the field, and the 1982 census in China employed 6 million workers (Bulmer 1983).

A major advantage of the social survey is that interviewers can be much more intensively trained than census workers, and so can be expected to produce higher quality data. Moreover, the greater training of field staff and smaller size of the study permits the use of more complex questionnaires. The length of interviews can be considerably greater than what is feasible in a census. Finally, a sample survey imposes upon public goodwill much less than a census, and is less likely to arouse opposition or accusation of invasion of privacy (Bulmer 1983: 31).

Social surveys in developing countries are confronted with a number of pitfalls:

- Basic data needed for survey research may be lacking.
- Concepts and terms which are familiar from use in the industrialized countries cannot automatically be transferred for use in survey work in a developing country.

- Available sampling frames are often inadequate.
- Regional variations in methods and procedures used may reduce the comparability of the data.
- Field staff and respondents are often unfamiliar with standard attitude measures and have difficulties in interpreting them.
- Responses to questionnaire items are strongly influenced by the culture of the respondent, with resulting problems of translation from one culture to another.
- Trained personnel are scarce and rarely combine field experience with academic knowledge.
- Data processing equipment is often limited or antiquated.

Employment surveys can illustrate these pitfalls. In most rural areas in developing countries, concepts like *employment* and *unemployment* are by no means clear. Is a person who is in *debt bondage* to be considered employed, unemployed or underemployed? This person is certainly not looking for work on the labour market. At the same time, the individual concerned may suffer all the disadvantages traditionally linked to underemployment.

Also, fertility surveys pose serious methodological problems. A popular form of survey instrument for family planning investigations in the Third World has been the so-called KAP (Knowledge–Attitude–Practice) Survey (Mukherjee 1975). These surveys have typically asked questions about respondents' knowledge of family planning methods, their attitudes towards family limitation and their birth control practices. KAP surveys are prone to response errors because, in most cases, little attention is given to the relation between verbal responses and actual behaviour. Evaluations of the reliability and validity of data from KAP fertility surveys suggest that there is more consistency in responses to factual information than to questions about desires, ideals and attitudes. Items like the number of children in the family, number of pregnancies experienced by the wife, age, religion, language and occupation yield more reliable results than questions about knowledge of contraceptive methods, ideals of reproduction and attitudes toward family planning programmes and abortion. Responses to such items as professed desire for additional children may fluctuate erratically over a period as short as a few months. To some extent, respondents appear to be unsure about the number of children they want. It seems reasonable to conclude that information from KAP surveys on desired family size "is so liable to error and uncertainty that it can be confusing and misleading if used for policy formulation and implementation" (Mukherjee 1975: 141).

8.2.4 Integrating research methodologies

Since the early 1980s, there has been a growing recognition of the need for merging two or more research methodologies in the same study. This approach is called *triangulation*. Integrating a number of research methodologies implies the ability to handle overlapping data sources. Quantitative survey data will have to be combined with qualitative data from group discussions or participant observation.

Warwick (1983) cites a study by Whyte and Alberti (1976) in highland Peru. In an effort to understand the sources of conflict, co-operation, and other aspects of community behaviour, the authors and their collaborators made use of both anthropological research and sample surveys to gather data on key topics. In addition, they drew on historical materials as well as administrative records to provide a broader perspective on community life.

A second example is the Development Program Implementation Study (DPIS) carried out in Indonesia by the Harvard Institute for International Development and several national counterpart organizations. The main purpose of that study was to identify the factors explaining why some large-scale development programmes are more successfully implemented than others, and why even the same programme varies in its success across different regions of the country. The research covers four nationwide development programmes: (1) family planning; (2) primary education; (3) rice intensification; and (4) village public works. All four of these programmes reach from the central government to the villages, have mass coverage rather than being aimed at special groups and are concerned with social services or community development rather than with just physical construction. The reason for choosing four different programmes was to permit the study to explore the effects of such influences as the task to be accomplished, organizational structure and management systems, client demand and the motivation of field implementers.

The first source of data was an organizational analysis. A key aim of the study was to understand how the organizational context of a given programme affected its implementation. Toward that end, the DPIS conducted interviews with about 500 public officials and other programme implementers in the four provinces chosen for detailed research. Respondents were asked about the history of the programme in their region; how it was carried out, and by whom; the main successes as well as obstacles in implementation; how obstacles were overcome; who supported, criticized, or opposed the programme, and suggestions for improvement. The theory behind these interviews was that field implementers could provide valid information about those aspects of implementation with which they were most familiar, especially their own immediate work.

The second data source was a set of anthropological studies conducted in four villages and their corresponding subdistrict capitals. Researchers lived in each village from six months to a year or more and gathered various kinds of data. In addition to recording their observations on programme implementation and community life more generally, they conducted a complete census of village households and then a sample survey of about 150 households per village. They also prepared life histories on between 20 and 30 villagers, with particular emphasis on their experience with the programme under study. They also carried out interviews with implementers working at that level. The observers in the subdistrict capitals likewise interviewed key implementers and watched them in action where possible. The assumption behind this approach was that the anthropological data would be particularly useful in understanding who participates in the four programmes and why; who receives more and less benefits from each; how implementation relates to local patterns of decision-making; and how clients react to the programmes overall and the specific services delivered.

The third source of data and an additional perspective on implementation came from what was called *economic studies*. In addition to providing an economic viewpoint that pervaded many aspects of design and analysis, this component involved three specific contributions to the research. The first was the collection and analysis of secondary data, including statistics on programme inputs and outputs. The main objective was to shed light on the cost-effectiveness of the programme under investigation. The second source of economic data was interviews with programme implementers and other officials. The focus was on how financial administration operates for each programme and its consequences for implementation. The third kind of economic data included information on programme efficiency at the local level.

The research design provided for substantial, though not total, overlap among the three data sources. All three kinds of analysis were carried out in the same provinces and in certain cases the same districts, but not necessarily the same villages. Hence the design of the organizational studies involved data collection in the same district as the anthropological studies, but not in the same villages and subdistricts. The main reason for this separation was to avoid the saturation of the anthropological field sites by too many outsiders. Similarly, the economic studies overlapped with both the organizational and economic studies, but not completely. The DPIS has been an ambitious attempt at methodological integration in the developing countries (cited by Warwick 1983).

According to Warwick, there are six main reasons for bringing together two or more data sources in the same study. The first and most obvious reason for expanding the number of data sources is to obtain crucial information that is not available from a single method. In the DPIS, the research team sought data on the costs per unit of service delivered and similar kinds of financial information. Neither the anthropological research nor the survey of field implementers supplied the required financial data. Hence, the specifications also called for a third component, called *economic analysis*, to gather information on costs and expenditure patterns for the programme covered. A second reason for combining data sources is to increase confidence in the accuracy of measurements or observations made on a given phenomenon. As used here, accuracy can be defined as the generalizability of the measurements or observations made of one phenomenon to all the measures or observations that might have been made of the same phenomenon at the same time. A third reason is to acquire qualitative depth. A common lament about quantitative data is that it lacks depth and meaning. Integrating survey data and statements gathered by qualitative approaches can overcome this handicap. A fourth reason for combining research methods in a single study is to augment the possibilities of generalizing the results to a broader population. By using a representative sample of individuals, survey research aims to collect data that can

199

be used for drawing conclusions about the population in question. In the DPIS, the research team applied the basic procedures of probability sampling to the selection of villages for intensive study. As a fifth reason, Warwick proposes historical interpretation. In certain kinds of research, it is crucial to explain events or situations in the present by reconstructing the past. The sixth reason is to test associations. Creating the possibility for the systematic exploration of associations is usually the principal reason for conducting a sample survey, but the same reason likewise arises in qualitative research. *Inter alia* in research trying to answer questions like, who participates? who benefits? and who is harmed by a given situation or intervention? It is precisely in developing a more effective approach to testing associations that creative combinations of research methods come into play.

Barriers to integration of methods are: limited competence of social scientists engaged in research, disciplinary ethnocentrism, costs and lack of suitable projects for combining methods (Warwick 1983: 293–6).

8.3 Meso-level SIA in a number of developing countries

The main example to be used in this chapter is the resettlement of communities, which usually occurs because a reservoir project requires the evacuation of the population of the area to be inundated. As a starting point for the discussion, I take the guidelines for management of water projects published by OECD in 1985 and already mentioned in Chapter 2. In these guidelines, a chapter is dedicated to problems related to resettlement.

Resettlement is a transition process which may take up to 15 years. The process starts as soon as the first rumours about the possibility of relocation occur. It peaks when the people are officially informed, when the moving takes place and during the time immediately following the relocation. It ends when the relocatees have adjusted to their new environment. Seven broad categories of people who are likely to be relocated or otherwise affected as a consequence of the reservoir project may be distinguished:

1. *Displaced people*: Those who must be relocated because their homes will be flooded.

2. *Host community*: People resident in the area where the displaced people are relocated to.
3. *Family and friends*: Extended family members and other social contacts of the people to be relocated but who themselves do not live in the area to be flooded. Relocation of the displaced people could affect their social ties, especially if relocation is to be a considerable distance away from their original home.
4. *Fringe dwellers*: Those original inhabitants of the area near the site to be flooded who do not have to move, but whose lives will change as a result of changing land-use and economic prosperity. Often they will be the same as the people in the category above, the extended family and social network of the displaced people.
5. *Economic immigrants*: Those who will enter the new lake basin to seek new economic opportunities, often imposing on the fringe dwellers.
6. *Neighbouring population*: People living in downstream or other areas, being economically dependent on the river basin to be flooded.
7. *Transients*: Those who come along for recreation or as tourists.

We have to keep in mind that usually whole communities have to be relocated. In Africa, for example, about 56,000 people were relocated during the 1950s in connection with the Kariba dam in Zambia and Rhodesia, over 70,000 people were resettled because of the Volta dam in Ghana and 42,000 people were moved as a result of Nigeria's Kainji dam. In Egypt and Sudan, more than 100,000 relocatees had to leave their homes when the Aswan dam was constructed. Within such a community, all kinds of formal and informal relationships exist which have their specific meaning for the members of such a community. Kinship, religion and agriculture are only a few topics that the resettlement agency will have to consider. Because of resettlement, people often have to change their habits completely and adjust to new and different environments and living conditions. Farmers may have to become fishermen; the dead must be left behind; religious customs may have to be changed (OECD 1985: 176).

Resettlement assessment and planning is a complex, time-consuming and expensive process. The experience with resettlement processes shows that often the time allocated for planning and executing resettlement has been completely inadequate. Planning for resettlement is seldom initiated at an early enough stage. In connection with the Kossou dam in the Ivory Coast in Africa, the agency responsible for the resettlement planning was not established until the dam was already half a year under construction. In such circumstances, it is hard to avoid tension-laden crash programmes and traumatic experiences (OECD 1985: 177).

Resettlement planning is expensive. It is expensive in terms of finance, personnel and equipment. It is not unusual for the total final cash costs to be double the original estimates. Besides these costs there are, of course, the human costs that are a result of the resettlement process. Tension and stress cannot be completely avoided, but ways to cope with them must be incorporated into a resettlement planning process.

Resettlement planning requires public information, involvement and participation. Both relocatees and hosts must be involved in a continual two-way communication process, which must be the basis of the whole resettlement planning process. Conflicting behavioural patterns and goals must be understood, so that severe conflicts can be avoided. The OECD (1985: 178) concludes:

> Resettlement planning must provide a framework to make this two-way communication effective. Resettlement planning must be organised in a way that those who are most directly affected can be informed so that they are not suddenly confronted with the loss of homes and lands. Resettlement planning must also be open to local opinions and initiatives. Local individuals and groups must be able to make a meaningful contribution to the total effort. Communication facilities must be created: the resettlement agency should be receptive to the ideas coming from future resettlers, hosts and immigrants. At least some local leaders should be involved in the planning. Effective resettlement planning can only be open participatory planning.

The movement of people to new areas is a difficult and hazardous process that should be prepared in an extremely cautious way. First of all, the moment of transfer must be chosen judiciously. Usually the best moment for moving into a new area will be after the farmers have harvested their crops. Then they can take the largest possible supply of food. Food shortage is a well-known problem which is directly related to the evacuation process. A second aspect that has to be dealt with in the social assessment of the resettlement process is connected with the health problems which arise from major resettlements. Mass movements may be followed by catastrophic epidemics. Preliminary health surveys make it possible to recognize potential medical problems before evacuation begins. After the evacuation, medical control surveys must be continued and the health facilities of the evacuation stage will have to be phased into the health facilities of the new settlements (OECD 1985: 179).

Very important for a successful resettlement planning is an integral programme for the planning of the resettlement areas. First of all, the project authorities have to take the responsibility for developing new economic opportunities for the relocatees. An important part of these opportunities will be related to agriculture. Special assistance is to be provided to those who use resettlement as a chance to change their occupation.

The OECD guidelines have been based on the evaluation of projects in many countries and they have been tested in the field in more than ten countries (Becker et al. 1986; OECD 1985). With regard to resettlement, these guidelines represent experiences gained up to the mid-1980s in more than ten developing countries. In 1994, the World Bank published a review of projects involving involuntary resettlement in the years 1986–93. This review provides a follow-up of the OECD manual. According to the World Bank, considerable improvements in the preparation and appraisal of projects involving resettlement were implemented between 1986 and 1993, bringing quality markedly above the levels found by the 1986 resettlement review. But some work processes and procedures were found not to have been fully carried out by borrowers from the bank. Specific problems that were found to recur, particularly in the early part of the review period, were: (a) failure by many borrowing agencies to prepare satisfactory resettlement plans (quality at entry); (b) laxness in fulfilling in-house responsibilities for review and clearance in early project stages; (c) irregular or insufficient project supervision; and (d) insufficient follow-up actions by borrowers and the bank when implementation problems were identified.

For sound project preparation and execution, the World Bank defines four elements as mandatory for projects entailing displacement: (1) population and income surveys; (2) resettlement plans and development packages; (3) resettlement timetables synchronized with civil works; and (4) distinct resettlement budgets for financing compensation and resettlement-related investments. With significant regularity, according to the World Bank, the failures in implementation and in restoring income can be traced to poor work processes particularly in early project stages during project identification, preparation, and appraisal.

The greatest initial difficulty in many instances is that borrowing agencies undercount the affected population in project preparation and provide inaccurate information to appraisal missions. Incorrectly assessed displacement sizes result in project underdesign, inadequate cost estimates, resource shortfalls, institutional inability to prepare adequate solutions and the impoverishment of resettlers.

Appraisal missions of the World Bank should not proceed to the field unless the borrower has submitted a resettlement plan to the Bank that will allow the Bank to appraise resettlement feasibility and cost in the context of the full project. Substantial progress has been made since the 1986 resettlement review, which found that only 14 per cent of the then active projects had prepared resettlement plans that included the minimum requirements of a baseline survey, timetable, budget and a set of rehabilitation proposals. For the 1986–93 period, an average of about 55 per cent of Bank-assisted projects could claim to have appraised full resettlement plans.

The quality and adequacy of resettlement planning have varied widely. Despite an overall objective of restoring incomes and living standards for displaced families, less than 30 per cent of the resettlement plans have made income restoration a primary goal. This has affected performance.

A comparative study by the World Bank of involuntary and voluntary settlement programmes highlighted the significant contrast between the resources and approaches used to prepare settlement programmes where development is the main objective, and programmes where involuntary resettlement is a subordinated component. The institutional and development packages of projects assisting voluntary settlements offer valuable models that can be adapted and emulated in involuntary resettlement projects. Furthermore, the large size of some involuntary resettlement operations, treated as project components ancillary to civil works, typically exceeds the capacity and expertise of the engineering entities that manage infrastructural projects. An innovative solution was introduced in 1994, wherein China's Xiaolangdi dam and the resettlement it caused are treated as two interrelated but distinct projects: one for the dam and the other for resettlement as a full-scale development project. This allowed the resettlement project to fully plan and design, in well-specified steps, its redevelopment approach, based on differential packages tailored to the incomes and potential of the affected population, category by category (World Bank 1994: xiv).

Good practice prudently spreads massive relocations over the entire duration of the project, carrying out resettlement a step in advance of civil works to avoid bunching at the end of a project. Poor practice leaves the bulk of the population transfer for the last one or two years of a project's 8–10-year lifetime, subjecting resettlers to increased risks. Explicit resettlement timetables, synchronized with civil works, were found to be missing from more than half of the ongoing projects (World Bank 1994: xv).

Inadequate financial planning has been a major problem in resettlement, explaining much of the uneven performance. Many borrowing agencies do not recognize and calculate all the costs of displacement incurred by the people affected and do not incorporate full resettlement and rehabilitation costs in overall project expenditures. This leaves resettlement underfinanced. The distinction between compensation costs for lost assets and the costs of new investments needed for re-establishing resettlers on a productive basis, with adequate shelter and services, has seldom been made, and such investment costs have not been budgeted. When the costs of relocating public sector infrastructure and settlers are consolidated, lack of distinction tends to mask low per capita allocations to displaced families. The overall result: resources earmarked for resettlement fall short of what is needed (World Bank 1994: XV).

Both the OECD guidelines and the review by the World Bank show that methods for SIA of development projects requiring resettlement of whole communities can be substantially improved by field testing and ex-post evaluation. Experiences gained in the past can be used as checklists in new SIAs.

Both studies also document improvements in the resettlement

processes themselves. Relocatees are handled with more care in recent projects. Furthermore, both analyses show that projects are too small a basis for SIAs of resettlement processes and that strategic IA is required, covering the whole process of change.

8.4 Macro-level SIA in a number of developing countries

In many such cases, SIA is still restricted to the analysis of social indicators (Soderstrom 1981), and has not yet progressed towards systems analysis. As discussed in the previous section, problems encountered in this research explain why SIA in these countries is often still in its infancy.

8.4.1 Population growth and the environment

My first example of SIA in developing countries is related to the relationship between population growth and the environment. Although population growth is but one of many factors that undermine the environmental resource base upon which sustainable development ultimately depends, it is an exceptionally significant factor. In many of the countries involved, there is a pronounced imbalance between the growth of population, on the one hand, and the natural resource base needed to support it, on the other hand (United Nations 1994). This applies to developed and developing countries alike, but in developing countries the imbalance is more marked. The interaction of population, consumption (or production) patterns and technology in producing environmental impacts or pollution is often encapsulated in the $I = PAT$ equation (Goodland 1994). In this equation I is environmental impact; P is population; A is affluence measured as per capita consumption; and T is technology level and measured as the environmental damage done by technology employed in supplying each unit of consumption. The equation might be interpreted as conveying the notion that consumption and production patterns are proximate factors of environmental deterioration that channel the underlying impacts of ultimate causes, which are the number of consumers (or producers) and their effective demand for goods and services.

The equation illustrates why developing countries with a large population but limited economic advancement can have a vast impact on the environment. Some objections have been raised to the $I = PAT$ equation, suggesting that the real relations between population and the environment are more complex than the postulated linear interactions. For instance, the equation does not take into account the possible detrimental impact of population growth on per capita consumption. Furthermore, institutions are a key variable in determining whether societies would be successful in equilibrating population levels with the availability of resources and economic growth while ensuring sound environmental management. Reciprocity of obligations in the case of population-induced environmental degradation is contingent upon cultural nuances of social expectations. Similarly, whereas technologies differ in their capacity for environmental damage and repair, social attitudes and systems help to determine the costs of environmental preservation or degradation and hence the type of technology employed (United Nations 1994).

A technology-driven explanation has been offered to show how population coupled with the level of technological development in a given society interacts to produce economic development and/or environmental degradation. In that analysis, development and degradation have been linked in a relative fashion. The level of development is determined to a large extent by the level of technology, which in turn affects lifestyles and consumption patterns and determines environmental impact. In that case, population is seen as a peripheral factor rather than a central part of the equation and technology becomes the more important multiplier (United Nations 1994).

Although demographic, economic and ecological processes are inextricably interrelated, the magnitude of the reciprocal impacts in different socio-cultural and ecological settings has not been sufficiently documented, the report by the UN concluded. Thus, to promote sustainable development, there is urgent need to strengthen data collection and research efforts in that domain and to test the efficacy of proposed policies and strategies in concrete settings.

8.4.2 Policy impacts on the dynamics of the population

There is a growing concern with rapid population growth in developing countries, in particular because of the likelihood that high fertility among the poor deepens and prolongs the battle against poverty and the possibility that rapid population growth, particularly in poor countries, exacerbates local environmental problems. While in the mid-1990s, the birthrate has decreased in virtually all developing countries, zero population growth in developing countries is not demographically possible before at least 2040, however, even if fertility were to fall immediately to replacement level, itself also a virtual impossibility. Which policy activities have an impact on fertility in developing countries?

Summers (1992), based on econometric studies at the country level of the effects of female education on fertility, concluded that one additional year of female schooling reduces fertility by between 5 and 10 per cent. The effect is probably closer to 10 per cent where fertility is relatively high. In Kenya, for example, where the total fertility rate is 6.5, a woman with secondary education has one fewer children than a woman with from five to eight years of education (Summers 1992); in Colombia in 1976 a woman with one to three years of education had almost seven births, compared with six births for a woman with from four to six years of education (World Bank 1985).

According to Birdsall (1994), the most careful single estimate of the cost of averting a birth is provided in a paper by Cochrane and Sai (1991). They first calculated the costs for a couple for a year of contraception for a range of contraception methods on the basis of information at the country level. These costs vary from about $3 per year of contraception for female sterilization in Indonesia to about $25 for pill use in Honduras and Morocco. To translate costs per year of contraception into costs of a birth averted, they assume that the foregone fertility of users is equal to the actual fertility of all women of the same age in the particular country.

These examples illustrate good research practice concerning macro-level SIA studies directed at developing countries in an adequate way. More examples can be found, inter alia, in the volume edited by Vanclay and Bronstein (1995).

8.5 Settings for SIA in developing countries

In 1994, a UN expert group, having studied the relationship between population, environment and development, in particular in developing countries, formulated a set of recommendations, of which I list a few:

1. Because there are strong linkages between population, development and the environment, governments are urged to establish or strengthen mechanisms to co-ordinate policies and programmes and to give unified direction for integrating environmental and population concerns into development policy-making and planning. In particular, governments are urged, when formulating their social and economic policies, plans and programmes in any sector, to take fully into account the implications of projected demographic trends and patterns of production and consumption, for the protection of the environment and the conservation of natural resources. Governments should incorporate these population concerns into national conservation strategies.

12. International governmental and nongovernmental organizations are urged to intensify and increase their efforts in promoting and understanding the severe impacts on health of environmental degradation and in transferring appropriate technologies for monitoring and minimizing such impacts to countries in need of them.

13. International organizations should increase their assistance to countries in the fields of population, sustainable development and environment, especially in training, research, policy formulation and the integration of population and environment-related factors into national planning.

14. International organizations, governments and nongovernmental organizations should increase their efforts to create greater awareness of the interrelated issues of population, environment and development. This should be done through the formal education system, existing demographic training institutions and collaborative training and educational programmes of nongovernmental organizations.

15. In order to address the relations between population, environment, economic growth and sustainable development issues,

databases should be strengthened and developed so as to promote an understanding of these issues and to make them
available and accessible to policy-makers and programme
managers.

16. Policy-oriented research should be undertaken to identify critically endangered areas beset by population pressure, destruction
of the ecosystem and degradation of resources and to determine
how these factors interact.

17. In devising strategies for sustainable development, special attention should be given to improving the plight of indigenous
populations. Their accumulated knowledge and methods for
sustainable exploitation should be taken into account.

18. In order to implement these recommendations, governments and
international organizations should identify and openly analyze
the conflicting goals between countries, regions and groups so as
to make fruitful negotiation possible and to create solutions with
mutual gains.

These recommendations are applicable to SIA and related action
research in developing countries in general. In addition to these
recommendations, I want to draw attention to the required transition
from project appraisal to strategic IA. I already elaborated upon this
transition in Chapter 7. Strategic IA has to ensure that the boundaries of
a SIA study are not drawn too narrowly. If individuals and communities
that will be afflicted by a policy activity are left out of the SIA study,
relevant positive and negative impacts will not be accessed, resulting in
the risk of protest later on in the development process.

8.6 Summary

Social analysis in developing countries requires methods of research
used in the developed and in the developing world. It would be a
mistake, however, to draw too sharp a distinction between both types of
methods. In social analysis in developing countries primarily administrative data, population censuses and social surveys are applied.
Pitfalls in surveys in developing countries, *inter alia*: basic data needed

for survey research are lacking, and concepts and terms used in industrialized countries cannot automatically be transferred for use in survey work in a developing country. There has been a growing recognition of the need for merging two or more research methodologies in the same study, in other words the need for triangulation.

Micro-level SIA is still scarce in developing countries. On a meso-level we find project assessment more and more replaced by strategic assessment. On a macro-level, mainly DIA is applied. Settings for SIA in developing countries have to be improved, a UN expert group concludes. The group advocates *inter alia* that governments and international organizations should identify and openly analyze the conflicting goals between countries, regions and groups so as to make fruitful negotiation possible and to create solutions with mutual gains.

CHAPTER 9

Conclusions, discussion and implications

9.1 Introduction

In this chapter, I will take a second look at the issues or questions formulated in the first chapter. I will summarize the answers to those questions which were provided in the preceding chapters. Following this, I will utilize the scientific convention of having a free-ranging discussion of the implications of the results of a study, which follows the strict reporting of those results. This ancient tradition in science may be new to some readers and for this reason it is worth describing in some detail. In the very last part of a publication (journal article), in a section usually labelled *Discussion*, an author (scientist) would usually try to identify the impact the publication is likely to have on the intended readership. The author would also try to stimulate positive impacts and to mitigate negative impacts. It is no coincidence, therefore, that I characterize the section called discussion in terms of an IA. Finally I will discuss the implications for SIA in the next decades.

9.2 Conclusions

My first question read: *What are the main characteristics of social impact assessment?* I can summarize the vital aspects of SIA as follows:

- SIA can be defined as the process of identifying the future consequences on individuals, organizations and social macro-systems of a current or proposed action.

- SIA is practised in the form of an SIA study, consisting of a preliminary phase and a main phase, with each phase requiring a number of steps.
- The typology of SIA specifies micro-, meso-, and macro-studies.
- SIA can be seen as instant, medium-sized and macro-studies, and as action research (strategic learning).
- SIA is closely related to oriented basic research.
- SIA is unfolding, gradually being adopted in all areas of society.
- SIA is frequently applied in combination with environment impact assessment (EIA), technology assessment (TA) and economic IA, however, without losing its identity.

The second question asked was : *What has been the historical development of SIA?* The dynamics of SIA show that:

- Contrary to some notions that locate SIA with the passage of the NEPA in the USA, the beginning of SIA can be located in the seventeenth century, introducing demographic impact assessment (DIA) and health IA.
- SIA has profited substantially from military simulations, the theory of games and systems thinking.
- SIA has been stimulated by planning disasters like the *War on Poverty* in the USA in the 1960s.
- Achievements in oriented basic research, theory formation and research methodology in the social sciences have resulted in achievements in SIA.
- SIA is applied increasingly by government, commercial and non-profit organizations, *inter alia* as a result of formal requirements.

The third question read: *What are the main methods used in SIA?* My answer is, in short:

- Problem analysis.
- Social survey, secondary analysis, and to a lesser extent, observation.
- Explanation and interpretation.
- The testing of predictions related to intervention hypotheses, in other words the classical approach in scientific advising and counselling.

- The design of possible future contexts for human action.
- The simulation of impacts of contexts on strategies, and strategies on target variables.
- Action research, including strategic learning.

The fourth question was: *What are the experiences gained from SIA in Europe, North America and a number of developing countries, and what pitfalls have been encountered?* A summary of the answers reads:

- There is clear evidence that SIA has enhanced the quality of decision-making;
- In Europe and North America, most governments are obliged by law to apply SIA to their own policies, partly because of the view that public spending has to be curbed. However, compliance with legal requirements is poor, but improving, albeit very slowly.
- In developing countries, SIA is stimulated because funding agencies require pretesting of innovations.
- The major pitfalls encountered are insufficient communication between central and target actors and underutilization of the outcomes of SIA.

The fifth question read: *What is the state-of-the-art in SIA?*

- Research methodology has been advanced far enough to be able to comply with most requests in contemporary SIA research practice; this favourable situation has emerged because all steps in a SIA project can profit from research techniques developed and tested in other types of policy-oriented social research.
- Oriented basic research should contribute more to the empirical and methodological basis of SIA.

The sixth and final question was: *Which normative and practical aspects of SIA give rise to concern?*

- There do not yet exist a code of ethics and rules of conduct for IA practitioners, including SIA practitioners; a normative framework will have to be elaborated and institutionalized in the near future.
- Often central actors do not inform relevant actors about SIA projects and their outcomes, resulting in a low democratic quality of decision-making.

- Often central actors do not carry out SIA because they presume this type of policy-oriented research is relatively expensive and time-consuming.
- access of SIA practitioners to policy-makers is too limited.
- SIA practitioners often lack adequate training.

9.3 Discussion

All kinds of futures analysis suffer from a number of misunderstandings, frequently to be observed in many circles. SIA requires the analysis of developments and situations situated in the future, and therefore SIA is one of the victims of the misunderstandings concerning futures research. With regard to SIA, I expect in the years to come, notwithstanding numerous warnings, a persistence of the argument that it is impossible to predict the future because predictions of future developments have been inaccurate many times. This erroneous argument overlooks the point that future developments and situations are related to variables that show substantial differences in predictability. As an example I take demographic processes. In countries with little migration and a stable mortality rate, the number of inhabitants between, for instance, 20 and 60 years of age can be forecasted for the next five to ten years in a relatively accurate way. In the same countries, however, the number of men and women 100 years and older cannot be forecasted in an accurate way for the next decades because the mortality rates for the very old contain a considerable amount of systems noise.

The misunderstanding implies that futures researchers including SIA practitioners have a communications problem with a lot of their fellow scientists. In my experience this communications gap can be bridged, albeit not in all cases. How can this be accomplished? As mentioned before, systems thinking provides a language that is understood in all scientific disciplines. SIA practitioners are advised to refer to the distinction between closed and open systems, and to systems noise operating in open systems. If SIA practitioners can argue that hypotheses related to specific social systems have been tested in a methodologically adequate way, scientists coming from other disciplines can be convinced in most cases that the outcomes of the testings are relevant, and that systems noise cannot be reduced further, at least not in the short term. Fellow scientists, in most cases, are also willing to accept that in a SIA study only a limited set of variables can be measured perfectly and that theoretical explanation has to be restricted to these variables. Those fellow scientists are furthermore in most cases reasonable enough to accept that other variables, that is, variables that have not been measured in a precise way, can best be handled by interpretation.

In this book, I have focused on good research practice, and I have tried to select the best available examples. Consequently this book does not present a representative sample of research practice in SIA in general. An evaluation of everyday research practice would require a different book. An evaluation study like this would certainly meet a need, and a number of evaluations are available already (e.g. Vanclay & Bronstein 1995). In my book, I have tried to bridge the gap between ideas about good research, and everyday research practice, by providing overviews of pitfalls. By focusing in this book on methodology in use in good research practice, I run the risk of being criticized for painting too favourable a picture of SIA. I am aware of this risk, but I hope serious readers will understand my motives and my approach.

I assume in this book that policy-makers, that is, central actors, are willing to have SIA projects done and to use all or part of the outcomes. Many readers will contest this assumption, and indeed only a few sections in society show substantial use of SIA. This number is increasing, however. As I argued before, as soon as pioneers in a sector are successful in using SIA, other actors will follow. Illustrations have been provided in preceding chapters concerning, *inter alia*, health care policy. Also, illustrations have been given of the emergence of legal requirements, making SIA mandatory in government systems.

Specifying methods for applied research and action research often leads to the criticism that it is inappropriate to approach nonrational behaviour by rational methodology. This kind of criticism is based on a misunderstanding. I have advocated an approach based on utilitarian individualism that assumes that actors try to achieve their goals. These goals will often be emotional, biased and contradictory. Nevertheless we can identify the goals actors want to achieve, we can observe how they try to achieve these goals and we can establish whether or not they achieve them. We can also find out which constraints have confronted actors during the behavioural process. Utilitarian individualism assumes that the actor is not insane, but it does not exclude irrational goals from its explanatory model.

Furthermore, research methodology as described in this book is criticized frequently for being overoptimistic regarding the opportunities for quantifying statements about observations. This again introduces a misunderstanding. Utilitarian individualism advocates both explanation and understanding, that is, both a (quasi)experimental approach and an holistic approach, the latter based on taking the role of the other (e.g. Esser 1993). Utilitarian individualism has also developed rules for when to use quantitative methods and when to use qualitative methods (e.g. Abell 1990). As an example I take the impact in the 1990s of social security policy on the behaviour of individual members of society. The impact of these policies greatly depends on what these individuals have experienced in their formative years. Individuals born between 1910 and 1930 experienced the depression of the 1930s in their formative years. The only way to reconstruct these experiences is by retrospective interviews and oral history approaches. Individuals born between 1955 and 1970 experienced the economic recession of 1975–85 in their formative period. Concerning the members of the latter cohorts, structured interviewing is an adequate approach. In an SIA like this, combining qualitative and quantitative methods is possible and evidently makes sense.

Closely related to this criticism is the idea that research methodology as described in this book is based on a natural science bias. Regarding this line of reasoning, we have to keep in mind that in the natural sciences too a distinction is made between open and closed systems, and that systems noise is a concept used in the natural sciences too. The natural sciences have concentrated for a long time on cyclical processes, showing little systems noise. Recently they have broadened their perspective, including noncyclical processes in their research. Regarding noncyclical research, they are aware of the fact that they are confronted with a lot of systems noise. I conclude that the methodology described in this book is typical for scientific research focusing on relatively open systems showing a relatively large amount of systems noise. This category of disciplines houses meteorology, the life sciences, the behavioural sciences and the social sciences, to give some examples. As a specific example, I take epidemiological research, which has studied the impact of the Second World War on women who were pregnant during that time. A sample of those women were interviewed in 1990 with regard to their diet during their pregnancy. Did they experience hunger? Was their diet unbalanced? This information was combined with information about their children to provide answers about the relationship between maternal health and children's health in later life. Nevertheless there are some methodological problems. What the women remember of what they ate some 50 years ago will be relatively unreliable and imprecise, in other words, full of systems noise. Nevertheless, this kind of epidemiological research is evidently worthwhile. Social impact assessors are frequently confronted with research data that show about the same degree of systems noise as data of epidemiological researchers. If both types of researchers work according to the standards of their disciplines, discussions about a *natural science bias* in the work of the social scientist would be as irrelevant as a discussion about a *social science bias* in the work of the epidemiologist. The latter discussion is never heard.

A criticism of a different kind suggests that SIA exhibits a conservative bias. SIA certainly can lead to an unmasking of rash reform ideas, in particular if the interventions proposed lack a specification of the resources needed to accomplish them. But this is not the same as a conservative bias. In general, SIA is capable of assisting both conservative and progressive actors by telling them what to expect in terms of consequences of current or future actions. If a social impact assessor is in doubt whether the proposed research activities are in harmony with the requirements of democracy, they are advised to simulate a session of parliament that decides upon the action under consideration. Would the action get a majority vote? In that case, the social impact assessor has a moral justification for studying future consequences of actions. We have to keep in mind also that formalized ethical codes and rules of conduct for scientists (e.g. doctors, lawyers) derive their justification from laws passed by parliament.

9.4 Implications for the future

I assume that SIA will be confronted with: (a) an increase in competition between actor systems, (b) an increase in external control of actor systems, (c) an increase in the demand for flexibility and innovation in actor systems, and (d) an increase in the application of science by actor systems.

The acceleration of competition between actor systems can be interpreted as part of the process of modernization, in particular of rationalization. In former times, a certain amount of slack was normal in most organizations, but gradually the drive for rationalization has led to an increase of efficiency. We see this happen in business enterprises because they introduce internal quality control. We also observe this in the area of government. In many countries in the West, government organizations have adopted internal quality control. Nonprofit organizations follow the same strategy, as we saw when developments in hospital organizations were discussed earlier. In many actor systems, input, throughput and output are measured and evaluated, followed by efficiency drives. If one organization in a sector of society is successful in systematically increasing its efficiency, other organizations in the sector will have to try to imitate this success.

The spread of external control of actor systems is a consequence of changes in the political system and the mass media. In the political system, opposition parties increasingly use external control of government organizations as a weapon to attack the governing parties. The opposition parties try to establish that the activities of the governing parties are undemocratic, inefficient or a waste of taxpayers' money. In order to achieve this effect, opposition parties pretest actions of their opponents with regard to future consequences, wait for the actions to be put into practice, evaluate the consequences and sum up with the statement, *I told you so*. The mass media have also adopted this strategy with regard to acts of government. Unmasking government makes newspaper articles and television programmes successful. The mass media also have discovered the advantages of unmasking business enterprises and nonprofit organizations. They have commercial products and services tested, followed by publicity about the outcomes. Nonprofit organizations are also targeted for ex-ante and ex-post evaluations. Mass media have health care tested by open or unobtrusive observation. They have services rendered by universities tested, followed by publications showing the ranking of the education provided and the outcomes of research published by departments in all kinds of disciplines and institutions. External evaluation forces actor systems to improve their ways and to watch their reputation.

CONCLUSIONS, DISCUSSION AND IMPLICATIONS

The demand for flexibility and innovation in actor systems is increasing because these systems have to survive in a quickly changing environment, confronting them with, *inter alia*, increasing cultural diversity of the population and demands for emancipation of women and minorities. They have to change to new instruments and procedures, and they have to cope with more and more complexity. These developments put pressure on human resources management. Actor systems have to keep their staff flexible, *inter alia* by running training programmes and ultimately forcing into retirement employees who are not able to keep up with change. These developments also require adjustments of equipment and procedures. Frequently actor systems must renew their technical infrastructure, in particular with regard to information systems. When new procedures are introduced in their sector of society, they are forced in most cases to adopt these procedures. Competition and external control pressure them to take the demands for flexibility and innovation seriously. The number of niches that permit actor systems to hide from external pressure is diminishing. Actor systems have to cope with permanent reorganization.

In all scientific disciplines that can offer their outcomes for practical use, methods for the application of science are improving and applicable knowledge is generated as much as possible. This is because social responsibility is taken seriously, but also because retrenchments in academic and related research force scientists to enter the market, to make profit and to finance part of their basic research out of these profits. At the same time, actor systems are increasing the application of science in order to improve their production systems, organizational systems and social systems. They try to produce goods and services more efficiently by adopting scientific procedures. They streamline their organization according to scientific insights. They utilize the scientific knowledge of their staff. Since ancient times, the medical system and the military have applied science (Bernal 1969). In the nineteenth century, industry and other commercial sectors followed their example. In the twentieth century, all other sectors have also been affected by science. For instance, the arts have started to innovate design procedures by studying the work of artists and focusing on success criteria (Hekkert 1995). In professional sports, athletes are trained and instructed according to insights derived from scientific research, with competition at the Olympic Games as the ultimate example of this type of application of scientific knowledge. Also universities are striving for excellence, applying scientific procedures to the improvement of educational processes and to the production of knowledge. The science of education and the science of science each have created a substantial system of applied science. We have to keep in mind that actor systems in most cases remain sceptical with regard to the benefits of applying science. Their attitude can best be characterized as one of ambivalence. They are aware of the shortcomings of scientists, at the same time however continuing to contract scientists in order to profit from their expertise.

The perspectives of SIA as a type of research, sometimes of action research, depend not only on advancements in SIA but also on the ability of social impact asssessors to bridge the communications gap between outsiders and social impact assessors. The best way to do this is to present examples of good research practice and successful implementations. We can assume that sooner or later decision-makers will react, because it is in their interest to identify in each problematic situation a least-regret strategy, and to implement this strategy. However, the perspectives of SIA are not only dependent on self-interest of decision-makers. Its future also rests on moral arguments, proposed by consequentialism. Decision-makers are confronted with a moral obligation to identify the future consequences of current or proposed actions, and to take knowledge about these consequences into consideration whenever they act.

Cases and exercises

General introduction

The six cases and matching exercises presented below are based on the practical experience of the author in co-ordinating training courses on strategic learning as a consultant, and teaching seminars on SIA in higher education. The cases cover situations in developed and developing countries. They deal with problems in government agencies, commercial enterprises and nongovernmental organizations. Consultants and teachers can apply the cases as they are described, and they can use the descriptions as a stepping stone for designing their own cases.

The first two cases can be used as soon as the participants have studied the first four chapters of the book. The remaining four cases require that participants are knowledgable about subjects dealt with in Chapters 5 and 6 too, and that they have enough information about the remaining chapters to be able to look up, study and apply the examples, theories and methods dealt with in these chapters.

The cases can be used in post-experience training activities, for instance, in an in-service training course in an organization. They can also be used in graduate education, in a seminar with one co-ordinating (assistant) professor and (for example) 18 graduate students. The following description is based on usage of the case in higher education. The assumption is that, during the case, students receive three contact hours twice each week and that they have to spend an additional 14 hours a week on homework, and discussions in small groups. (Students attend a parallel seminar on a different subject each week, also requiring 20 hours).

At the end of the description of each case instructions are provided for readers who prefer to use the cases and do the exercises on their own. The use of the cases and exercises in a group of up to five participants is also dealt with.

Case 1: SIA and advanced negotiations and decision-making

Preparation

The co-ordinator will have to obtain from two to three life insurance companies copies of the last issues of their annual business report and annual social report. In most countries reports like these are unclassified documents.

Case description

The setting of the case is the same as that of the illustration provided in section 1.2. We are dealing with a (fictitious) life insurance company selling life insurance and investment arrangements to private customers. Three problems are on the agenda of a specific board meeting. First, an expansion of the market. Second, the situation in an ongoing merger with another life insurance company. Third, kindergarten provisions for young children of female employees.

First seminar session

Following a short presentation of the case and the information provided by the (two to three) real-life insurance companies, in a plenary session a *conceptual map* is designed of the central actor system and its target system. Each of the three items on the agenda are dealt with in a submap. After one hour the participants split up into three groups. Each group will be held responsible for preparing negotiations and decision-making regarding one of the issues on the agenda of the board. Each group elaborates the part of the conceptual map dealing with its specific assignment. Special attention is given to future consequences of current and proposed actions. Finally a plenary meeting is held to discuss the next step.

First period of study

The three groups elaborate the conceptual map into a memorandum providing a *problem analysis*. They discuss two to three alternative *strategies* and their *consequences*. Copies of the memoranda are distributed to all participants.

Second seminar session

The memoranda providing the problem analysis and describing three strategies are discussed in a plenary meeting. Following this three *scenarios* are designed. Next a *scenario-to-strategy* workshop is held, with special emphasis on the identification of *strategies and their consequences*. Finally the next step is discussed.

Second period of study

The three groups elaborate a document on the outcomes of the scenario-to-strategy workshop, including social impact assessments. Each document will have to prepare the members of the board for negotiations and decision-making during the board meeting. The documents are distributed to all participants.

Third seminar meeting

The *board meeting* is simulated. Participants play roles: chairperson, head and representatives of the marketing department, the operations department and the personnel department, members of a staff unit, and so on. Special attention is given to the characteristics of the information used during negotiations and decision-making. Which part of the information is quantitative, hard, highly accurate? Which part is qualit ative, soft, less accurate?

Third period of study

The three groups write evaluation reports on negotiations and decision-making in the board meeting. The groups provide suggestions for improvements of the SIAs and the policy formation.

Fourth seminar meeting

In a plenary session the evaluation reports are discussed. The co-ordinator provides a debriefing.

Use of the case by one person (or a few persons)

If one person works on the case and the exercises, he or she will only write the documents. In a very small seminar group of two to five participants, all meetings will be held plenary. Only one problem will be dealt with.

Case 2: SIA and regional development planning

Preparation

The co-ordinator will have to trace documentation on one or more descriptions of large-dam projects, dealing with economic, environmental and social issues. These documents will be made available to the participants at the very end of the seminar.

Case description

The case deals with a large-dam project in a developing country. A valley will be inundated after a large dam has been built. The water of the artificial lake will be used for irrigation and for the production of electricity. The lake will be used for fishing and tourism. The inhabitants of 70 villages will have to be evacuated. The villagers now earn a living in agriculture. The resettlement will afflict 35,000 individuals. Resettlement will take place in an area about 20km from the lake. Downstream 5,000 individuals will be confronted with the loss of 50 per cent of their agricultural land.

The project will take ten years to complete. At the moment of the case exercise the decision to build the dam has already been taken. The inhabitants of the area to be inundated have been consulted. Of the adult inhabitants 35 per cent have voted against the development project, 45 per cent voted in favour of the project and 30 per cent abstained from voting.

The problem to be analyzed is related to the planning of the evacuation and the resettlement process. Between the time of the case exercise and the completion of the dam a period of three years elapsed. Villagers to be resettled will get a financial compensation that covers about 60 per cent of the costs they have to pay to rebuild an agricultural enterprise in the resettlement area.

Baseline information coming from one or more development projects will be provided by the co-ordinator of the seminar. Participants in the seminar will be invited to formulate additional baseline information.

First seminar meeting

An introductory presentation will be held. Following this participants will design a *conceptual map*, with special emphasis on providing an arrows scheme. Next three groups of participants will each be made responsible for writing a document on one of the problem areas in the case. Group 1 will look at economic and related social issues (rebuilding farms, retraining villages in new occupational skills, etc.). Group 2 will deal with commercial fishing and tourism as new sources of income. Group 3 will look at social networks, family ties, the young and the old, etc. Each group will draft a document providing a *problem analysis*, with special emphasis on the assessments of social impacts.

First period of study

Each group elaborates a document with a problem analysis, at least three strategies and an exploration of their consequences. The documents are distributed.

Second seminar meeting

A set of three *scenarios* is elaborated, focusing on changes in political, economic, environmental and social issues. Following this a *scenario-to-strategy workshop* is held. The co-ordinator introduces two critical incidents dealing with social aspects of the development project.

Second period of study

Each group elaborates a document on outcomes of the scenario-to-strategy workshop, focusing on the problem it has to deal with. The documents are distributed.

Third seminar meeting

A *meeting* of the co-ordinating board of the development project is simulated. Participants play roles, including the role of representatives of the area to be inundated and the area downstream that is also afflicted by the artificial lake.

Third period of study

Each group writes an evaluation report on negotiations and decision-making in the meeting of the co-ordinating board. The groups deal with an additional two critical incidents presented by the co-ordinator of the seminar. Distribution of documents.

Fourth seminar meeting

In a plenary session the evaluation reports are discussed. Special attention is given to the moral aspects of the development project. Have arguments of legal and social justice been adequately taken into account?

Use of the case by one person, or a small seminar group

If one person wants to use the case, only the reports will be produced. In a small seminar group, having up to five participants, all meetings will be held plenary.

Case 3: SIA and the art-science of management

Preparation

The co-ordinator identifies one or a few modern handbooks on methods of advanced management. Below a number of examples are provided:

- Stephen P. Robbins & Mary Coultar 1996. *Management*, 5th edn. New York: Prentice Hall.
- Don Hellriegel and John W. Slocum Jr 1996. *Management*, 7th edn. Cincinnati: South-Western College Publishing.
- Gary Hamel and C. K. Prahalad 1994. *Competing for the future: breakthrough strategies for seizing control of industry and creating markets of tomorrow*. Boston, MA: Harvard Business School Press.
- Francis J. Gouillart and James N. Kelly 1995. *Transforming the organization*. New York: McGraw-Hill.

Case description

We may expect that modern handbooks on methods of advanced management deal with strategic learning and related approaches, including SIA. We also expect them to inform their readership about the main characteristics of quantitative (hard) and qualitative (soft) knowledge and the synthesis of hard and soft information in negotiations and decision-making. We evaluate one or a few of these handbooks with regard to these aspects. In most cases the evaluation ends in disappointment. The handbooks either ignore these issues or treat them in passing. In this case the participants will draft a chapter or section in addition to the handbook they evaluated. In the additional text they will discuss strategic learning, including SIA. They will also write about the main types of information and their synthesis in negotiations and decision-making.

First seminar session

Discuss the book(s) you selected. Elaborate the criteria concerning the description of strategic learning and types of information you would like to apply. Allocate tasks to three groups of participants in the seminar.

First period of study

Each group drafts an abstract of the text it wants to write. It formulates the questions to be dealt with. It specifies headings of sections, etc. Documents are distributed.

Second seminar meeting

Participants discuss the abstracts. Each group gets comments from the two other groups. A conceptual map of the text to be written is drafted.

Second period of study

Additional sources are identified and additional reading is accomplished. The draft abstracts are elaborated. The new documents are distributed.

Third seminar meeting

Two to three *devil's advocates* are invited to provide critical comments on the documents that have been distributed.

Third period of study

Each group writes the final draft of its text. The outcomes are distributed.

Fourth seminar meeting

A discussion of the final drafts is staged. The final editing of the texts is organized. The final texts will be put on the Internet, making them available to disappointed readers of the management handbooks that have been evaluated.

Use of the case by one person, or a small seminar group

If one person has to do all the work, only the documents will be produced and one or two *devil's advocates* will be employed. A small seminar group can restrict discussions and writing to plenary meetings.

Case 4: SIA and the integration of Europe[1]

Preparation

The co-ordinator of the seminar is advised to identify and study a number of documents on the integration of Europe. A number of examples are provided below:

- European Commission, 1985. *Completing the internal market: White Paper from the Commission to the European Council*. Luxembourg.

- L. Betten (ed.) 1991. *The future of European social policy*, Deventer/ Boston, MA.
- H. Mosley 1990. The social dimension of European integration. *International Labour Review*, **2**, 147–64.

Description

In 1986 the Council of the European Community decided that the integration of the markets of the member countries into one market had to be finished in 1992. This decision has been taken in 1986 because the Council was convinced that the economic depression had been overcome and a period of economic growth seemed to have began. In the mid-1980s the integration of Europe has been subjected to a number of IAs. This huge intervention of deregulation has been pretested by economic and fiscal IA, *inter alia* by analyzing what would happen if Europe would not be transformed into an integrated economic system. It has to be admitted that these pretests are slightly biased, however. They border on advocacy planning because they focus on variables that promise a positive outcome of the analysis. Nevertheless these IAs provide a valuable overview of what had to be expected in an economic and fiscal sense.

The plans for a common market in Europe included a free circulation of man and woman power. At this point SIA enters the scene. What will be the future consequences of current or proposed actions in this area? The case invites participants to explore these impacts.

First seminar session

The participants discuss the problem of a free circulation of the working population in Europe. A *problem analysis* is elaborated, based on a *conceptual map*. Gradually the discussion is focused on a limited number of problems. For instance, the free circulation of professionals and semiprofessionals, medical experts and nurses, engineers and technicians.

CASES AND EXERCISES

First period of study

A document on the problem analysis is drafted. How are professional and occupational educations and degrees to be treated? Which social security arrangements will have to be continued and which will have to be changed? Will regulations concerning the maximum number of working hours have to be harmonized between countries? The document is distributed.

Second seminar session

The economic boom that started in the mid-1980s is not to last for ever, we assume. The political willingness to co-operate will show ups and downs, we assume. The external context of an integrated Europe will show continuous and discontinuous change. How are we to incorporate these developments in our analysis? A set of *scenarios* has to be designed. We also have to look at *strategies* and their *consequences*. Three groups are made responsible for exploring three aspects of the problem.

Second period of study

Each group has to come forward with a *SWOT analysis* of the EU with regard to the free circulation of professional and occupational manpower and to identify the consequences. The results are distributed.

Third seminar session

A *scenario-to-strategy workshop* is held.

Third period of study

The outcomes of the scenario-to-strategy workshop are evaluated. The prioritization of strategies is analyzed, applying multiple-criteria analysis. The document is distributed.

CASES AND EXERCISES

Fourth seminar meeting

The documents presenting the strategies and their consequences, analyzed with regard to their relationships with scenarios, are discussed. The co-ordinator will present a debriefing.

Use of the case by one person, or a small seminar group

Restrict the case to the elaboration of documents if one person has to do the job. Eliminate groups and concentrate on plenary meetings if the number of participants is five or less.

Note

1. The author gratefully acknowledges the help of Jan Simonis in writing this case instruction.

Case 5: SIA and the prospects of the women's movement

Preparation

The co-ordinator will have to study some background publications on social movements, the diffusion of innovations and the women's movement. For example:

- S. Tarrow 1996. *Power in Movement: Social Movements, Collective Action and Politics*. Cambridge: Cambridge University Press. Includes some information on the women's movement.
- E.M. Rogers 1996. *Diffusion of Innovations*. New York. The Free Press, Fourth Edition.

Case description

To what extent is it possible to identify the future consequences of collective action and social movements? This question requires focusing on a specific case. What about the consequences of action directed at the emancipation of women?

First seminar session

Participants will design a *conceptual map* about the women's movement and emancipation policy directed at women. They will also discuss the theory of collective action and theories about social movements. Next they will focus on a specific aspect of the women's movement, for instance female academics at universities. They will design an explanatory and interpretive model concerning this specific aspect.

First period of study

Three groups of participants will each elaborate a *problem analysis* with regard to the specific aspect. They will also draft the outlines of a *baseline analysis* and a *systems analysis*. The documents will be distributed.

Second seminar session

The three documents are discussed. *Scenarios* are designed. *Strategies* are elaborated.

Second period of study

Three groups elaborate a *scenario analysis* and a *social impact assessment*. The outcomes are distributed.

Third seminar session

The documents are discussed. The strategies are redesigned in order to mitigate negative impacts. Scenario analysis and SIA are repeated.

Strategies are ranked according to criteria of priority selected by the participants.

Third period of study

The three groups are instructed by the co-ordinator to analyze the impacts of two critical incidents. Scenario analysis and SIA are repeated. Ranking is repeated. Documents are distributed.

Fourth seminar meeting

Evaluation of the case and the exercise. Design of an ex ante evaluation of the strategies elaborated in the third period of study.

Use of the case by one person or a seminar with up to five participants

If one person only is involved, only the documents are produced. The case focuses on the application of theory and the mitigation of negative impacts of strategies. In a small group all activities take place in plenary meetings.

Case 6: SIA and the fight against addictions

Preparations

The co-ordinator will trace documents on compulsive gambling and actions to reduce this type of addiction. The co-ordinator will also trace documents on drugs abuse, both soft and hard drugs, dealing with France, Sweden and the Netherlands. Furthermore documentation on action to reduce or eliminate the use of drugs will be provided to the participants.

Next the co-ordinator will provide documentation of institutional change, focusing on changing government systems (Putnam 1993).

Case description

Compulsive gambling has been a grave concern for municipal governments for many centuries. This can be illustrated by an example. When in the past the government of Venice for the umpteeth time interdicted all gambling, the players took refuge in small rooms at the back of coffee houses on the San Marco Scquare. These small rooms were called casini. That's how the casino of today acquired its name. After a while the government of Venice revoked the interdiction, primarily because gambling continued anyway, albeit now in secrecy, and the municipal government regretted that it had forgone revenues, because illegal gambling cannot be taxed.

Policy-makers who react to addictions like compulsive gambling are said to do so on the basis of either the domino theory or the safety valve theory. The domino theory leads to the prediction that each leniency with regard to gambling will end in a spreading of this social disease. The safety valve theory owes its name to a safety device attached to the boilers of steam engines. If an excessive amount of steam is produced, part of the steam will escape through the safety valve. If the safety valve is shut off, the boiler can explode. The safety valve theory leads to the prediction that suppression of opportunities for acting out will lead to social conflict, without solving the problem. Adherents to the safety valve theory advocated some lenience with regard to gambling in order to avoid social conflicts and to facilitate monitoring and containment.

Sometimes government actions to curb addiction to drugs are explained in a similar way. This theoretical perspective leads to the following argument. If a specific government applies the domino theory, it is likely to treat the sale and use of drugs as a criminal offence. Often an additional theory, the stepping-stone theory, is applied. This theory predicts that use of soft drugs is a stepping stone on the way to hard drugs. If, on the other hand a government applies the safety valve theory, it will react more flexibly, and perhaps tolerate a limited use of soft drugs like hashish.

In France the sale and use of all kinds of drugs is illegal. Dealers and users have retreated to remote areas like urban slums. It is relatively difficult to acquire clean syringes, for instance. In the Netherlands the sale and use of soft drugs is tolerated within certain limits. Dealers and users of soft drugs have not gone in hiding. Addicts to hard drugs can obtain clean syringes without difficulty. In Sweden a policy to curb the sales and use of drugs is in operation that combines elements from both the French and the Dutch approach.

This case focuses on a problem that can easily be seen as the most difficult one in SIA today. Participants in a seminar are invited to come forward with answers to two questions. What are the consequences of the French, Dutch and Swedish approach to fight the taking of soft and hard drugs? What would be the consequences of taking the French approach to fight the taking of soft and hard drugs and introduce it in the Netherlands?

First seminar session

Participants design a *conceptual map*, elaborating the example provided in the book. They elaborate the conceptual model into a *problem analysis*. Following this they focus on a *systems analysis*, including a critical discussion of theories (domino theory, stepping-stone theory, safety valve theory).

First period of study

Three groups evaluate *trend analyses* and *monitoring systems* nowadays in use in France, Sweden and the Netherlands. Each group designs improvements to both components of a SIA project. Documents are distributed.

Second seminar session

Documents are discussed. Next, participants elaborate scenarios and strategies.

Second period of study

Three groups study the literature on the consequences of anti-addiction policies. They also study the literature on institutional change in government systems (*inter alia* Putnam 1993). Documents are distributed.

Third seminar session

Participants discuss the memoranda. Next they elaborate a scenario-to-strategy analysis. They try to mitigate the negative consequences of preliminary strategies.

Third period of study

Three groups elaborate the set of strategies and assess their consequences in detail. They search for a least-regret strategy. Memoranda are distributed.

Fourth seminar meeting

The co-ordinator invites two to three experts to play the role of *devil's advocates*. Participants and outsiders discuss the outcomes of the exercises in the seminar.

Use of the case by one person or a seminar with five participants or less

In this case specific attention is given to systems analysis and theoretical explanation. Also trend analysis and monitoring get special attention. Finally the contribution of *devil's advocates* is explored. If a single person uses the case, maybe at least one devil's advocate can be found. In a small seminar discussion and elaboration is restricted to activities of the group as a whole.

Glossary

Action research Policy-oriented research combined with an action; (a) data gathering and other components of social research are used to intervene in a target system, (b) policy-oriented research is carried out in close co-operation with an actor system.

Analytical tradition An approach in the social sciences applying the covering law model (*see also* covering law model; interpretive tradition).

Art-science An action that requires the application of scientific knowledge and the use of professional intuition.

Baseline analysis Analysis of the history of the problem to be analyzed in the impact assessment.

Basic research Experimental or theoretical work undertaken primarily to acquire new knowledge of the underlying foundations of phenomena and observable facts, without any particular application or use in view (*see also* oriented basic research; policy-oriented research).

Central actor The person whom the impact assessor has taken as the central decision-maker in the social system to be analyzed (*see also* target actor).

Conceptual map Schematic overview of issues relevant to a problem, sometimes including arrows hypothesizing the direction of causal relationships.

Consequentialism Tradition in moral philosophy advocating the assessment of the consequences of human actions, and taking responsibility for the consequences.

Cost-benefit analysis An analysis in financial terms of the costs and

240

benefits of a current or proposed action (*see also* multiple-criteria analysis).

Covering law approach Approximating a causal analysis as closely as possible (*see also* analytical tradition).

Critical incident A subscenario; an event in possible future contexts for the actor system and the target system, in most cases characterized by low probability and high impact (*see also* scenario).

Delphi An expert opinion survey with three characteristics: anonymity among participants, statistical treatment of responses and iterative polling with feedback.

Demographic impact assessment The process of identifying the future consequences of a current or proposed action that may have an impact on demographic processes or on issues related to demographic processes.

Economic impact assessment The process of identifying the future consequences of a current or proposed action which are related to economic situations and developments.

Environmental impact assessment The process of identifying the future consequences of a current or proposed action which are related to the environment.

Evaluation research The process of identifying the working of an action, and its consequences (also called ex-post evaluation, *see also* formative evaluation; summative evaluation; program evaluation).

Formative evaluation The process of identifying the working of an action, and its consequences, combined with using the outcomes of the identification to intervene in the action (*see also* evaluation research; programme evalaution; summative evaluation).

Game theory A model based on game theory is a mathematical representation of rational decision-making involving two or more actors.

Impact assessment The process of identifying the future consequences of a current or proposed action (also called ex-ante evaluation, pretesting of actions, analysis of consequences).

Interpretive tradition An approach in the social sciences applying *Verstehen* as advocated by Weber (*see also* analytical tradition).

Least-regret strategy Strategy that minimizes the risk of a suboptimal decision by a policy-maker.

Micro-simulation   simulation based on data about individuals, e.g. person-period files (*see also* simulation).

Monitoring   The process of identifying the consequences of an action during the action.

Multiple-criteria analysis   An analysis in other than financial terms of the cost and benefits of a current or proposed action (*see also* cost-benefit analysis).

Oriented basic research   Basis research oriented or directed towards some broad field of general interest (*see also* basic research).

Policy-oriented research   The sort that is directed primarily towards a specific practical aim or objective (*see also* basic research; oriented basic research).

Postdiction   Predicting past developments in a system in order to develop and test a model that in turn can be used to predict future developments.

Problem   A discrepancy between a desired situation or process and an actual situation of process.

Programme evaluation   The process of identifying the working of an action, and its consequences, with regard to one or more phases in an action, combined with identifying the future consequences of one or more phases in that action (*see also* evaluation research; formative evaluation; summative evaluation).

Risk   an event with known probability (also called statistical uncertainty; *see* uncertainty).

Risk assessment   The process of identifying risk associated with a current or future action (*see* risk).

Risk management   mitigating risk, e.g. by monitoring, information (reducing subjective risk) and increase of safety (reducing objective risk).

Scenario   A sketch of a possible future context for the actor system and the target system.

Scenario-to-strategy workshop   A step in strategic learning; a workshop, in which strategies are pre-tested by identifying their future consequences in a number of scenarios.

Simulation   (a) Running a nonlinear, dynamic model; (b) the process of pretesting actions in an artifical setting in order to gather information about possible consequences.

Social auditing Checking on the working of an action and its consequences.

Social impact assessment The process of identifying the future consequences of a current or proposed action which are related to individuals, organizations and social macro-systems.

Social technology Intervention techniques (e.g. deregulation, decentralization), and auxiliaries in policy-making (e.g. network planning).

Strategic learning The process in which a central actor formulates problems, analyzes his or her past, identifies possible future contexts, designs and pretests strategies and involves all relevant members of the actor system in turning the organization into a social system responsive to developments in its context (also called organizational learning).

Strategy Course of action concerning the main aspects of an intervention (*see also* tactic).

Strengths-weaknesses-opportunities-threats analysis Analysis of strong and weak aspects of a central actor and his action, of opportunities and threats involved (called SWOT analysis).

Summative evaluation The process of identifying the working of an action, and its consequences, in order to use the outcomes of the identification to asses the action (*see also* evaluation research; programme evaluation; summative evaluation).

Systems noise Unpredictable situations and processes in a system.

Tactics Course of action concerning details of an intervention (*see also* strategy).

Target actor Actor whom the impact assessor has taken as an actor at whom the action is directed (*see also* central actor).

Technology assessment The process of identifying the future consequences of a current or proposed action which are related to technology.

Typology A symbolic representation of two or more phenomena on a relatively high level of abstraction.

Uncertainty An event with unknown probability (also called indeterminacy; *see also* risk).

Bibliography

Abell, P. 1990. Methodological achievements in sociology over the past few decades with special reference to interplay of quantitative and qualitative methods. In *What has sociology achieved?* C. G. A. Bryant & H. A. Becker (eds), 8–30. London: Macmillan.

Allison, G. T. 1971. *Essence of decision explaining the Cuban missile crisis.* Boston, MA: Little, Brown.

American Psychological Association 1992. *The ethical principles of psychologists and code of conduct.* Bingamton, New York: Haworth Press.

Andersen, O. 1991. Occupational impacts on mortality declines in the Nordic countries. See Lutz (1991), 41–55. London: Academic Press.

Ascher, W. 1978. *Forecasting: an appraisal for policy-makers and planners.* Baltimore, MD: Johns Hopkins University Press.

Beaujot, R. 1991. Immigration policy and sociodemographic change: the Canadian case. See Lutz (1991), 359–79. London: Academic Press.

Beck, U. 1992. *Risk society: towards a new modernity.* London: Sage.

Becker, H. A. 1987a. Social scenarios of sea level rise, *Project Appraisal* **2** (2), 91–6.

— 1987b. International assessment of water projects, *Impact Assessment Bulletin*, **5** (3), 111–21.

— 1990. Achievement in the analytical tradition in sociology. In *What has sociology achieved?*, C. G. A. Bryant & H. A. Becker (eds), 8–30. London: Macmillan.

— 1992. *Generaties en hun kansen*, Amsterdam: Meulenhoff (Dutch only).

— 1995. Demographic impact assessment. See Vanclay & Bronstein (1995), 141–51. Chichester: Wiley.

Becker, H. A. & F. L. Leeuw 1994. Contemporary sociology in the Netherlands. In *International handbook of contemporary developments in sociology*, R. P. Mohan & A. S. Wilke (eds), 153–84. Westport, CT: Greenwood Press.

Becker, H. A., H. De Vries, P. Thoenes (eds) 1981. *Handleiding voor het ontwerpen van scenario's.* Utrecht: Department of Planning and Policy Analysis, University of Utrecht. (Dutch only.)

Becker, H. A., J. van Doorn, F. van Vught 1986. Producing detailed guidelines for appraisals. *Project Appraisal* **1** (1), 21–31.

Berger, T. R. 1983. Resources, development and human values. *Impact Assessment Bulletin* **2** (2), 129–48.

Bernal, J. W. 1969. *Science in history*. London: Watts.

Birdsall, N. 1994. Another look at population and global warming. In *Population, environment and development*, United Nations, 39–55. New York: Department of Economic and Social Information and Policy Analysis.

Blake, R. R. & J. S. Mouton 1976. *Consultation*. Reading: Addison-Wesley.

Boothroyd, P. 1995. Policy Assessment. See Vanclay & Bronstein (1995), 83–126. Chichester: John Wiley.

Bryant, C. G. A. 1995. *Practical sociology: post-empiricism and the reconstruction of theory and application*. London: Polity Press.

Bryant, C. G. A. & H. A. Becker 1990. *What has sociology achieved?* London: Macmillan.

Buckley, R. 1995. Environmental auditing See Vanclay, & Bronstein (1995), 283–301. Chichester: Wiley.

Bulmer, M. 1982. *The uses of social research: social investigation in public policy-making*. London: Allen & Unwin.

—1983. General introduction. In *Social research in developing countries*, M. Bulmer & D. P. Warwick (eds), 3–26. Chichester: Wiley.

Burdge, R. J. 1994a. *A community guide to social impact assessment*. Middleton: Social Ecology Press.

—1994b. *A conceptual approach to social impact assessment: collection of writings by Rabel Burdge and Colleagues*. Middleton: Social Ecology Press.

Burdge, R. J. & R. A. Robertson 1994. Social impact assessment and the public involvement process, *Environmental Impact Assessment Review*, **10** (1/2), 81–90.

Burdge, R. J. & F. Vanclay 1995. Social impact assessment. See Vanclay & Bronstein (1995), 31–65. Chichester: John Wiley.

Burdge, R. J., D. R. Fields, S. R. Wells 1988. Utilizing social history to identify impacts of resource development on isolated communities: the case of Skagway, Alaska. *Impact Assessment Bulletin* **6** (2), 37–55.

Canter, L. W. 1996. *Environmental impact assessment*. New York: MacGraw Hill.

Carley, M. J. & E. S. Bustelo 1974. Social impact assessment: the state-of-the-art. In *Social Impact Assessment*, C. P. Wolf (ed.). Washington, DC: Environmental Design Research Association.

Carley, M. J. & E. S. Bustelo 1984. *Social impact assessment and monitoring*. Boulder, CO: Westview Press.

Carpenter, R. A. 1995. Risk assessment. See Vanclay & Bronstein (eds), 193–219. Chichester: John Wiley.

Carson, R. 1962. *Silent spring*. London: Penguin.

Central Planning Bureau 1992. *Scanning the future: a long-term scenario study of the world economy, 1990–2015*. The Hague: Sdu Publishers.

Cernea, M. (ed.) 1991. *Putting people first: sociological variables in rural development*, 2nd edn. New York: Oxford University Press.

Chambers, R. 1991. Shortcut and participatory methods for gaining social information for projects. In *Putting people first: sociological variables in rural development*, 2nd edn, M. M. Cernea (ed), 515–37. New York: Oxford University Press.

Coates, J. F. 1976. Technology assessment: a tool kit. *Chemtech* (June), 372–83.

Cochrane, S. H. & F. T. Sai 1991. *Health sector priorities review: excess fertility*. Washington: World Bank.

Coile, R. C. 1986. *The new hospital: future strategies for a changing industry* Rockville, MD: Aspen Publishers.

Commoner, B. 1994. Population, development and the environment: trend and key issues in the developed countries. In *Population, environment and development*, United Nations, 39–55. New York: department of economic and social information and policy analysis.

Condorcet, M. J. A. N. C. 1793. A general view of the science of social mathematics, in *Condorcet: Selected writings*. K. M. Baker (ed), 183–206. Indianapolis. IN: Bobbs-Merrill, University of Chicago, 1976.

Copi, I. M. 1978. *Introduction to logic*. New York: Macmillan.

Courgeau, D. & E. Lelière 1992. *Event history analysis in demography*. Oxford: Clarendon Press.

Dasgupta, A. K. & D. W. Pearce 1978. *Cost-benefit analysis: theory and practice*. London: Macmillan.

Derman, W. & S. Whiteford (eds) 1985. *Social impact analysis and development planning in the Third World*. Boulder, CO: Westview.

DeSola Pool, I. & R. P. Abelson 1961. The simulmatics project. *Public Opinion Quarterly* **25**, 167–70.

DeTombe, D. J. 1994. *Defining complex interdisciplinary societal problems: a theoretical study for constructing a co-operative problem analyzing method: the method COMPRAM*. Amsterdam: Thesis Publishers.

DeTombe, D. J. & C. Van Dijkum (eds) 1996. *Analysing complex societal problems: a methodological approach*. München and Mering: Rainer Hampp Verlag.

Dewulf, G. 1991. *Limits to forecasting: towards a theory of forecast errors*. Amsterdam: Thesis Publishers.

Dewulf, G. & H. A. Becker 1993. Cohort replacement in industrialised and developing countries: a social impact assessment, *Project appraisal* **8** (4), 225–231.

Doelen, F. C. J. van der 1992. Beleidsinstrumenten in soorten: zwepen, wortels en preken. In *28Hb Beleidsvoering overheid* **3**, 1–33. (Dutch only.)

Donahue, J. D. 1989. *The privatization decision: public ends, private means*. New York: Basic Books.

Dunn, W. N., A. M. Hagedus, B. Holzner 1988. Science impact assessment and public policy. *Impact Assessment Bulletin* **6** (3–4), 146–54.

Edelstein, M. R. 1984. Social impacts and social change: some initial thoughts on the emergence of a toxic victim movement. *Impact Assessment Bulletin* **3** (3), 7–18.

Epstein, R. A. 1992. Justice across the generations. In *Justice between age groups and generations*. P. Laslett & J. S. Fishkin (eds) 84–106. New Haven, CT: Yale University Press.

Esser, H. 1993. *Soziologie*. Frankfurt am Main: Campus Verlag.

Ester, P., L. Halman, R. De Moor (1993). *The individualizing society: value change in Europe and North America*. Tilburg: Tilburg University Press.

Fearnside, P. M. 1994. The Canadian feasibility study of the Three Gorges dam proposed for China's Yangzi River: a grave embarrassment to the impact assessment profession *Impact Assessment* **12** (1), 21–59.

Fernandes, A. J. 1990. Introducing social evaluation for improved project performance: a suggested checklist approach. *Project Appraisal* **5** (1), 11–19.

Finsterbusch, K. 1995. In praise of SIA: a personal review of the field of social impact assessment: evaluation, role, history, practice, methods, issues and future. *Impact Assessment* **13** (3), 229–52.

Finsterbusch, K. & C. P. Wolf (eds) 1981. *Methodology of social impact assessment*, 2nd edn. Stroudsburg: Hutchinson Ross.

Finsterbusch, K., J. Ingersoll, L. Llewellyn (eds) 1990. *Methods for social analysis in developing countries*. Boulder: Westview.

Finsterbusch, K., L. G. Llewellyn, C. P. Wolf (eds) 1983. *Social impact assessment methods*. Los Angeles: Sage.

Fisher, R. & W. L. Ury 1981. *Getting to yes: negotiating agreement without giving in*. Boston: Houghton Mifflin.

Forrester, J. 1971, *World dynamics*. Cambridge: Wright-Allen.

Gershefski, G. W. 1970. Corporate models: the state of the art. In *Corporate simulation models*, A. N. Schrieber (ed.), 26–42. Washington, Seattle: University of Washington Printing Plant.

Gianotten, V., V. Gorverman, E. van Walsum, L. Zuidberg 1994. *Assessing the gender impact of development projects: case studies from Bolivia, Burkino Faso and India*. London: Intermediate Technology Publications.

Gibbs, G. I. 1978. *Dictionary of gaming, modelling and simulation*. London: E. & F. N. Spon.

Gilley, J. W. & S. A. Eggland 1989. *Principles of human resource development*. Reading, Massachusetts: Addison-Wesley.

Glaser, B. G. & A. L. Strauss 1974. *Awareness of dying*. Chicago: Aldine.

Gondolf, E. 1986. A rapid assessment of community education in India: constraints, criteria, and method. *Impact Assessment Bulletin* **3** (4), 32–47.

Goodland, R. 1994. Environmental sustainability and the power sector. *Impact Assessment* **12** (3), 275–304.

Groves, R. M. & R. L. Kahn 1979. *Surveys by telephone, a national comparison with personal interviews*. New York: Academic Press.

Halstead, J., T. Johnson & L. Leistritz 1991. The role of fiscal impact models on impact assessment. *Impact Assessment Bulletin* **9** (3), 43–55.

Hanneman, R. A. 1988. *Computer-assisted theory building, modelling dynamic social systems*. London: Sage.

Hardin, R. 1988. *Morality within the limits of reason*, Chicago: University of Chicago Press.

BIBLIOGRAPHY

Harrod, R. F. 1951. *The life of John Maynard Keynes*. London: Macmillan.

Heilig, G. 1991. The Possible impact of AIDS on future mortality. See Lutz (1991), 71–96. London: Academic Press.

Hekkert, P. 1995. *Artful judgments, a psychological inquiry into aesthetic preference for visual patterns*. Doctoral dissertation, Technical University Delft, the Netherlands.

Herrera, A. O., H. D. Scolnik, G. Chichilnisky 1978. *Catastrophe or a new society?: a Latin American world model*. Ottawa, Canada: International Development Research Centre. (Buenos Aires: Fondación Bariloche.)

Höhn, C. 1991. Policies relevant to fertility. See Lutz (1991), 247–56. London: Academic Press.

Hollander, C. F. & H. A. Becker (eds) 1987. *Growing old in the future: scenarios on health and ageing, 1984–2000*. Dordrecht: Martinus Nijhoff Publishers.

Iedema, J., H. A. Becker, K. Sanders 1996. Transitions into independence: a comparison of cohorts born since 1930 in the Netherlands. *European Sociological Review*, in press.

Ingersoll, J. 1990. Social analysis in AID and the World Bank. In *Methods for social analysis in developing countries*, K. Finsterbusch, J. Ingersoll, L. Llewellyn (eds), 19–36. Boulder, CO: Westview Press.

Inskeep, E. 1991. *Tourism planning: an integrated and sustainable development approach*. New York: Van Nostrand Reinhold.

Inter-organizational Committee on Guidelines and Principles 1994. *Guidelines and principles for social impact assessment*. Washington, DC: Department of Commerce.

Jenkins, W. I. 1978. *Policy analysis, a political and organisational perspective*, London: Martin Robertson.

Jiggins, J. 1995. Development impact assessment: impact assessment of aid projects in nonwestern countries. See Vanclay & Bronstein (eds), 265–83. Chichester: John Wiley.

Jolly, D. 1988. *L'hôpital au XXIe siècle*, Paris: Economica.

Julien, P. -A., P. Lamonde, D. Latouche 1975. *La méthode des scénarios, une réflexion sur la démarche et la théorie de la prospective*. Quebec, Canada: Institut National de la Recherche Scientifique du Québec.

Juslén, J. 1995. Social impact assessment: a look at Finnish experiences. *Project Appraisal* **10** (3), 163–71.

Kahn, H. & A. J. Wiener 1967. *The Year 2000, A framework for speculation on the next thirty-three years*. New York: Macmillan.

Kay, J., C. Mayer, D. Thompson (eds) 1986. *Privatisation and regulation*: the UK experience. Oxford: Clarendon Press.

Keilman, N. W. 1990. *Uncertainty in national population forecasting: issues, measurements, backgrounds, recommendations*. Amsterdam: Swets & Zeitlinger.

Kemp, A. A. M. de & C. Sips 1994. *Prospects for European integration and consequences for social security policy in the Netherlands: a qualitative analysis*. Dutch Department of Social Affairs and Employment, The Hague: Vuga.

Keynes, J. M. 1919. *The economic consequences of the peace*. London: Macmillan.

Keynes, J. M. 1936. *The general theory of employment, interest and money*. London: Macmillan.

Knight, J. 1994. *Institutions and social conflict*. Cambridge: Cambridge University Press.

Lagergren, M., L. Lundh, C. Sanne 1984. *Time to care: a report prepared for the Swedish Secretariat for Future Studies*. Oxford: Pergamon Press.

Leeuw, F. L., R. C. Rist, R. C. Sonnichsen 1994. *Can governments learn?: comparative perspectives on evaluation and organizational learning*. New Brunswick: Transaction Publishers.

Leistritz, F. L. 1995. Economic and fiscal impact assessment. See Vanclay, F. & Bronstein (1995), 129–39. Chichester: John Wiley.

Lemons, K. E. 1992. A comparative study of impact assessment, *Impact Assessment Bulletin* 10 (3), 57–67.

Linstone, H. A. & M. Turrof (eds) 1975. *The delphi method: techniques and applications*. London: Addison-Wesley.

Lutz, W. (ed.) 1991. *Future demographic trends in Europe and North America: what can we assume today?* London: Academic Press.

Majone, G. & E. S. Quade (eds) 1980. *Pitfalls of analysis*. Chichester: John Wiley.

Manton, K. G. 1991. New biotechnologies and the limits of life expectancy. See Lutz (1991), 97–117. London: Academic Press.

March, J. G. & H. A. Simon 1958. *Organizations*. New York. John Wiley.

Martino, J. P. 1972. *Technological forecasting for decisionmaking*. New York, John Wiley.

McPherson, J. 1986. Social impact assessment in New Zealand. *Impact Assessment Bulletin* 4 (1–2), 261–71.

Meadows, D. H. 1972. *Limits to growth*. New York: Universe Books.

Meadows, D. H., J. Richardson, G. Bruckmann 1982. *Groping in the dark: the first decade of global modelling*. Chichester: John Wiley.

Meadows, D. H., D. L. Meadows, J. Randers 1991. *Beyond the limits: confronting global collapse: envisioning a sustainable future*. London: Earthscan Publications.

Mitchell, T. R. & R. J. Ebert 1975. *Organizational decision processes: concepts and analysis*. New York: Crane, Russak.

Mohan, R. 1994. *Understanding the developing metropolis: lessons from the city study of Bogot and Cali, Colombia*. Oxford: Oxford University Press.

Mohan, P. & A. S. Wilke (eds) 1994. *International handbook of contemporary developments in sociology*. Westport, CT: Greenwood.

Mukherjee, B. N. 1975. Reliability estimates of some survey data on family planning. *Population Studies* 29, 127–42.

Nelissen, J. H. M. 1993. *The redistributive impact of social security schemes on lifetime labour income*. Tilburg: Tisser.

Newell, A. & H. A. Simon 1972. *Human problem solving*. Englewood Cliffs, NJ: Prentice-Hall.

Nijkamp, P. 1986. Multiple criteria analysis and integrated impact analysis. *Impact Assessment Bulletin* 4 (3/4), 220–61.

—1991. Climate change, sea-level rise and Dutch defence strategies. *Project Appraisal* 6 (3), 143–49.

Nijkamp, P. & J. Spronk (eds) 1981. *Multiple criteria analysis: operational methods.* Aldershot: Gower.

OECD 1981. *Frascati manual: the measurement of scientific and technical activities.* Paris: OECD.

—1985. *Management of water projects: decision-making and investment appraisal.* Paris: OECD.

Ortolano, L. & A. Shepherd 1995. Environmental impact assessment. See Vanclay & Bronstein (1995), 3–30. Chichester: John Wiley.

Osborne, D. E. & T. Gaebler 1992. *Reinventing government: how the entrepreneurial spirit is transforming the public sector.* Reading, MA: Addison-Wesley.

Peters, D. 1994. Social impact assessment of the Ranomafan National Park project of Madagascar. *Impact Assessment* 12 (4), 385–409.

Pinho, P. & A. R. Pires 1991. Social impact analysis in environmental impact assessment: a Portuguese agricultural case study. *Project Appraisal* 6 (1), 2–7.

Porter, A. L. 1995. Technology assessment. See Vanclay & Bronstein (1995), 67–81. Chichester: John Wiley.

Porter, A. L. & F. A. Rossini (eds) 1983. *Why integrated impact assessment?* New York: North Holland.

Porter, A. L., F. A. Rossini, S. R. Carpenter, A. T. Roper (eds) 1980. *A guidebook for technology assessment and impact assessment.* New York: North Holland.

Prendergast, C. 1989. Condorcet's Canal study: the beginnings of social impact assessment. *Impact Assessment Bulletin* 7 (4), 25–37.

Priscoli, J. D. 1982. Social impact assessment research at the U.S. Army Corps of Engineers. *Impact Assessment Bulletin* 1 (4), 20–30.

Putnam, R. D. 1993. *Making democracy work: civic traditions in modern Italy.* Princeton, NJ: Princeton University Press.

Rahman, M. 1993. Disaster mitigation in Bangladesh: peasants' perceptions and aspirations. *Impact Assessment* 11 (1), 57–87.

Raser, J. R. 1969. *Simulation and society, an exploration of scientific gaming.* Boston, MA: Allyn and Bacon.

Ratcliffe, J. 1995. The measurement of indirect costs and benefits in health care evaluation: a critical review. *Project Appraisal* 10 (1), 13–19.

Rawls, J. 1971. *A theory of justice.* Oxford: Oxford University Press.

Rivers, M. J. & D. Buchan 1995. Social assessment and consultation: New Zealand cases *Project Appraisal* 10 (3), 181–89.

Roberts, R. 1995. Public involvement: from consultation to participation. See Vanclay & Bronstein (1995), 221–46. Chichester: Wiley.

Roebig, J.H. 1983. An aesthetic impact assessment technique. *Impact Assessment Bulletin* 2 (3), 29–41.

Rogers, E. M. 1995. *Diffusion of innovations,* 4th edn. New York: Free Press.

Rubington, E. & M. S. Weinberg (eds) 1981. *The study of social problems: five perspectives,* 3rd edn. Oxford: Oxford University Press.

Sackman, H. 1974. *Delphi assessment: expert opinion forecasting and group processes: a report prepared for United States Air Force Project Rand.* Santa Monica: Rand Corporation.

Sanders, K. & H. A. Becker 1994. The transition from education to work and social indepdenance: a comparison between the United States, The Netherlands, West Germany, and the United Kingdom. *European Sociological Review* 10 (2), 135–54.

Schoonenboom, J. & H. M. Langeveld 1990. De emancipatie van de vrouw, een zelfevaluatie. In *Terugkijken op Toekomstonderzoek,* H. A. Becker & G. Dewulf (eds), 317–50. Utrecht: ISOR Publications. (Dutch only.)

Schwarz, B. 1972. S.O.M.: an education simulation model. In *Developments in simulation and gaming,* H. A. Becker & H. M. Goudappel (eds), 47–73. Meppel: Boom.

Senge, P. M. 1990. *The fifth discipline: the art and practice of the learning organization.* New York: Doubleday.

Shannon, R. E. 1975. *Systems simulation: the art and science.* Englewood Cliffs, NJ: Prentice Hall.

Smith, M. A. 1995. Community impact agreements, mechanisms for change management: the Niagara experience. *Project Appraisal* 10 (3), 189–97.

Snijders, C. 1996. *Trust and commitments.* PhD Thesis, Utrecht University.

Soderstrom, E. J. 1981. *Social impact assessment: experimental methods and approaches.* New York: Praeger.

Steinman, G. 1991. Immigration as a remedy for the birth dearth: the case of West Germany. See Lutz (1991), 337–59. London: Academic Press.

Stevens, R. 1989. *In sickness and in wealth: American hospitals in the twentieth century.* New York: Basic Books.

Summers, L. 1992. Investing in all people. Paper prepared for the QuadiAzam Lecture at the Eighth Annual General Meeting of the Pakistan Society of Development Economists, Islamabad.

Taplin, R. & R. Braaf 1995. Climate impact assessment, In *Environmental and social impact assessment,* F. Vanclay & Bronstein (eds), 249–81. Chichester: John Wiley.

Tarrow, S. 1996. *Power in movement: social movements, collective action and politics.* Cambridge: Cambridge University Press.

Taylor, C. N., C. H. Bryan, C. G. Goodrich, 1990. *Social assessment: theory, process and techniques,* 2nd edn. Lincoln: Taylor Baines Associates.

Taylor, C. N., C. G. Goodrich, C. H. Bryan 1995. Issues-oriented approach to social assessment and project appraisal. *Project Appraisal* 10 (3), 142–55.

Thompson, J. G. & D. Bryant 1992. Fiscal impact in a Western boomtown: unmet expectations. *Impact Assessment Bulletin* 10 (3), 3–23.

Thompson, J. G. & G. Williams 1992. Social assessment: roles for practitioners and the need for stronger mandates. *Impact Assessment Bulletin* 10 (3), 43–57.

Thurow, L. 1992. *Head to head: the coming economic battle among Japan, Europe, and America.* New York: Morrow.

Treweek, J. 1995. Ecological impact assessment. In *Environmental and social impact assessment,* F. Vanclay & D. A. Bronstein (eds), 171–91. Chichester: John Wiley.

Turner, B. S. 1987. *Medical power and social knowledge*. London: Sage.

Twomey, J. & J. M. Tomkins 1993. Evaluation of health promotion. *Project Appraisal* **8** (1), 23–31.

United Nations, 1994. *Population, environment and development: proceedings of the United Nations expert group meeting on population, environment and development*. New York: Department for Economic and Social Information and Policy Analysis.

Valkonen, T. 1991. Assumptions about mortality trends in industrialized countries: a survey. See Lutz (1991), 3–27. London: Academic Press.

Vanclay, F. (1989–96). *Social impact assessment bibliography*. Wagga Wagga, NSW, Australia: Centre for Rural Social Research, Charles Sturt University.

Vanclay, F. & D. A. Bronstein (eds) 1995. Editor's preface: the state of the art of impact assessment, In *Environmental and social impact assessment*, xi–xiii. Chichester: John Wiley.

Vanclay, F. & G. Lawrence 1995. *The environmental imperative: ecosocial concerns for Australian agriculture*. Rockhampton: Central Queensland University Press.

Van Deth, J. W. & E. Scarbrough (eds) 1995. *The impact of values*. Oxford: Clarendon Press.

Van Herwijnen, M., R. Janssen, P. Nijkamp 1993. A multi-criteria decision support model and geographic information system for sustainable development planning of the Greek islands. *Project Appraisal* **8** (1). 9–23.

Vennix, J. A. M. 1996. *Group model building: facilitating team learning using system dynamics*. Chichester: John Wiley.

Verloo, M. & C. Roggeband 1996. Gender impact assessment: the development of a new instrument in The Netherlands. *Impact Assessment* **14** (1), 3–20.

Vlek, C. A. J. 1986. Rise, decline and aftermath of the Dutch societal discussion on (nuclear) energy policy 1981–1983. In *Impact assessment today*, H. A. Becker & A. L. Porter (eds), 141–88. Utrecht: Van Arkel.

Von Newmann, J. & O. Morgenstern 1943. *Theory of games and economic behaviour*. New York: John Wiley.

Voogd, J. de, J. de Koning, M. M. J. Leenders, A. Gelderbom, N. Mahieu 1995. *Guaranteed minimum income arrangements in the Netherlands, Belgium, Denmark, France, Germany and Great Britain*. Department of Social Affairs and Employment, Department of Labour-Market and Education. The Hague: Vuga.

Warwick, D. P. 1983. On methodological integration in social research. In *Social research in developing countries*, M. Bulmer and P. D. Warwick (eds). Chichester: Wiley.

Weber, Max 1968. *Methodologische Schriften*, Frankfurt am Main: S. Fischer Verlag.

Weesie, J. 1988. *Mathematical models for competition, cooperation, and social networks*. Doctoral dissertation, Utrecht University.

Wenner, L. N. 1986. Social impact analysis in retrospect: was it useful? *Impact Assessment Bulletin* **3** (4). 11–25.

Westhoff, C. F. 1991. The return to replacement fertility: a magnetic force? See Lutz (1991), 227–35. London: Academic Press.

Whyte, W. F. & G. Alberti 1976. *Power, politics and progress*. New York: Elsevier.

Williams, W. 1971. *Social policy research and analysis: the experience in the Federal social agencies*. New York: Elsevier.

Wind, H. G. (ed.) 1987. *Impact of sea level rise on society*. Rotterdam: A. A. Balkema.

Wolf, C. P. 1974. Social impact assessment: the state-of-the-art. In *Social impact assessment*, C. P. Wolf (ed.). Washington: Environmental Design Research Association.

— 1981. Social impact assessment. *Impact Assessment Bulletin* **1** (1), 9–20.

World Bank 1985. *Population change and economic development*. New York: Oxford University Press.

— 1991. *Environmental assessment sourcebook* [3 volumes]. Washington, DC: World Bank.

— 1994. *Resettlement and development: the bankwide review of projects involving involuntary resettlement, 1986–1993*. Washington, DC: World Bank.

World Commission on Environment and Development (WCED) 1987. *Our common future* (Brundtland Report). Oxford: Oxford University Press.

World Health Organization 1986. *Health projections in Europe: methods and applications*. Copenhagen: WHO.

Index

254

bargaining) and models on a relatively low level of abstraction. High-level models provide an insight in long-term problems and their possible mitigation or solution. Low-level models provide a framework for understanding behaviour in specific social settings.

Reviewing old forecasts has turned into a specific research programme, as we saw in Chapter 2. The outcomes of these ex-post evaluations are relevant to impact assessors because IA requires trend analyses. Similar to the explanation of mistakes in old problem analyses, we find theories that explain the degree of accuracy in trend analyses. The degree of accuracy in old trend analyses can be explained by theories about characteristics of researchers and their organizational setting, data acquisition, theories in use and pressure from decision-makers, the press and protest movements. Accuracy of forecasting ranges from high to low, related to the variables that are involved. In demographic forecasting, for instance, predictions for the next five years of the number of inhabitants of a country between 20 and 70 years old will turn out to be highly accurate. On the other hand, predictions of the number of children born each year, or of the number of people of more than 100 years old, will turn out to be highly inaccurate.

Reviewing old futures explorations, like scenario analyses, is still in its infancy, because only a few old scenario reports are available yet. Nevertheless, a number of old world models using scenarios has been evaluated already. The outcomes of these reviews are in line with those of the reviews summarized above. If the relative predicability of each variable is taken into account, scenario analysis elucidates future developments and events in a way that is highly relevant to policy-making. If the predicability of developments in a specific category of variables is low, the quest for planning is high. Disaster relief co-ordination illustrates this. Because the time and place of disasters are characterized by low predicability, disaster relief requires preparation, including the establishment of disaster relief units that can come to the rescue of victims at short notice.

Reviewing old SIAs has not been practised on a large scale either. An exception is the ex-post evaluation of the emancipation of women and related policy actions mentioned in Chapter 2. In the next years, more old reports will become available. Ex-post evaluations of old SIAs will provide a major contribution to the improvement of SIA methodology. The SIA community must be able to rely on their colleagues in universities and related research institutes for this kind of oriented basic research.

In preceding chapters, I already touched upon ex-post evaluation of social technology. Now I want to look into this subject in more detail. Social technology, as we saw, consists of policy instruments for launching innovations and for managing organizations and social networks. It also covers instruments for activities of a more practical nature: network planning, public relations, etc. Each of these instruments has been applied already, activities have been evaluated, sometimes even on a large scale, and the evaluations have been followed by improvements of the instruments. SIA always includes the design and pretesting of actions using instruments. For this reason, social technology is of strategic importance to SIA.

As an example of systematically improving social technology, I will discuss the ex-post evaluation and reorientation of privatization. Privatization constitutes a broad-ranging example. This type of political activity has been practised in many countries since the early 1980s, primarily because it was supposed to contribute to the economic and social revitalization of western countries. The USA was the first to launch large-scale privatizations. Donahue (1989) argued that the early 1980s brought a virtually worldwide cooling toward collectivism and a growing readiness to experiment with market approaches. Accompanying this enthusiasm for private enterprise was an enduring, deficit-induced imperative to limit government spending. The term privatization has two meanings. The first meaning involves removing certain responsibilities, activities or assets from the collective realm. This is the chief meaning of privatization in countries retreating from postwar, post-colonial experiences with socialism, as they separate factories, mines, airlines and railroads from public control. The second meaning implies retaining collective financing but delegating delivery to the private sector. There is a large element of nonsense in the privatization debate, Donahue concluded. Proponents are fond of invoking the efficiency that characterizes well-run companies in competitive markets and then, not troubling with any intervening logical steps, trumpeting the conclusions that private firms will excel in public undertakings as well. At the same time, it would be perverse to reject privatization simply because some enthusiasts favour it for the wrong reasons.

The first lesson from the evaluation of privatization concerns the